BŚT 31.87

Cambridge Studies in Social Anthropology

General Editor: Jack Goody

33

WHY MARRY HER?

This book is published as part of the joint publishing agreement established in 1977 between the Fondation de la Maison des Sciences de l'Homme and the Press Syndicate of the University of Cambridge. Titles published under this arrangement may appear in any European language or, in the case of volumes of collected essays, in several languages.

New books will appear either as individual titles or in one of the series which the Maison des Sciences de l'Homme and the Cambridge University Press have jointly agreed to publish. All books published jointly by the Maison des Sciences de l'Homme and the Cambridge University Press will be distributed by the Press throughout the world.

Why Marry Her?

Society and symbolic structures

LUC DE HEUSCH

Translated by JANET LLOYD

CAMBRIDGE UNIVERSITY PRESS

Cambridge
London   New York   New Rochelle   Melbourne   Sydney

and

EDITIONS DE LA MAISON DES SCIENCES DE L'HOMME

Paris

Published by the Press Syndicate of the University of Cambridge
The Pitt Building, Trumpington Street, Cambridge CB2 1RP
32 East 57th Street, New York, NY 10022, USA
296 Beaconsfield Parade, Middle Park, Melbourne 3206, Australia
and Editions de la Maison des Sciences de l'Homme
54 Boulevard Raspail, 75270 Paris Cedex 06

Ch. 2 except postscript and chs. 4–6 first published 1971 by
Editions Gallimard, Paris, in *Pourquoi l'épouser?*
Ch. 3 except postscript first published 1974 in *Man*, n.s. 9, 4
Bibliography and English translation of introduction, chs. 1–2,
postscript to ch. 3 and chs. 4–6 first published 1981

Printed in Great Britain at the University Press, Cambridge

British Library cataloguing in publication data
Heusch, Luc de
Why marry her? – (Cambridge studies in social
anthropology; 33).
1. Social Structure – Addresses, essays,
lectures
I. Title II. Series
301.4′008   HM131   80-41710
ISBN 0 521 22460 8

Contents

v

Preface

The main body of this volume is composed of four of twelve studies published by Gallimard under the title *Pourquoi l'épouser? et autres essais* (1971). 'Possession et chamanisme' and 'La folie des dieux et la raison des hommes' appear here in their original form. The author has thought it opportune to introduce a number of slight alterations to 'Structure et praxis sociales chez les Lele du Kasai' and to follow this text with a new commentary in which he discusses the analysis of the Lele kinship system that Lévi-Strauss undertook in 1973 in *Anthropologie structurale deux*. This appendix will only be intelligible if the reader first reads the first chapter in this volume, 'A defence and illustration of the structures of kinship', which, like the Introduction, has never been published in French. Chapter 4, 'Structure and history', gives a fuller version of a substantial part of the study published in *Pourquoi l'épouser?* under the title 'Signes, réciprocité et marxisme'. In the present volume the author devotes his attention entirely to Kachin society as described by Edmund Leach.

Finally, this volume also includes an article originally published in *Man* (new series, 9, 4, 1974); 'The debt of the maternal uncle', and adds a postscript on the subject of the systems known as the 'Omaha systems'.

The publisher wishes to thank the Royal Anthropological Institute of Great Britain and Northern Ireland for permission to reproduce chapter 3, 'The debt of the maternal uncle', first published in *Man* (new series, 9, 4, 1974).

Introduction: travel memories

Through the dark years of the Nazi occupation I discovered, one after the other, Rimbaud, Freud, Malinowski, Frazer and the poetic brilliance of surrealism. In 1947 I rushed to Paris to meet André Breton. I was twenty years old. He received me in his customary grave, friendly way, surrounded by Hopi dolls and marvellous paintings that, in my eagerness, I scarcely noticed. Unhesitatingly, he directed my hesitant steps in the direction of the man who was, in a way, the shaman of the group: Pierre Mabille, doctor, psychologist, sociologist and seer, and just back from Haiti, filled with wonder at the diversity of the human race, whether seen individually or collectively. It was he, with his supremely liberated spirit and an intelligence never divorced from sensibility, who more than anyone else cultivated my burgeoning taste for anthropology while at the same time putting me on my guard against an excessive solemnity.

I spent very little time in the University of Brussels, preferring the company of the painters and poets who had grouped themselves together under the geographical and mythical sign of COBRA.[1] Rashly, I undertook to defend a lyrical totemism, as a reaction to my aversion to industrial society. After all, had not René Char written: 'Long ago the grass was good to fools and hostile to the executioner' (*Jadis l'herbe était bonne aux fous et hostile au bourreau*)?

I decided to travel. In those days escape led, alas, to the colonies — or rather, *the* colony, the Belgian Congo. In the early fifties, the Institute of Scientific Research in Central Africa, recently created, was recruiting its first professional anthropologists. Frans Olbrechts, the godfather of this emerging Belgian school, generously asked me where I would like to pursue my scientific education.[2] Maquet, Vansina and Biebuyck had all three decided on London. I chose Paris. And so it was that I became a pupil of Marcel Griaule, who himself had recently trained under Ogotemmêli.

I was fascinated by the teaching of Griaule, who, scorning all theories, was engaged in revealing the sinuous paths by which the creation of the world had proceeded. Jacques Maquet, recently hailed as grand master in London, suggested that my young wife and I should drive with him from Brussels to Bukavu. In those days this represented quite an adventure, despite the robust nature of our

1

reinforced and specially outfitted 1952 Studebaker. For reasons that will ever remain a mystery, the British consul refused me a transit visa for Nigeria. We decided to take a chance with fate, if not with the authority of the young queen of England, who was certainly not aware of the injustice being done to me, and to cross the Sahara. Jacques Maquet, even while at the wheel, proceeded to initiate me into the work of Radcliffe-Brown and filled in a number of sociological lacunae for me. I for my part tried to pass on to him some of my enthusiasm for Dogon thought which was at that time considered in London to be some kind of anthropological mystification. In short, we attempted over a whole month to set up a dialogue between the venerable British school of social anthropology and the young French school of ethnography — each equally entrenched in its rebarbative isolation — meanwhile admiring the changing scenery through which we passed without significant mishap. The doors to Nigeria opened before us. It turned out that I was innocent after all.

My orders were to proceed to the Tetela of the Kasai, where a Catholic bishop had produced a dictionary which my linguist colleague, John Jacobs, had the task of perfecting. On the subject of colonisation, Monsignor told me bluntly, 'You can't make an omelette without breaking eggs.' I was the first white man in living memory who declined to go to Mass at Tshumbe Sainte-Marie. I got a cold reception, for I was compromising the colonial order. My wife's hair was red and the rumour went round that she was the devil. I was saddened by the stupidity of the *pax belgica* which had put an end to the never very dangerous warlike ardour of the Tetela, although I certainly suffered less from it than did an obscure employee in the postal administration, a native of the region, who eight years later was to become the first prime minister of the Congolese republic. Patrice Lumumba was at that time kicking his heels in Stanleyville, not yet caught up in his meteoric and tragic destiny. I tried, as conscientiously as possible, to describe the tradition bequeathed by his ancestors. I found myself plunged into an unexpected world of conflict that encompassed genealogical quarrels, an intense circulation of bride-wealth, competition for prestige and justifiable dissatisfaction with the enforced cultivation of cotton. This 'educational work' was regarded by the Tetela quite purely and simply as slavery. Their religious preoccupations were decidedly embryonic. In reply to my incessant questions on cosmogonical matters, one sage replied, during a burial, 'If you really want to know what the moon is, take an aeroplane and go and have a look.'

I was intrigued by some mysterious figures who, despite the fact that the savanna was crossed only by a few thin strips of trees, declared themselves to be the masters of the forest (*nkum'okunda*). Neither their necklaces made from leopard teeth — the traditional attribute of lineage chiefs — nor their chants, whose rhythm was beaten out by drumsticks sounding upon a clapperless metal bell (*elundja*) regarded as their own particular attribute, were taken very seriously by the Tetela. But they all agreed that this male society, with its jealously guarded secrets, wielded considerable authority further to the north, among the

2

Hamba. One member of this brotherhood of ill-determined status was Okito-sumba, a most intelligent man. He had been a village chief but, for reasons none too clear, he had lost this function. It was to increase his prestige that, having become an initiate in a neighbouring group, he had introduced the *elundja* bell in Kalema. I determined to follow his example in order to learn more about it.

The Hamba comprise a group of small tribes closely related to the Tetela. At some point in the past, they separated from their brothers on the savanna and went off into the forest. I journeyed north as far as I could into a cul-de-sac. In this geographical position I enjoyed the illusion of having reached the end of the world, of having gone back through time right to the threshold of primitive life. But it was only an illusion. The Djumbusanga, who make up a small community of some two thousand souls, were as welcoming as they were cheerful and still liked to wear the traditional raffia garments that had disappeared among the Tetela of the savanna. They delighted in adorning themselves with copper bracelets and covering their bodies with red powder. The *nkum'okunda* did indeed wield great authority. They often met together to settle disputes and to dance in imitation of the animals of the forest. They would willingly travel to visit their colleagues in distant villages, so that this association was rather like an intertribal freemasonry. But it was just as much a male recreational club as a collective organ of power. In order to climb up through the hierarchy and gain the right to wear some new insignia of dignity, it was each time necessary to make a solemn offer of a considerable quantity of riches to the assembled body of the brotherhood, gathered in a circle in the shade of a palm tree. Was I confronted with a plutocracy? Or with an assembly of priests with some secret knowledge?

One day I was at last allowed to enter their sanctuary; the entry to it was barred by a palm leaf placed across a path which gave on to the road some kilometres from the village. We went in backwards and found ourselves in a first enclosure. In the centre there stood a mast topped with a spike stuck into a lump of the red paste extracted from the ngula tree and used for body painting. The neophyte is told to climb up and get this mysterious object, but he must be sure not to comply with this order. What he must do in order to be allowed to proceed further is approach the palms of his two hands several times towards the mast without touching it. As far as I can judge, after having visited a large number of lodges, no esoteric teaching lies behind these signs of recognition. Confronted with this enigma, the question rather seems to be whether one does or does not belong here among the powerful.

I was both disappointed and amazed. Normally, some preliminary rough joking takes place in this first enclosure. I was grateful to my guide for sparing me this. A second palm leaf separated us from the larger enclosure where the masters of the forest were awaiting me, singing joyfully. My heart was beating fast. I thought I was passing through the door into another world, penetrating to the heart of the sacred. I was mistaken yet again. However, more and more signs were manifesting themselves. Perhaps strangest of all were the leaves and feathers stuck into the ground, which were mechanically waving to and fro in a mysterious fashion. I was very frightened (and I had to be to play my role correctly) when my initiator lifted up a lump of termite's nest, revealing a hole into which he invited me to plunge my arm. Luckily, a substitute was designated to take my place, to whom, happily and cravenly, I agreed to pay a goat. His arm was seized and soon he was writhing in pain, pinned to the ground, in the power of some invisible force. One or two initiates of high rank soon let me into the secret. A tunnel had been dug under the enclosure, emerging on the other side of the wall of foliage which marked out the zone for the mysteries in which we were absorbed; a fellow member of the brotherhood was acting in the name of the spirits of the underground world. And it was also he who was shaking the leaves and bird feathers. I will at this point cut short this list of signs or symbols, call them what you will; they varied from one lodge to another, as did the arrangement of the enclosures. Instead of acceding to a myth – or at the very least to the first stage of an initiatory questioning – I had discovered a lighthearted political mystification. The power it served was, however, a most respectable one. For these masters of the forest (who had for the first time agreed to accept a white man among them, being correctly convinced that I was in league with neither the government nor the clergy nor the detested cotton company) wielded with moderation and wisdom a collegial power from which no tyrant could possibly emerge. The joking did not prevent them from dispensing justice correctly or from maintaining peace across the tribal boundaries.

From then on, I shared appreciable hunting dues with my colleagues, but I was in despair at their lack of metaphysical concern. They purveyed no teaching and practised no magico-religious rites. They were content simply to introduce a measure of lighthearted ceremonial into collective life, leaving the relentless task of pursuing sorcerers to the *wetshi*, the diviners and healers. No more than the Tetela of the savanna were the Hamba concerned to organise rites of passage in accordance with the precepts of Van Gennep, nor to set up an ancestor cult or even rites for the increase of game, as one might have expected. There were no masks, no sacrifices, no possession. No symbolical activity at all. I wondered anxiously what Griaule would think of the report of such an insignificant mission. The points of reference he had taught me to look for seemed to have been effaced from my territory by some mischievous spirit whom I persisted in pursuing over a wide area. Once I had been initiated among the Djumbusanga, I enjoyed an international passport permitting me to visit a large number of lodges. Each one has elaborated in its own way secrets and signs which depended at least in part on an esoteric code of circulation that made it possible for those in the know to avoid falling into a trap as they entered the enclosure.

But I persisted in my quest for a meaning, a quest which, in the eyes of the Hamba, had no meaning at all. Step by step, I worked my way back to the presumed origins of the institution which had, over the last months, become the

4

main focus of my attentions. All the threads in this piece of detective work led to the Nkutshu. They raised no difficulties in accepting my status as a 'full' (*manyi*) master of the forest. Here the tunnel that I had first learned to recognise among the Djumbusanga changed its function, but was just as worrying. Instead of being the secret place *par excellence*, hidden from the sight of the neophytes, here it became the compulsory way in. You had to crawl along it, confronting naked, threatening men there, in order to accede to the sanctuary under the open sky, protected as always by a circular palisade of foliage. Here the new-comers were subjected to practical joking of a somewhat rougher kind than I had seen inflicted more moderately elsewhere. Two wooden statuettes, one male and the other female, bearing the insignia of power, were enthroned in the centre of the enclosure. Among the Djumbusanga, the masters of the forest had contented themselves with exhibiting in a miniature hut a single statuette referred to as the elder (*enundu*). More or less everywhere these quite crudely carved objects constituted the centre of the initiatory mystery. Nothing was said about them at all. They were the mystical masters of the brotherhood, and that was enough.

After all my investigations, I had not discovered mythical thought, but I was learning to discover history. What confronted me was the recent political history of the Tetela and the Hamba. Faithful to the teaching of Boas, I had worked my way back along the development of a new institution of social control, intro-duced only a few generations ago, which had rapidly eclipsed the traditional power of the lineage chiefs, still alive among the Tetela of the savanna. The Nkutshu claimed that an ancestor had instituted the association of the masters of the forest so as to impose male law, judged to be natural, more successfully upon the women, who had become very unruly. This sociological fable is easy to decipher. All these mysteries, which I knew to be no more than tricks, signs of recognition, made it possible to operate a distinction between the men, who were included, and the women, who were excluded, to oppose the forest and the village. Both the hidden explanation for the paucity of symbolism and its *raison d'être* at last dawned on me: the initiation simulated an alliance between the male power, the strong men, and the powers of the forest even though the beliefs of the Hamba and the Tetela exclude the possibility of any ritual pact with the disquieting world of the spirits (*edimu*). Perhaps in this way the *nkum'okunda* managed to persuade others that they were making effective inter-ventions with the spirits in order to ensure success in hunting, but I never heard them make such extravagant claims in my presence.

While the association of the masters of the forest spread among the Hamba tribes, creating new bonds between them, magnificent dancers, their faces painted with many-coloured, perfectly symmetrical designs, appeared on the ceremonial scene, there to embody the 'total social reality' so dear to Marcel Mauss.[3] When mourning for one or several great *nkum'okunda* comes to an end, these figures appear out of the forest wearing headdresses of eagles' feathers, their torsos covered with red powder. Amid the din of the drums beating out the *lukutu* rhythm, they make no sound: a needle stuck through their lips forces them to keep silent. They make their way, in little leaps, to the centre of the village. After this choreographic display they go and sit quietly upon upturned mortars set up by the elders of the maximal lineages. Then follows a veritable potlatch. Over the past few days all those who have received in marriage a daughter belonging to one of the organising lineages have gathered in the village. At this solemn moment these sons-in-law arrange themselves in a single file, accompanied by their wives, and each in turn presents himself before his father-in-law, his arms laden with gifts. They place at his feet copper bracelets, banknotes and bales of cotton, in the presence of a herald whose function is to make known to the crowd the generosity of each son-in-law. All quarrelling is forbidden. The beauty of the dancers, now sitting motionless on their lineage thrones, sets the seal upon the fragile equilibrium of a society founded upon the interplay of matrimonial alliances. Here art is hyperfunctional and ceremonial is fully significant. I felt myself at peace with Durkheim. My enquiry was certainly taking a new turn. Was I about to be converted to functionalism?

Let us take a look at the economics of the situation.[4] Up until the installation of a number of European shops in the region, the Hamba and the Tetela had disdained any form of market economy. The circulation of rare wealth objects was their passion: in addition to the traditional goats and iron and copper 'currency', these now included the colonial money that a powerful cotton company was dispensing in dribs and drabs. This company enjoyed a comfortable monopoly over the purchase of the cotton: it enjoyed the support of the administration, which had decreed cotton cultivation to be compulsory in order to advance these 'savages' along the road to civilisation. The government, the church and the business world had, it goes without saying, defined the path to be followed once and for all. This noble educative effort was, in fact, extremely profitable for those in control. For their part, the Tetela–Hamba were not interested in investments (how could they have been?); they were content simply to introduce the Congolese franc into the matrimonial circuits, and this occasioned formidable inflation. The capitalist economy in no way altered the status of the son-in-law, who remained permanently in debt to the relatives of his wife. Wives simply started to insist on imported cotton fabrics from their husbands. The young men, who in the old days were condemned to a prolonged celibacy, became the rivals of the older, polygamous, men, and the demand for women went through an inevitable crisis about which the older men openly complained. The divorce rate increased. The structure, however, stood up to this crisis admirably.

Vastly oversimplifying, you could say that both the Tetela and the Hamba constitute in different but comparable forms small societies based upon potlatch and big-men (in the Melanesian sense of the word). In both cases what matters most is the acquisition of prestige. How should we interpret this system of values, for which I know of no other example so radical in Africa? Is this an economico-political strategy susceptible to Marxist analysis? That seems very doubtful despite the fact that the masters of the forest who have honoured all the payments demanded by their colleagues are assured of a relative material comfort: the many hunting dues that they receive are augmented by fines that they collectively impose when they preside at tribunals ... and then there are also the contributions from new members or from those acceding to new levels in the hierarchy. A curious plutocracy this, where accession to power involves squandering one's wealth. My old friend Edinga was well aware of the dilemma. Although he was a member whose opinion was respected in the brotherhood of the *nkum'okunda*, he preferred to help his sons to marry rather than to accede to a higher level.

The personal ambitions of the Tetela of the savanna take a quite different form. They can only be realised within a strictly lineage structure, not in a brotherhood theoretically open to any head of family. The figure of the chief takes on a certain importance in these southern tribes where huge communities sometimes comprising several thousand men and women, all actually or fictitiously the issue of a common ancestor, consider themselves to be autonomous groups.[5] Here political organisation depends upon the common genealogical charter. In theory, seniority defines the locus of power. But this must be confirmed by potlatch. The chief of a political-cum-family community is chosen from the eldest segment of the eldest lineage descended from the common ancestor; but at each level in the lineage segmentation the man who occupies a homologous position may be defined as the elder (*enundu*) of the group, or as its chief (*owandji*). The chiefs of the maximal lineages then compete for prestige. When it comes to his investiture, the chief of the largest independent unit (or tribe) can only win public ratification for his title at the cost of a fantastic outlay of wealth through which matrimonial wealth is redistributed throughout all segments of the society. The candidate then has the right to dance the dance of the leopard in the company of his close relations. However, the prestige thus won does not confer upon him any rights over agricultural production. As a 'master of the earth', *owandji wa nkete*, the main chief (elder of the eldest lineage) can only demand a hunting due. To consolidate his position he must also demonstrate another talent, on which he is constantly expending his energies. The extensive polygamy of the chief is explicitly thought of as the means of ensuring this statutory generosity, 'the chief's work', which is proverbially represented as never-ending (*nkumi hashile*). However, he receives no wives as tribute. The chief, just like any other man, is permanent debtor to his father-in-law and his brothers-in-law. The chiefs of the other senior lineages who are in a junior position to their genealogical elder may set themselves up as his rivals. They, in their turn, try to organise a great potlatch of outstanding proportions which will establish their prestige in the region: the chiefs of neighbouring communities are invited as well as the elders of the various lineage segments of their own tribe. This institutional rivalry clearly accounts for the permanent

7

scissions that continuously fragment Tetela society, which, in fact, sees itself as one vast family that has burst apart but that stems from a single genealogy.

The acquisition of prestige appears, in the last analysis, to be functionally dependent on the circulation of the rare wealth objects distributed by the matrimonial chain. Elders who are ambitious capitalise on their wealth for a while but then redistribute it throughout the society as a whole. Here again, the introduction of the currency issued by the colonial power has had no effect whatsoever upon this remarkably stable aspiration. At this point we notice a basic structure that is common to the Tetela and the Hamba. The appearance of the *lukutu* dancers, the impassive inaugurators of a peaceful potlatch, gives a ceremonial impetus to the process of distributing matrimonial wealth in the same way as does the leopard dance which the Tetela chief has the right to perform once he has dispensed a veritable fortune previously accumulated through the combined efforts of the family as a whole together with its various networks of matrimonial alliances.

There are many points of correspondence between the two institutions: the *lukutu* dancer of the Hamba is chosen from a junior segment, and the Tetela chief belongs to an elder branch, but each represents his lineage. The former appears at irregular intervals, before the potlatch is organised; the latter makes only one ceremonial appearance, surrounded by his wives and relatives after having distributed all his capital. In the first case, the beneficiaries of the operation are all the individual members of the lineage (enriched by a direct and personal acquisition of matrimonial wealth publicly handed over by their sons-in-law); in the second, the wealth distributed by the lineage chief is diffused throughout the lineage community as a whole through the intermediary of the elders of the various constituent segments. During a recent visit to the Kasai, after an absence of twenty years,[6] I noticed that the dramatic economic crisis that Zaïre is experiencing and that has had the effect of isolating the Tetela–Hamba communities from all the commercial networks set up by colonisation has brought about a reduction in ceremonial life. These communities are no longer fuelled by money. It is strange that the decomposition of capitalism should affect the non-commercial traditional circuits that had allowed themselves to be flooded by its currency even though those who manipulated it were unaware of its particular economic significance. For the Tetela and the Hamba it was indeed all a nonsense.

A time for reflection

I was confronted with societies whose passion was for the circulation of rare wealth objects devoid of any economic meaning. The significance of Marcel Mauss's and Lévi-Strauss's theses concerning archaic exchange became increasingly evident to me. The constant circulation of matrimonial wealth belongs to the complex structure of marriage, which ethnographers in the past were overhasty in defining as 'marriage by purchase', if indeed they did not appeal to the fallacious concept of the 'dowry'. Among the Tetela, power rests on the rules of filiation and the interplay of alliances: it is a function derived from these two indissociable structural phenomena. The great polygamy of the chiefs is explicitly conceived as the instrument *par excellence* of a political system based upon generosity rather than domination or control over rituals. Among the Hamba, the rare wealth objects are redistributed periodically within the lineage framework through the *lukutu* festival and within a closed male society, the *nkum'okunda*. In both cases the institutions oppose both the formation of any dominant social class and the exercise of political tyranny, whatever the gerontocratic tendencies of the system.

I had long been intrigued by the fact that religious activity hardly existed (with the exception of investiture rites for the diviners, involving blacksmiths). I now believe that social life among the Tetela–Hamba belongs more to ceremonialism than to ritualism. By ceremonialism I mean a certain codified presentation of social roles, in the sense used by Max Gluckman.[7] Comparing this state of affairs with that which prevails in the other societies that belong to the great Mongo linguistic group, it is impossible not to come to the following conclusion: that the Tetela–Hamba's almost all-engrossing passion for the manipulation of rare wealth objects and their considered desire to convert these riches symbolising women into signs of prestige, without bothering to establish communication with their ancestors or with the spirits of nature, involve a loss — a loss which cannot be explained by colonisation alone. I must confess to having felt a certain lassitude when it came to recording the minute inventory of gifts and counter-gifts stored for as long as possible in the family memory in the way that, elsewhere, the exploits of the gods or civilising heroes are collated. Here, despite the dearth of epic brilliance, the interminable genealogical charter and the account of migrations and segmentations assume the function of myth.

This situation is all the more remarkable given that, at that very period, Mary Douglas and Victor Turner were discovering the richness and complexity of the magico-religious thought of other Bantu societies, the Lele and the Ndembu. The society of the Pangolin Men, who control fertility rituals among the Lele, in no way resembles the Hamba brotherhood of the masters of the forest. The latter treat the pangolin (and the leopard) with a ceremonial respect, while the former make this animal the primary symbolic focus for ritual activity that demands a full exercise of classificatory thought (see Chapter 2). Most investigators who have studied the Bantu linguistic zone in central Africa are in agreement in recognising that mythical discourse constituted as such is rare. But today we know that this does not necessarily imply an impoverishment of symbolic thought. Lévi-Strauss has made the timely suggestion that we should describe as 'implicit mythology' this speculative backcloth to which the commentaries and interpretations of the ritualists refer.[8]

I had already been aware of the presence of this latent discourse at the time I

9

was preparing my doctoral thesis on the subject of royal incest in Africa, in particular in the civilisation in the Great Lakes region.[9] I had pursued my investigations by examining the epic accounts relating to the founding of the state bequeathed by the oral traditions of the Luba, the Bemba and the Kuba. As I did so, remarkable symbolic relations between these epics and the body of rituals and beliefs as a whole became apparent. The application of the structuralist method in central Africa which I attempted in *Le roi ivre, ou l'origine de l'Etat* turned out to be fruitful.[10]

At a time when many scholars in France were striving to show that structuralism was a dangerous philosophy — putting the independence of the movers of history at risk in favour of a blind, anonymous system or, on the contrary, threatening the determinism of history seen as the bearer of a meaning — I myself persisted in seeing it as nothing but an innocent method that was extraordinarily effective in the understanding of kinship, myths and rituals. In my view, the structuralist hypothesis did not exhaust the entire anthropological field of investigation nor, *a fortiori*, the sociological one. I did not believe it had any terrorist intentions. Even the historians were becoming interested in it: André Burguière concluded a serious article with the words: 'A little structuralism leads us away from history; more of it leads us back' (*Un peu de structuralisme éloigne de l'histoire; beaucoup de structuralisme y ramène*).[11]

As is well known, this intellectual adventure has made little impact in the Anglo-Saxon circles to which this book is directed. Divergent philosophical traditions have certainly not made scientific relations between the two sides of the Channel — that imposing cultural frontier — any easier. How can we make ourselves understood to one another when there have been so many misunderstandings despite an increasing number of translations? I should like to try to dispel a few of them, at the risk of sometimes displeasing and mindful of all that I owe to the critical, courteous, if sharp, minds of the many colleagues with whom I established friendly relations in the course of two fruitful visits to England: in 1973, at the invitation of the British Academy, and in 1975, as the Simon Visiting Professor at the University of Manchester. I should also like to express my gratitude here to Mary Douglas, Jack Goody and the friendly shade of the great Max Gluckman.

To be honest, I must confess that I do not really understand the preoccupations of those who propose to 'rethink' kinship. All theory appears to be systematically banned — and reviled — by the very heirs to the great school of anthropology which, from Frazer to Meyer Fortes, was bold enough to carry out a number of comparative studies. The fact that these were undertaken from very different points of view could only be stimulating. No doubt Leach was right to tax certain English typologists with having collected into the same boxes butterflies of the same colour under the illusion that they were constructing a natural science of societies. But was the ambition of Radcliffe-Brown (whose advocate, in opposition to his own lineage, I now paradoxically find myself to be) funda-

10

mentally unreasonable? If we abandon his project it should at the very least be replaced with one that is more consistent. I confess that I do not always fully understand the fluctuating theoretical position of Edmund Leach. Nevertheless, the great merit of his masterpiece, *Political Systems of Highland Burma*, is that it calls for a number of different types of readings. I shall, at my own risk, be hazarding a suggestion in the hope of underlining one point in the case of a particular example: namely, the kind of resistance with which an archaic social structure may oppose the historical upheavals that threaten it both from within and from without (Chapter 4). In following this line of argument, I shall naturally not overlook the ever-present possibility of catastrophe. But catastrophe itself, in its turn, calls, as in mathematics, for a new theory and, when all is said and done, historical materialism amounts to no more than an often misleading approximation to one.

The *volte-face* of Needham, who did so much to introduce structuralist thought to Great Britain, perplexes me. The distinction that he has thought it necessary to introduce between matrimonial systems governed by prescriptive marriages on the one hand and by preferential marriages on the other seems to me far from convincing. It is the source of a considerable number of misunderstandings and misinterpretations where the work of Lévi-Strauss is concerned (see Chapter 1). As I proceed, I shall be discussing the unconvincing line of argument developed in that anti-structuralist manifesto, the introduction to *Rethinking Kinship and Marriage.*[12] Generally speaking, the extremely eminent authors collaborating in this work seem to be making an irritated return to traditional empiricism. They also seem to be the more or less willing participants in a communal festival in which the ritual victims finally thrown together in the holocaust are Radcliffe-Brown and Lévi-Strauss. Needham appears to have common sense on his side. 'We should pay first attention to the analysis of particular cases and extract the theoretical lessons progressively from these', he declares.[13] This clearly presents us with a philosophical choice. I would point out, however, that the radical method proposed by Needham recoils against him when he states from a theoretical point of view that marriage with a female patrilateral cross cousin cannot be the basis for any systematisation, despite the fact that the empirical evidence indicates precisely the contrary. I shall be devoting a considerable part of my first chapter to this demonstration, at the same time showing that the various types of patrilateral marriage in the matrilinear societies of central Africa stem quite clearly from a definitely structural framework.

From an epistemological point of view, I for my part doubt whether any theoretical illumination can result from a simple juxtaposition of concrete societies when it has from the start been decided that they are intractable to any organising principle. This is clearly not the way that contemporary physicists and biologists have proceeded. Is the creative imagination required in these fields to become blind and unfruitful where the human sciences are concerned? I will leave to others the task of demonstrating the specious nature of the analysis proposed by F. Korn, who strives to show that the multiplicity of preferential unions among the Iatmul of New Guinea definitively destroys Lévi-Strauss's theory.[14] I shall be concerned, rather, to show that similar alternatives also exist in central Africa and that what needs to be done in such a case is to find the canonical preferential union in relation to which all the other options in the system are organised (see Chapter 1). The fundamental bases of Lévi-Strauss's programme seem to resist all these concerted attacks.

Clearly, the matrimonial systems in which there are many options do not present the quasi-crystalline structure of matrimonial classes where restricted exchange operates, nor the organic flexibility of generalised exchange governed by the sole rule of marriage with the daughter of the maternal uncle. The patri-lateral systems that we shall be examining in the first chapter present a large measure of fluidity even while limited by precise residential constraints. But unfortunately anthropology has not yet discovered any model capable of con-veying the evolution of these systems that are open to change. The false antinomy between prescriptive and preferential marriages could take on a new significance once structuralism is in a position to submit itself to diachronic investigations, just as biology has.

Functionalism tried hard to exorcise the demon of history. But it was not long before it infiltrated anthropology surreptitiously via studies devoted to social change. There followed a demand for an ethno-history that would apply the rigour of textual criticism to oral traditions. Both procedures indubitably had great merits. However, the first stems mainly from a desire to understand the immediate present, while the second has the disadvantage of encapsulating the diachronic development of societies in a new kind of micro-history haunted by chronology. The investigator seldom finds himself in a position to reconstitute the structural changes or even the socio-economic upheavals that have a pro-found effect upon the life of societies. The strategic position of the anthro-pologist faced with this complex task is assuredly infinitely more uncomfortable than that of the historian. The latter explores the 'long periods' (*temps longs*), to borrow Braudel's expression, as do anthropologists defining a 'civilisation' in synchrony as a system of symbolic values and of production and exchange; but the historian is also always alert to the underlying shifts or even disturbances of various kinds by which a more or less durable equilibrium is always threatened. The Annals School has found a way of exploiting to advantage this double view that the anthropologist is, more often than not, denied. On the other hand, the comparative method of structural anthropology offers an advantage of a special kind. Although the question Lévi-Strauss poses may not be of a historical nature, this is not because history itself is rejected. While he may decide quite deliber-ately to isolate the phenomena which he analyses from their context — that is, the spatio-temporal dimension — he does so rather in the manner in which physicists proceed when they create a vacuum in a literal sense; he does so in order to isolate a certain number of recurrent properties that belong to a certain type of socio-economic structure, the type to which we crudely apply the term 'archaic'. It is thus that Lévi-Strauss eventually disengages from the historical context the particular subjects of his own research, that is to say the laws of kinship and of symbolic thought, while at the same time condemning the functionalists for allowing concrete social systems to float in a historical (and no longer experimental) vacuum.[15]

The analytical concept of 'transformation' proposed by Lévi-Strauss can be interpreted in several ways, as was clearly perceived by Jean Pouillon.[16] It may denote the general system of structural constraints that govern a certain type of organisation; Lévi-Strauss's theory of kinship belongs to this general, transhistorical level. But a 'transformation' may equally well be the concrete historical process by which one particular kinship system is converted into another in one particular place. Finally, a number of different historically related forms all belonging to a single structural family may coexist within the same cultural region; in this case the 'system of transformations' is a spatial one, 'like so many dialects in a single ideological language'.[17]

These various interpretations are neither contradictory nor incompatible. The Pende of Zaïre declare categorically that in the old days they used to marry their paternal aunt, not — as they do today — her daughter. It is possible to show that the two preferential marriages are situated within the same structural field, and corresponding converse forms of them can be found among the Amerindians (see Chapter 1). But it so happens that other variants of this structural field are to be found in the neighbourhood of the Pende, in the western region of the 'matrilinear belt' of central Africa. This time a comparative analysis refers us to the cultural history of a vast area. With such a view in mind, Lévi-Strauss in *La pensée sauvage* envisaged an even more ambitious programme of research for Australia. He expressed the hope that 'the day may come when all the available documentation on Australian tribes is transferred to punched cards and with the help of a computer their entire techno-economic, social and religious structure can be shown to be like a vast group of transformations'.[18]

In connection with one particular problem of the anthropology of religion, I have been able to show that structural analysis is capable of illuminating the historical process.[19] A cult of possession, the Kubandwa, suddenly made its appearance in Rwanda and Burundi, probably in the seventeenth century. This is the very period when the mythical hero, Ryangombe, in whose name the rituals are performed, first appears in a dynastic chronicle. The cult extends, in various forms, throughout practically the whole Great Lakes region. The myths and rituals can be divided into two large groups, one relating to the northern region, the other to the southern, and it is possible to show that the chronicle of King Ryangombe peculiar to the Rwanda and the Burundi is related to a whole corpus of legends with a historical purpose, telling of the tragic end of the powerful Chwezi dynasty, believed to have reigned over the Bunyoro and the Ankole. The link between these two mythical corpora can be seen very clearly among the Buhaya where the chronicle describing the disappearance of Wamara, the last Chwezi sovereign, corresponds term for term with the account of the tragic end of the hero Ryangombe. Among the Rwanda, the myth of Ryangombe, which is a transformation of the myth of Wamara, establishes a religious counter-order within the royal order, from which it borrows, and inverts, a number of features. But here a much wider problem arises: the theme of the hunter-king, the founder of a kingdom, either real or imaginary, pervades the whole of Africa. In this respect the chronicle of Ryangombe, the chimerical king who demands a religious initiation for his devotees, can also be deciphered as a more distant transformation of the chronicles of the foundation of the Luba and Lunda kingdoms that I studied in *Le roi ivre*, but this time it is impossible to establish any direct historical link. It would thus appear that huge, coherent symbolical systems from widely flung places correspond with one another, just as Lévi-Strauss established in the case of the Amerindian civilisations. In Africa, the work of collecting these systems has barely begun. The many studies being pursued today in western Africa, prompted in the first instance by Marcel Griaule and Germaine Dieterlen, are revealing increasingly clearly that sophisticated, pre-Islamic symbolical systems are to be found in the entire Mande area for which we have evidence and that, in relation to these, peripheral peoples such as the Minyanka of Mali are currently undergoing a process of transformation which has not yet been fully analysed.[20] As I pursued my own research in the Bantu linguistic zone, I noticed that the magico-religious system of the peoples of the Kongo language stems from a quite different set of problems from that revealed further to the east, among the Kuba, the Luba and the Lunda. On the other hand, it presents a number of remarkable features that connect it with the mythical thought of western Africa.[21] I am wary of jumping to any definite conclusions. However, I am sure that, as increasing numbers of systematic enquiries are undertaken into the systems of thought that are too often neglected by the various schools of sociology, we shall be in a position to produce maps indicating their distribution and that these will throw a new light on the history of African civilisation itself. These zones of distribution will certainly not coincide with linguistic charts, or will seldom do so; nevertheless, a comparison between the two sets of data cannot fail to be stimulating.

Finally, a recent programme of investigation showed me that certain institutions might have a structural history. In *Le roi ivre* I made a start on a symbolic analysis of the rites of circumcision prevalent in the region where the Lunda cultural influence was detectable. I later discovered that an analogous symbolic system had developed in southern Africa among the Sotho, the Tsonga, the Venda etc. Despite the transformations undergone by certain features, the resemblance between the forms taken by the two systems was so striking that for a moment I thought that, despite the geographical and historical distance, the two cultural zones had preserved a common Bantu heritage. However, a rapid survey soon convinced me that collective rites of circumcision were not to be found anywhere else in this precise form. What is more, many Bantu peoples are entirely unfamiliar with even the physical operation. To my great surprise, I then learned, from consulting the nineteenth-century historical information, that a Sotho conqueror called Sebetwane, fleeing from the Zulu invasions, had made a fantastic journey with his people, across Botswana and the Kalahari, to the banks of the Zambezi, where, in 1832, he appeared at the head of a powerful army that overthrew the dynasty then established in Barotseland. A whole body of data suggests that circumcision camps, the fundamental basis of the military education of Sotho youths, were firmly established in the region during the thirty years of the Sotho (Kololo) domination. The institution, associated with a similar symbolic schema, was probably first copied by the Lunda of the south (and in particular by the Ndembu), subsequently spreading rapidly among the Lwena, the Lovale, the Chokwe, the Yaka, the Pende etc. Fortuitously, and against all expectations, the history of the events that actually took place corroborates the conclusions of the structural analysis in which the importance of the latent diachronic dimension is, for once, clear to me.

Economics, politics

Towards 1970, Marxist anthropological thought appeared to be at last stirring from its dogmatic torpor. I conceived the hope that this new line of enquiry would make it possible to conduct a fruitful comparison between the structuralist method and the dialectic of the social classes. After all, Lévi-Strauss himself suggested that a distinction might be made between the 'cold' or 'stationary' history characteristic of a certain number of societies — which he saw as no more than 'a history of symbols and signs' — and 'hot' and 'cumulative' history in which 'caste and class differentiations are pursued relentlessly to generate change and energy'.[22] And conversely, had not Marx himself, as early as 1858, freely suggested a programme for anthropological research? When he defined the tribal or natural community as 'the community of blood, language and customs etc.', he explicitly warned against any attempt to reduce these phenomena, the foundations of social life, to relations of production.[23] He discovered a number of types of problems posed by the archaic State before the appearance of social classes and all the diversity of their historical forms. He was even aware of the existence of a period that was not dialectical, since he describes (although not without a certain disdain characteristic of his time) those 'little communities that lead a vegetative existence, independent of each other'.[24] It is all too easy to push aside this embarrassing text, which resolutely turns its back on the unilinear concept of evolution, by insisting — as does Meillassoux — that it still bears the mark of 'bourgeois ideology'.[25] In doing so, one condemns oneself to

15

the purely scholastic task of cutting up history, now promoted to the status of metaphysics, into arbitrary 'periods' in the face of a certain amount of ethnographic counter-evidence.

The proposal put forward by Godelier is surely more interesting. It is to make an enquiry into the various modes of production characteristic of archaic societies and to consider them as a hierarchy of so many 'networks of structural causality'.[26] However, the end result of his actually applying this method to the Mbuti hunters of central Africa was to subordinate all social and religious life to the constraints of the ecosystem. Now there is no evidence at all to support the idea that the complex exogamy that governs the circulation of women among the Mbuti results from the 'constraint' of the dispersion of groups and the 'constraint' of fluidity which is supposed to affect them by reason of the environment and techniques of trapping with a net. It is apparent that among the Mbuti matrimonial alliance sometimes plays a role that is the opposite of that which Godelier assigns it. Turnbull tells us that a hunter by the name of Cephalus was attempting to attach himself to two other families with whom he had matrimonial links in order to form an autonomous band. Because Cephalus had exchanged sisters with them, these two families could not reject him even though their own group was already sufficiently large. So he set up his camp a little way away from them.[27] Does it not appear that the obligations of hospitality that stem from marriage might disrupt relations of production just as much as they facilitate them?

The circulation of men is, in fact, facilitated by the exogamy practised by the Mbuti, where the son-in-law is prepared to hunt with his father-in-law. But no necessary bond exists between the rules of exogamy and the constraint of production. The former cannot be reduced to the latter. It is perfectly possible for them to operate at different levels. Jacques Monod was well aware of this in the discussion that followed Godelier's talk given at the Colloque of Royaumont.[28] The famous Arapesh aphorism that forbids the eating of one's own mother, one's own sister, one's own pigs and one's own yams and prescribes the consumption of the mother, sister, pigs and yams of others reflects no more than a desire to see men working for one another in a Utopian world which, as we shall see, bears little resemblance to the reality of the domestic mode of production.

There would not seem to be any advantage in presenting kinship as both an infrastructure and a superstructure in order to safeguard historical materialism at any cost.[29] Godelier introduces into the classic functionalist approach a dialectical dimension that still does not manage to seize upon the elusive 'last resort' determinism. I, for my part, have suggested that kinship should be interpreted resolutely as an infrastructure: the means whereby man organises his own reproduction through a symbolic system that promotes the exchange of what are the fundamental objects of value — namely women. In and through exogamy, the human race finds a number of solutions, mediated through the group, to the demands of his own biological nature. This basic link of man with

16

nature cannot be reduced to the process of work except by means of some rhetorical ploy whereby reproduction is reduced to production, as if the symbolic process were negligible.

But what do we mean by production in these primitive hunting or farming societies? It is surely not necessary to burn Marx at the stake — Marx who remains one of the best anthropologists of the capitalist society (although not the only one: Max Weber is also worth reading) — to discover that Marxism was for a long time at fault in its various attempts to fit into its general view of history 'the ancient society that rested on blood links' that was already fascinating Engels (who was smarter than is often thought).[30] The meticulous comparative analyses carried out by Marshall Sahlins currently seem to me most convincing. The arbitrary balance sheets established by international pressures and expressed in ethnocentric dollars have little meaning from an anthropological point of view unless to show that poverty has been introduced more or less everywhere in the Third World, which a systematic economy of exploitation, reaching critical proportions, has turned into a veritably excluded world. The serious imbalance thus introduced into socio-economic structures that were formerly perfectly viable, together with the recent population explosion, are certainly contributory factors in a process of pauperisation that is as enormous as it is absolute, in an increasing number of tragic cases. Nevertheless, this bitter realisation does nothing to invalidate the conclusions put forward by Marshall Sahlins. Among primitive hunters, as among primitive farmers practising slash-and-burn cultivation, a remarkably stable and effective 'domestic mode of production' used to exist. Most often the unit of production was a 'household' based on a division of labour between the two sexes. Its form varied from one society to another, ranging from the nuclear to the extended family and including many different types, patrilocal, matrilocal, polygenous etc. Each household enjoyed autonomous access to the means of production. A number of concrete modes of domestic production are based on this model. At a higher level, various forms of cooperation are liable to appear. 'Certain projects are collectively undertaken by constituted groups such as lineages or village communities', but 'cooperation does not institute a *sui generis* production-structure with its own finality, different from and greater than the livelihood of the several domestic groups and dominant in the production process of the society'.[31] This economic system is centripetal, centring as it does on the needs of the household. But it is also centrifugal, if one considers the dispersal of the units of production and their natural disinclination to increase their productivity beyond a certain limit. This observation certainly also applies to the farmers of the Sudanese savanna where the unit of production and consumption is often a large patriarchal family or even, as among the Minyanka of Mali, a lineage segment devoted to 'an economy of auto-subsistence based on agriculture'.[32] The Minyanka establish a subtle equilibrium between work in the collective family fields and work in the field allotted to each conjugal unit. It would certainly be interesting to make a careful analysis of the various kinds of reasons which prompt so many societies in western Africa to organise work and the redistribution of food on wider community bases, presenting a striking contrast in this respect with most of the traditional peasant societies of central Africa. However that may be, the first systematic analyses undertaken by Sahlins show quite clearly that even in relatively favoured regions work is normally maintained at a lower level of production than would be possible in the particular environment. Sahlins takes up a firm position in opposition to the classic picture of the savage condemned to a pitiless and unceasing struggle for biological survival in a hostile environment that is favoured by contemporary American cultural anthropology.[33] The intensification of subsistence production is alien to the strategy of the domestic mode of production, as Sahlins shows in a number of convincing examples. Where exchanges do take place they are related to 'the simple circulation of merchandise' defined by Marx: 'like peasants, primitive people remain constant in their pursuit of use values, related always to exchange with an interest in consumption, so to produce with an interest in provisioning'.[34] Sahlins naturally excludes from his analysis the first steps towards a market economy that are characteristic of so many African societies. He also makes it clear that the archaic State which remodels production and exchange is hardly relevant to his subject. One of his major themes is precisely that only institutions that are external to the domestic mode of production are capable of disrupting the centrifugal movement which encourages a natural dispersion of households. In accordance with its greater or lesser powers of integration, the kinship system favours spatial concentration, although the economic activity of the household is never totally merged with that of the community thus constituted. Sahlins proceeds to conclude that the many interferences between kinship and the productive unit constitute 'a permanent contradiction of primitive society and economy', the source of tensions more or less disguised and suppressed by the ethic of generalised reciprocity.[35]

Sahlins then ascertains that the political relationships inscribed within kinship are liable to transmit an impulse to production. In many African chiefdoms and throughout Polynesia leadership is a higher form of reciprocity and liberality.[36] It is for this reason that polity generates a domestic surplus. This thesis obviously destroys the Marxist dogma according to which the economic forces would be determinant in archaic societies as well as in our own. Tetela is a perfect illustration of the situation described by Sahlins. The relative hierarchy of lineages according to the order of their ancestors' birth is a purely structural phenomenon devoid of any strictly economic significance. It is a political differentiation in the kinship order (to use one of Sahlins's general statements) that the Tetela introduce within their vast lineage organisation. On this basis, the Tetela have built chiefdoms of varying importance. But neither the elders of the tribal community nor the chiefs of the maximal lineages affirm their authority except by generously distributing food and prestigious goods. Chiefs do not collect agricultural tribute, nor do they impose collective work. Ritual activity, which in other societies implies considerable expenditures, is quasi-non-existent. Here political incitement to produce is at its weakest. Power among the Tetela is an almost judicial affair: it rules on conflicts and never interferes in the realm of domestic production. Great Tetela chiefs do not tally up their profits; on the contrary they pride themselves on the innumerable gifts they distributed during their investiture, the memory of which they carefully maintain.

Let us examine these facts more closely. Within the polygamous family, each household constitutes a unit of production and autonomous consumption, although even here generosity is required *vis-à-vis* close relatives and affines. The intense circulation of rare goods within the marriage circuits is not controlled by the lineages' elders. Lineage affiliation does not even determine the collective ownership of land: it instigates supple, local regroupings, but land is at the free disposal of all the tribe, i.e. a group of lineages. The fragility of the tribal structure, the constant process of fission that undermines it, is assuredly closely linked to the weakness of authority. One can only see in this a deliberate project, analogous *mutatis mutandis* to that of the Amerindian chiefdoms described by Pierre Clastres.[37] However, contrary to the Amazonian Indians, there are few African societies that are not profoundly marked by a familial hierarchy within the lineage. We shall see further on how kingship, far from springing naturally from this kinship order, introduces a radical rupture into it. I deeply regret that Marxist anthropologists, whose work is centred in Africa around the relationships senior—junior, have always limited themselves to a rigid schema that scarcely expresses the totality of concrete historical situations. I do not doubt that there are some places where the elders can be seen as the managers of production and/or of the circulation of women and rare wealth objects. But, at all events, it is somewhat misguided to believe that the advantages that they derive thereby stem from a mode of exploitation analogous to that which characterises class societies.

The question that is posed is rather to discover how — in what particular circumstances — a split appears between one lineage or aristocratic clan and the rest. I shall set out this problem as it concerns the Kachin, taking good care meanwhile not to suggest any general law of evolution. The dominance of the younger lordly lineage and the manipulation of the prestige wealth objects associated with this in the Highlands of Burma can hardly be seen as prefiguring an alleged 'Asiatic' and universal mode of production (see Chapter 4). Kachin society is incommensurable with the social structure of, for example, the Kukuya of central Africa. This was characterised at the end of the colonial period by the opposition and complementarity of, on the one hand, the 'lords of the sky' belonging to the predominantly patrilinear groups and, on the other, the 'lords of the earth', the chiefs of a collection of matrilinear lineages.[38] Bonnafé believes that the double Kukuya aristocracy that dominates the lineage organisation constitutes a 'lordly class' which accumulates prestige wealth for its own profit.

19

But this expression refers to an empirical reality quite different from that envisaged by Marx in his analyses of slave, feudal or capitalist societies. The concept of 'class' runs the risk of becoming a purely formal one — in defiance of the methodological requirements set out by Marx himself — and of becoming a quite vacuous one if it is applied indiscriminately to each and every hierarchical situation obtaining within a lineage order. Bonnafé suggests a better definition when he describes the social organisation of the Kukuya as a 'tributary system'. But in these circumstances it is the political dimension that needs to be studied anew or, to be more precise, the politico-religious dimension superimposed (in both senses of the word) upon a domestic economy. The opposition and the complementarity of the 'lords of the sky' and the 'lords of the earth' are only meaningful within a symbolic system which it would be foolhardy to interpret *a priori* as a superstructure.

Class societies and sacred kingship

The two major steps towards a class society are, without doubt, the introduction of slavery on the one hand, and the development of links of personal dependence on the other. However, as has been shown by the authors of a remarkable collective work devoted to slavery in precolonial Africa (*L'esclavage en Afrique précoloniale*), the first of these two types of alienation encompasses a number of extremely diverse data.[39] Some forms of the alienation of personal status are certainly not incompatible with lineage societies, as several studies in this collection show. I hope I may at this point be allowed to refer once again to my own enquiries. The Tetela 'slaves' were neither prisoners of war nor merchandise bought on the market place (such an institution being quite unknown). Their ancestors somehow placed themselves outside their own lineage. Following some serious misdemeanour, they were given as matrimonial wealth to some figure allied by marriage, but they are always eventually integrated into a new lineage system with the status of a younger brother, though they are deprived of the opportunity to take part in the competition for prestige. The Tetela tried in the long run to disguise such shameful origins. Among the matrilinear Pende, as we shall see, the initial slavery of the bought wife was subsequently converted into a relationship of matrimonial alliance; ultimately this situation was transformed into a fictional kinship relationship: the descendants of the slave ancestor became autonomous and were regarded as the 'grandsons' of the clan that had received them, having earlier been its 'sons' (see p. 74).

In both these cases slavery, far from being in contradiction to the kinship organisation, is absorbed by it. The intrusion of slavery into the domestic mode of production is without any dialectical effect. It is remarkable that a society as complex as the Kuba kingdom should take the form of a vast community of free men anxious to develop agricultural and artisan production for themselves. Vansina has calculated that slave labour represented little more than 6 per cent of the population.[40] Nevertheless, the core of a slave economy does develop around the royal family, as is often the case in societies of this type. But there are many examples to show that the political strategy of the sovereigns of western Africa is quite capable of giving power to the captives of that power, as Marc-Henri Piault neatly puts it, referring to peoples belonging to the Hausa cultural zone.[41]

Besides, it should also be remembered that the great empires of western Africa have for centuries been open to the strong currents of international commerce. Furthermore, everything goes to suggest that the development of domestic slavery in the matrilinear Bantu societies close to the Atlantic coast is directly linked with trafficking, that is to say with pressures from the external world and its devastating economy.

I have elsewhere analysed the complex problems posed by a number of stratified African societies too hastily defined as 'feudal'.[42] I suggested that the feudal phenomenon was, strictly speaking, simply one particular (typically European) historical example of a universal structure founded upon a formal relationship of exchange between two free partners in a hierarchical order: the relationship of clientship. Here the rupture in the lineage order undeniably constitutes the beginnings of a system of authentic social classes. These emerge as the result of unbalanced exchanges initiated or maintained by the network of links of personal dependence between herdsmen and farmers among the Rwanda and the Burundi. The lineage framework has lost its autonomy; it has become integrated into a new structure which itself rests upon the links of clientship that exist within the dominant class. This considerably raises the temperature of the waters of 'cold history'. The exchange structure to which any system of clientship refers in order to mask exploitation is amazingly poor at the level of structural transformation. On the other hand, it presents an extraordinary diversity of contingent historical modalities at the level of social praxis. The appearance of this socio-economic order, which henceforth links production and exchange to subordination, is the concomitant of the origin of the class system in central East Africa, but with its transformation in medieval Europe from the eighth to the eleventh centuries. It should be emphasised that, at the beginning of this period, western society had practically, and with few exceptions, regressed to an economic state of auto-subsistence.

Jack Goody has convincingly shown how difficult it is to reduce the modes of production, destruction and exchange, and likewise the government of complex African societies, to the empirical models of European or Asiatic history.[43] He rightly stresses the extreme diversity of the historical processes that have contributed towards the emergence of centralised governments in Africa. But he also considers — and here I must disagree with him — that the concept of kingship is too vague to serve as a useful basis for comparison; he adds that the adjective 'divine' is of no help to us whatsoever.[44] In my opinion it is rather the concept of the State that is equivocal. On the one hand it refers to western sociological and legal modes that are alien to the African reality; on the other, anthropologists apply it to widely differing political systems whose only common denominator is, in the last analysis, sacred kingship. All the typologies proposed have proved inadequate; they could not fail to be so given that they refer to empirical facts rather than to structural models. On the other hand, the historical variations of sacred kingship allow one to glimpse a symbolical field common to all of them that I have elsewhere attempted to describe from a number of points of view.[45] I should now like to suggest a provisional synthesis.

It is to Frazer that we owe the notable credit for making the first analysis of this politico-religious formula of government that he, quite mistakenly, judged to be representative of an age in which the human race was dominated by magical thought. I have no hesitation in saying that his views, all too often attacked in the name of fragile functionalist interpretations, today more than ever constitute the essential point of departure for any serious re-examination of the question, whatever their shortcomings may be.[46]

My earliest reflections on this theme took shape in the course of my first visit to the Rwanda, in 1949, and during a number of short stays there in 1953 and 1954. Kingship there was still flourishing and powerful. King Mutara IV had been converted to Catholicism and Abbé Kagame was, with his permission, starting to commit to writing, down to the last detail, the impressive secret oral tradition which governed the many ritual activities of the sovereign. This text of the first importance (*Ubwiru*) had not yet been published and commented on at the time when, taking as my starting point the popular traditions of the Rwanda, I set about writing my *Essais sur le symbolisme de l'inceste royal*. The Rwanda kingdom is bicephalous, closely associating the king and his mother — or mother substitute. A whole body of beliefs — that do not, in fact, appear in the esoteric code (the separation and rivalry between the reigning sovereign and his future heir, the ritual killing of the former before his strength declines) — were remarkably reminiscent of an Oedipean schema.[47] Similar features can be found throughout the entire Great Lakes region. I grant that in those days I probably exaggerated the importance of the psychological interpretation. Nevertheless R. Cohen's criticisms on that score, made in the name of an extremely sketchy functionalist interpretation,[48] neglect the essential point, namely the symbolic significance of the royal couple of mother and son and of the incest with a sister that in fact takes place in numerous regions of Africa. Why does sovereignty, which is defined first and foremost by its ritual power, so often lead to the establishment of a counter-order to that of the family, an order which, by denying them, transcends the fundamental ethical principles of lineage society whether these be patrilinear, as in the Rwanda, or matrilinear, as among the Kuba? Jan Vansina has provided important data concerning the latter kingdom that are worth consideration. At his enthronement the Kuba king forgoes all links with the clan. He has sexual relations with a sister and marries a great-niece belonging to the clan. He is assimilated to a dangerous sorcerer and is henceforth considered to be both unclean and also a spirit of nature (*ngesh*). His power is dangerous and yet indispensable to the successful functioning of the universe and of society.[49]

There are many similar examples. They all, in different ways, combine to establish that sacred kingship constitutes an autonomous symbolic structure, founded upon features that are remarkably constant despite a variety of economic, cultural and historical contexts. Alfred Adler, in an illuminating study, has recently stressed the importance of the network of prohibitions that surround the sovereign. He suggests that the killing of the king (the reality of which the functionalist school is mistaken in denying) constitutes the strongest mark of the prohibition that affects the sovereign as a unique being situated at the dangerous junction of nature and culture.[50] As do the incest and the royal sorcery, the prohibitions underline the fact that the basis for the magic sovereignty is a 'reversal' of the original symbolic order, that is to say the rules that govern a lineage society.

The acceptance of sacred kingship, the recognition of the magico-religious power of a unique and transcendent being over nature: here lies the decisive upsetting of archaic society. This change is of no little consequence: it implies the introduction of a tributary economy, it announces the end of the domestic mode of production and sooner or later it installs violence in the heart of the social project.

The novel thesis of Pierre Clastres must be reconsidered here. While presenting Sahlins's work to French readers, he proposed to define archaic society by its original political design, which is to impose on the leader a permanent debt, thus preventing him from transforming his prestige into power. In State societies, on the contrary, people are unceasingly in debt *vis-à-vis* the monarch, for to retain power, to impose tribute, is one and the same thing, and the first act of a despot consists in proclaiming the obligation to pay it.[51] How is such a drastic change possible? Should one, like Sahlins, assume the existence of a historical continuum, a genealogical process between these two radically opposed conceptions of polity? But, Clastres continues, how can one explain that a real power can spring from the quest for prestige undertaken by an ambitious man, whereas in Melanesia this project unfolds within a society that on the whole exploits the work of a minority that surrounds the big-man?[52] Should not one, on the contrary, suppose the existence of a historical hiatus? Clastres calls the 'State' (*l'Etat*) the instrument of this transformation. In my opinion he is on the wrong track. The State, as a coercive apparatus, implies the emergence of a politico-religious institution in a locus extraneous to kinship and liable to break the control of the latter over all social relations. This locus is called king. Sacralisation accompanies the development of power. This is why, long ago, I proposed to incorporate political science within the comparative history of religion, to take account of the birth of empires and the growing fascination exercised on men by the magic of power throughout history, whatever may be the socio-

23

economic formations.[53] But sacred kingship must not be confused with the State; it precedes the State and makes it possible. It is already germinating in a few small clannic societies of Africa, beside politically fully developed forms of the State. I shall ask the reader to refer to the pages I devote to the abortive attempt by the Tundu clan to seize power among the Lele of Kasai (Chapter 2). There is also the most singular case found among certain Pende groups in Zaïre, where the chief after being invested is condemned to wearing a penile sheath (*étui pénien*) that prohibits any sexual relations. It is as if the menace that sacred power puts on the family order, its mode of production, its ethics, must be carefully suppressed. And in fact, the Pende chief shows himself to be outside the cultural order by a worrying propensity to transform himself into a leopard, like the sacred king of the Kuba. In order to ward off this peril, in two Pende chiefdoms depressive drugs are periodically administered to the chief, suppressing any desire and temporarily inducing a torpid state.[54]

There is then a critical threshold where the recognition of a transcendent power, extraneous to society, is accompanied by the denial of the chief's procreative capacity. Now mystical control over fecundity is precisely one of the major characteristics of sacred kingship. Assuredly these facts betray a remarkable will to resist the stranglehold that power has upon the kingship order. A chief in the process of sacralisation finds himself marginalised, a prisoner of interdictions. This situation is in exact opposition to that of the elder of the lineage whose privileged status has nothing to do with sacred kingship, even if he is the preferential intermediary between the dead and the living. It is as if the budding sacred power was perceived as dangerous, in fact cursed, as an autonomous institution, separate from the hierarchical kinship order. This specific aspect remains present when the king, incestuous sorcerer, effectively takes power and finds himself at the head of a State machinery.

Africa constitutes a privileged field for the analysis of the multiple forms taken on by this process. In any royal symbolic structure, polity is indissolubly linked to a new ritual order, of which it constitutes the very foundation.

This ritual order is not affected by the size of the population of the society in which it arises. In this respect there is no common measure between the two million inhabitants in the Rwanda round about 1950 and the 70,000 souls in the Kuba kingdom at the same period or the 25,000 men over whom the Mundang king of Lere reigns at present.[55] There is no correlation between this structure and an unchanging type of status hierarchy nor with any particular existing form of government. In the nineteenth century the Rwanda kingship was totally despotic, and a system of social classes, setting in opposition the Tutsi herdsmen and the Hutu peasants, had become established. On a smaller scale, the Mundung king of Lere, who has at his disposal a formidable cavalry, nevertheless shares his power with those who are masters of the land and who represent the principal clans. Finally, the Kuba kingdom, with its subtle system of councils which control all political decisions can, in a world context, be seen as a

24

model of democracy; here no title was hereditary apart from the royal function itself.

Nevertheless, kingship, when founded on a transcendent basis, always introduces a threat of tyranny. Throughout history tyranny makes its appearance as soon as power has become sacred. Deleuze and Guattari, freely interpreting my analysis of the Great Lakes systems of royalty, have no hesitation in seeing royal incest as the very expression of the 'supercoding (*surcodage*) of the machine of despotism'.[56] In his impressive attack on French kingship in 1792, Saint-Just declared royalty to be an eternal crime and a king to be beyond the pale of nature. He thereby found himself in agreement with universal mythical discourse while reversing the terms it uses. For, strictly speaking, the African kings are outside culture and are directly associated with nature (or with divine transcendence). French society had difficulty in adapting itself to regicide, which, provided we keep a sense of proportion, can be seen as the distant echo of extremely ancient rituals. The revolution gave birth to an emperor who put Europe to fire and to the sword. Since that time new examples of charisma and of the sacralisation of power have deflected plenty of other revolutions from their natural courses, riding roughshod over any general consensus.

The African societies that adjusted to sacred kingship in the Utopian hope of increasing their control over the forces of nature remained, for their part, always dimly conscious of the fact that they were playing with fire.

PART I

Structure and social praxis

1

A defence and illustration of the structures of kinship[1]

On the structural reality of the patrilateral marriage

The theory of kinship developed by Lévi-Strauss has been the subject of so much polemical discussion on the part of so many schools of thought with diverging points of view that an entire work would be necessary to give a full account of the debate. I will limit myself here to raising two questions often debated in Anglo-Saxon circles and taken up, in France, by Dan Sperber. Should a radical distinction be made between prescriptive and preferential unions — and, if so, should one, following Needham, call into question the coherence of *The Elementary Structures of Kinship* and reject some of its models?

I shall attempt to convince the reader that there is no question of doing so and that matrimonial systems founded on a plurality of apparently contradictory preferential marriages can be harmoniously integrated into the general schema constructed by Lévi-Strauss.

Let us first remind ourselves of its fundamental elements. The extraordinary variety of empirical systems of kinship can only be understood by reducing them to a limited number of models. These, taken together, constitute a metasystem (a structure) within which — for reasons that usually escape us — each individual society retains its own individual form. Exogamy is the positive side to the prohibition of incest. It implies the need for an exchange of women, and this exchange is the determining principle for rules of marriage and kinship.

In elementary structures of kinship determined by preferential marriage (with a female relative who is designated by a kinship or class relationship) there are two major aspects to matrimonial exchange. Restricted exchange implicitly or explicitly calls for an even and limited number of exchanging units: between such groups reciprocity is immediate and permanent. In contrast, generalised exchange brings into play at least three exogamous units allied by a theoretically circular relationship, the simplest formula for which is as follows: A provides women for B, which provides women for C, which provides women for A. We should point out that this asymmetrical type, where reciprocity involves an element of risk, was clearly analysed as early as 1935 by the Dutch ethnologist

Van Wouden, who described it as 'the logical expression of systematic matrimonial circulation'.[2]

One of the strengths of Lévi-Strauss's thesis is his discovery that the introduction of a pertinent distinction between the two types of female cross cousins inaugurates generalised exchange. This type of alliance makes its appearance when the object of the preferential marriage is the daughter of the maternal uncle, to the exclusion of the daughter of the father's sister. The converse situation (marriage with the patrilateral cross cousin, to the exclusion of the matrilateral cross cousin) also implies generalised exchange but in a less risky form: the direction taken by the circulation of women between the groups is reversed every other generation so that the exchanges between the partners united by a deferred reciprocity balances out in the short term.

As is well known, Needham criticises Lévi-Strauss for not having distinguished between marriages that are prescriptive and those that are preferential. In his opinion, because of Lévi-Strauss's failure to make this distinction, his theory 'does not make sense'.[3] He suggests that it can only apply to systems that demand that the wife should be taken from one particular category of relations, and not to those that do no more than indicate a preference for such unions. Lévi-Strauss defended himself against this damaging interpretation in his preface to the second edition of *Elementary Structures*: 'Rather, let us own that the notions of prescriptive and preferential marriage are relative: a preferential system is prescriptive when envisaged at the model level; a prescriptive system must be preferential when envisaged on the level of reality, unless it is able to relax its rule to such an extent that, if one persists in preserving its so-called prescriptiveness (instead of paying heed, rightly, to its preferential aspect which is always apparent) it will finally mean nothing . . . The question of how far and in what proportion the members of a given society respect the norm is very interesting, but a different question to that of where this society should properly be placed in a typology. It is sufficient to acknowledge the likelihood that awareness of the rule inflects choices ever so little in the prescribed direction, and that the percentage of conventional marriages is higher than would be the case if marriages were made at random, to be able to recognise what might be called a matrilateral "operator" at work in this society and acting as pilot: certain alliances at least follow the path which it charts out for them, and this suffices to imprint a specific curve in the genealogical space.'[4]

By setting up a radical opposition between prescriptive and preferential marriages Needham not only establishes two artificial formal categories but furthermore makes the second quite unintelligible. On the basis of his arbitrary decision, Needham then goes on to show that patrilateral marriage can only exist in a preferential form: it can never take a truly prescriptive form.[5] So according to him this model does not exist structurally. This position, which Sperber later also adopts,[6] seems to me even more untenable than the earlier one, and I must now examine it further.

30

The principal basis for Needham's thesis is the fact that the female patrilateral cross cousin is necessarily also a matrilateral relation 'in one aspect of her status at least'.[7] So, he goes on to declare, there can be no purely patrilateral system: there are only two kinds of female cross cousins who can be married according to a prescriptive system — the matrilateral cousin and the bilateral cousin. Unfortunately, this is a specious argument. It is indeed true that in a system in which marriage takes place with the daughter of the paternal aunt, she is also the mother's mother's brother's daughter's daughter, as happens in the restricted exchange practised by the Australian Kariera. But this dual status in no way authorises us to deny the structural originality of patrilateral systems.

Let us examine the situation more closely. First let us take a society of Zaïre, the Pende. Their best ethnologist, Léon de Sousberghe, also attacks the structuralist thesis. According to him, the Pende say that there is no difference between the two forms of asymmetrical marriage that Lévi-Strauss believed he had isolated and opposed. De Sousberghe tries to show that 'any patrilateral system that is rigorously applied is bound to be bilateral'.[8] But the problem should be posed quite differently, as I have elsewhere explained.[9] What happens is that, far from being confused with patrilateral marriage, which is always to the fore in the social structure, a matrilateral marriage may sometimes succeed it. In every case the first type of marriage has priority from a structural point of view. De Sousberghe himself writes: 'marriage with the female patrilateral cross cousin remains pre-eminently to be preferred'.[10] Among the Pende of the Kasai, marriage with a classificatory matrilateral female cross cousin only takes place if nothing better is possible, if patrilateral marriage turns out to be impossible. The Pende of the former province of Leopoldville, for their part, tolerate marriage with a true matrilateral female cross cousin more generally, following a patrilateral marriage according to the rules. Whether one interprets this succession of preferential unions in terms of an exchange of male seed between matrilineal clans, as the Pende do, or — conversely — in terms of an exchange of women, it can be seen that the matrilateral marriage repeats the previous alliance in the same direction, whereas the primary system (patrilateral marriage) implies a switch in the direction taken by alliances from one generation to the next. I shall have more to say about this obviously exceptional feature of the Pende system later on.

Sperber acknowledges that this analysis, which I have already published in a more developed form, is an interesting one, but he takes me to task for not having understood the true significance of Needham's distinction between prescriptive marriages and preferential ones. Sperber thinks that, from a cognitive point of view, these unions 'do differ in nature, not just in degree' as I had held, 'since in a prescriptive system the way the alliance is represented is absolutely determined by the system of categories, even when practice no longer conforms with this, whereas in a preferential system the way the union is represented depends upon practice which is not presupposed by the categories. Only in

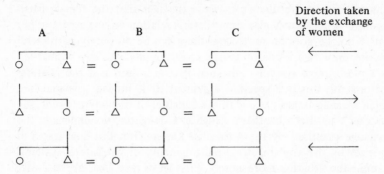

Fig. 1.1a   The classic marriage with a patrilateral female cross cousin

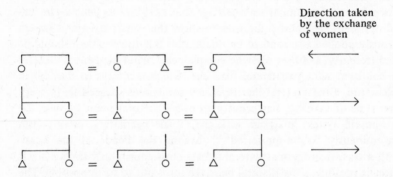

Fig. 1.1b   Marriage with a patrilateral female cross cousin is followed by a marriage with a matrilateral female cross cousin

prescriptive systems does the code of categories reflect an image of the network of alliances. Nobody has demonstrated this with greater force than Lévi-Strauss in *The Elementary Structures of Kinship*, even if, in his preface to the second edition, he ascribes more importance to the structure itself of the networks than to the link between the network and the code.'[11] Following Needham, Sperber thus makes a radical opposition between systems that imply recognition of groups which exchange and those which, through preferential marriages, set up privileged networks of matrimonial relations. I still believe that this is a difference of status that separates stable or rigid structures from structures that are more fluid or even labile. Clearly, the structural characteristic of patrilateral marriage itself — the alternating directions taken by the alliances — rules out the formation of fixed groups of 'receivers' and 'givers'. I shall be demonstrating that it is precisely this that accounts for the elasticity of the historical transformations of this system in central Africa.

However, I must start by saying that my incomprehension of the true nature of so-called prescriptive unions, which, according to Sperber, stems from the fact that I used this term 'in the normal sense rather than the technical one of "obligatory" ', certainly seems to be shared by Lévi-Strauss, who has no hesitation in understanding it in the same way, as can be seen from the passage quoted above. In any event, the doctrine of those who oppose prescriptive and preferential marriages is not firmly established, for Rivière and Carter Lane believe that a preferential system allows a choice between more than one category of relations.[12] This remark nevertheless has the merit of posing a new problem which does not seem to have attracted the attention of investigators. Why do some, particularly labile, matrimonial structures have a much more extensive range of modes than others? Does it, as F. Korn suggests in connection with the Iatmul, mean that the structural theory definitely will not work? This question is central to the new investigations that I here propose to carry out in the African domain.

Let us start by considering the Pende. If, as Sperber believes, the cognitive aspect – that is to say the way in which men think about their practice – is decisive, it is important to ask ourselves whether the kinship terminology is in harmony with the preferential marriage with a patrilateral female cross cousin that is the focus of Pende preoccupations. Let us examine what L. de Sousberghe has to tell us on this subject. The Pende of the Kasai, who rigorously apply patrilateral marriage, make a careful distinction between the two female cross cousins: only the patrilateral cousin is called *gisoni*, not the matrilateral one, whom one can neither marry nor call *gisoni*.[13] Matrilateral cross cousins belong to the category of 'sons' and 'daughters' because the clan of the male *ego* is seen as having 'engendered' them; patrilateral cross cousins, in contrast, are 'fathers', since *ego* has been engendered by their clan. And, as is consistent, *ego* is the 'father-in-law' (*uko* or *mukilo*) of the husband of his matrilateral female cross cousin. Fig. 1.2 illustrates this data.

These relations of paternity and descent between clans are naturally reversed in the following generation, and the Pende do not seem to be at all bothered by this alternation which, from a general theoretical point of view, embarrasses

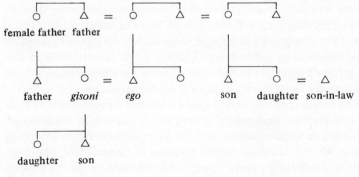

Fig. 1.2

Needham so much. One of his arguments against the existence of the patrilateral system is, in effect, that it would be impossible for it to preserve the terminological unity of the lineages involved.[14] The Pende are not unaware of the problem. Supposing *ego* not to have married his patrilateral female cross cousin, a particularly thorny problem clearly arises. On the question of his relations with the children of this potential wife (*gisoni*), one of de Sousberghe's informants said: 'When I turn my thoughts to the fact that I have played with their mother (in a joking relationship), they are my children but when I turn my thoughts to the fact that their *lemba* (maternal great-uncle) engendered me, I am their child.'[15] In order to resolve this equivocal situation it is customary to come down in favour of the first alternative; in this way the systematic alternation of relations of paternity and descent between the clans is preserved. The declaration that all members of the paternal clan can be called 'fathers' must therefore be regarded with some reservation. It is precisely this theoretical possibility (which would introduce a Crow-type terminology) that the informant mentioned above was considering and rejecting.

It is therefore clear that there does exist, among the Pende, a privileged matrimonial formula with which the terminology conforms: I shall henceforth use the term 'canonical' to describe this, in order to avoid the ambiguities of the term 'preferential'. This model expresses the alliance in the language of kinship: it assimilates the patrilateral female cross cousin, the ideal wife, to a female 'father' and the matrilateral female cross cousin, theoretically prohibited as a wife, to a 'daughter'.

If systematic marriage with the daughter of the paternal aunt happens in fact among the Pende, it is because it is empirically possible. Now, taking up Needham's line of argument, Dan Sperber on the contrary was of the completely arbitrary opinion that such could not be the case, since the inversion in the direction taken by alliances in each generation (see Fig. 1.1) 'would imply that a group A should at one and the same time both dominate a group B and be dominated by it'.[16] The fact is that the Pende are in no way concerned by this apparent contradiction for the very good reason that asymmetry in alliance relationships in no way implies any notion of inferiority or superiority. One can even go so far as to say that the patrilateral system tends to annul all hierarchical relationships between the groups in alliance, whereas hypogamy or hypergamy often takes over matrilateral systems (see Chapter 4). It is noticeable in this respect that in certain Pende groups marriage with the female matrilateral cross cousin associates master lineages with lineages of servile origin (see p. 40).

The appearance of marriage with the female matrilateral cross cousin in Pende society poses a new problem that cannot be avoided. The canonical terminology, the broad lines of which we have just recapitulated, applies as much to the Pende of the Kasai as to the Pende of the former province of Leopoldville. However, the latter allow that, following a correct patrilateral marriage, in the third generation the uterine nephew of *ego* may ask his uncle for a daughter in marriage.[17]

Several groups in this way allow a man to marry a cross cousin who is in the position of daughter (not 'female father'), whereas such a union remains strictly forbidden among the Pende of the Kasai. They insist that matrimonial practice should conform strictly with the terminological code, and only in exceptional circumstances do they allow a marriage with a matrilateral classificatory cross cousin: 'if the father cannot find a wife for his son within his clan, the latter will seek help from his maternal grandfather (*khaga wabutile gin'enji*: the grandfather who engendered his mother), asking him to find a wife for him from within his clan'.[18]

This occasional disagreement between the rigour of the canonical terminology and matrimonial practice deserves further examination, for it masks a new structural problem. We must introduce into the discussion a third type of preferential union: the right over his granddaughter that the Pende of the former province of Leopoldville – and they alone – give the grandfather.[19]

Grandparents and grandchildren use the term *mbai*, comrade, as a term of familiarity, when they are of the same sex.[20] The grandson enjoys a joking relationship with his grandfather (apparently with both his mother's father and his father's father). Furthermore, the Pende of the former province of Leopoldville, although not those of the Kasai, allow marriages between grandfather and granddaughter. To the extent that lineage endogamy is respected – and, as we shall see, it is not always – this matrimonial privilege can only concern the daughter's daughter. It is, in fact, immediately apparent from Fig. 1.3 that the son's daughter (*d*) belongs to the same matri-segment as the paternal grandfather (*ego*), who is also the maternal great-uncle, if marriage with the patrilateral cross cousin has been correctly applied.

L. de Sousberghe made a particularly careful study of the union between the grandfather and the granddaughter in the Moshinga chiefdom; there is no doubt that in this case it is specifically a matter of a privilege over the daughter's daughter (*c*). To understand the structural significance here, we must take into account the body of rules which accompany it. They are illustrated by Fig. 1.3.

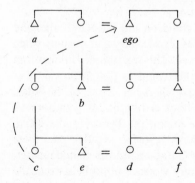

Fig. 1.3

After a first — canonical — marriage with the patrilateral cross cousin, thanks to which the son (*b*) 'returns the face' of his father to the latter's clan, the grandson (*e*) marries a woman (*d*) in the same group as his maternal uncle. As the Pende themselves say, 'the grandson returns to the *jigo* (lineage) of his (maternal) grandfathers to marry a girl'. The grandfather (*ego*), for his part, 'follows his granddaughter, his seed', and marries her.

So what conclusions may we draw?

The secondary union of the maternal grandfather (*ego*) with his daughter's daughter (*c*) is intimately connected with the primary marriage of the grandson (*e*) with his matrilateral cross cousin (*d*). Marriage with the maternal uncle's daughter, which always occurs in the third generation, in fact masks a reciprocal exchange between the maternal grandfather and his daughter's son: (*e*) gives his sister (*c*) to *ego*, from whom he then has the right to expect a great-niece (*d*). The development of the possibility of matrilateral marriage, far from being an aberration in the system or the result of some strange laxity, becomes under these conditions a necessity: the marriage with the daughter of the maternal uncle brings the cycle of alliances between the two lineages involved full circle through a pure and simple direct exchange, effected between alternate generations. The maternal grandfather's right to 'follow his seed' and marry his daughter's daughter is integrally linked with his obligation towards his daughter's son.

It is remarkable that the Pende of the Kasai, who rigorously practise marriage with the patrilateral female cross cousin, forbidding marriage with the matrilateral cross cousin, also forbid union with the granddaughter.[21] Here is *a contrario* proof of the essential association between the two non-canonical preferential unions. However, even among these purists of patrilateral marriage, a man who cannot find a patrilateral cross cousin may still turn to his maternal grandfather. We do not know whether the Pende of the Kasai, like the Pende of the former province of Leopoldville, used in the old days to combine this upsetting of the canonical patrilateral rule with the preferential union of the grandfather with his granddaughter. It should, however, be noted that, at all events, the former has a joking relationship with the latter and calls her 'wife'.[22]

The joking relations that exist between the grandson and the grandfather and that place them in the position of potential allies reveal significant nuances when the two regions under consideration are compared. This relationship implies that the grandson has the right to commit small thefts and to play practical jokes which sometimes take on a positively aggressive character. Thus, in the Ndala chiefdom, the grandson can with impunity shoot arrows at his grandfather's buttocks.[23] Now such behaviour is forbidden among the Pende of the Kasai, who allow only 'innocent teasing and little jokes'.[24] When we reflect that these same groups forbid any unions between the grandfather and the granddaughter, we cannot help but conclude that through the very violence of his behaviour, the grandson is expressing his claim for a wife in the face of the systematic right that the maternal grandfather assumes to claim his granddaughter for himself. This privilege wrongs first and foremost the son's son (*f* in Fig. 1.3), who should have received *c* if the marriage with the patrilateral cross cousin had been correctly applied. As we have seen, in the case of the daughter's son, this seizing of a wife is, on the contrary, directly compensated for, since the grandfather gives him a great-niece. We shall see later that the Lele of the Kasai, who base their matrimonial system on the maternal grandfather's right over his daughter's daughter, resolve the problem quite differently: *ego* cedes his right over *c* to his great-nephew *f*, and this inaugurates an original form of generalised exchange in which the same lineages intermarry every other generation. But this solution implies the prohibition of any marriage between cross cousins of the first generation (see pp. 96–9).

Let us return to the Pende problem. L. de Sousberghe does not make it clear whether the difference in status between the son's son and the daughter's son, which I have just described, is expressed by slight differences in their behaviour. Nor does he make it clear how *f* will marry when all the preferential formulae described have been brought into play. We can only suppose that he too will turn to his maternal grandfather, that he will marry the daughter of his maternal uncle and that in the third generation the whole chain of alliances will thus move in the same direction as in the preceding generation, thereby setting up a generalised exchange which, if de Sousberghe is right, could well come to dominate the matrimonial chain in several regions of the Pende area. Paradoxically then, the direct reciprocity effected in the former province of Leopoldville through the exchange between the grandfather and the grandson contains the possibility of a radical transformation in the canonical system constructed on the basis of the ideological primacy of patrilateral marriage.

The systematic practice of marriage with the daughter's daughter and that of marriage with the maternal uncle's daughter which is associated with it among the Pende of the former province of Leopoldville is certainly a source of tensions. We have only to introduce a third lineage into Fig. 1.3 for this to emerge clearly.

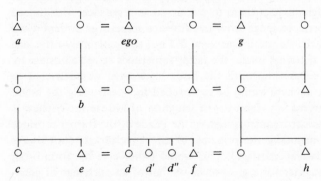

Fig. 1.3 (extended version)

The right that g, for his part, has over his granddaughter d is in danger of coming into conflict with the right that e can claim over the same woman; this contradiction can only be resolved harmoniously provided that a sister (d') to d is available. At all events, the maternal grandparents can be seen as seizers of women, since they are twice takers of wives from the same lineage. Furthermore, these practices are opposed to any repetition of canonical marriage with the patrilateral cross cousin in the third generation, namely for e, f, and h. For h to be able to marry in accordance with this rule, for example, a third woman (d'') would have to be available. Even supposing that such was the case, h and f would then purely and simply be exchanging sisters. Now there is no evidence at all for this practice among the Pende. Besides, it would not be compatible with the spirit of the system.

We must conclude then that the Pende of the former province of Leopoldville construct extremely short circuits of exchange, limited to three generations. This closed system can only open out into generalised exchange or strictly maintain the canonical rule of marriage with a patrilateral cross cousin by excluding all secondary rights of the maternal grandfather over his granddaughter. This is the firm choice made by the Pende of the Kasai, who simultaneously and for reasons that are now clear forbid marriage with a matrilateral female cross cousin.

The system becomes even more complicated in the Moshinga chiefdom. Here, to adopt de Sousberghe's expression, it seems to be governed by 'the grandfather's arbitrary power over his descent, among whom he chooses wives as he pleases, with no clearly defined rule of preference'.[25] Let us examine the situation more closely, clearly distinguishing between the different types of cases.

1. A patriarch can claim for himself the daughter of a uterine nephew. Thus, in Fig. 1.3, a claims d or one of her sisters. This situation obviously leads to another form of direct reciprocity. It will not be forgotten that *ego*, a's brother-in-law, can always claim c on the grounds that she is his daughter's daughter. But then all a and *ego* are doing is exchanging their respective great-nieces. The danger of this solution is clearly that it may once again wrong the generation of e and f etc. So we might expect them to put up some resistance. This indeed seems to be what happens, to judge from the violence sometimes evident when such rights are claimed. If the uterine nephew did not spontaneously offer one of his daughters to his maternal uncle, the latter sometimes seized a hostage by force and would not release him until the bride he wanted was delivered to him.[26] The recalcitrant nephew would be reproached for 'destroying the house of the seed'.[27] At all events, a's claim to the daughter of his uterine nephew is not an aberration in the matrimonial system of the Pende of the former province of Leopoldville, which maintains the principle of direct reciprocity (but always after a canonical patrilateral marriage). This would either take the form of an exchange of a granddaughter for a great-niece or that of an exchange of great-nieces.

2. In the same Moshinga chiefdom any man may also lay claim – if necessary by force – to 'the female descendants of his sons'.[28] In the Kianza chiefdom, the union of a man with his son's daughter appears to be 'perfectly legitimate'.[29] We have already pointed out that this union is strictly speaking incestuous if the canonical marriage with a female patrilateral cross cousin has been applied. De Sousberghe does not appear to notice that the formula of the command adopted by the grandfather 'to insist that his descendants should give him one of his granddaughters' really only applies, *stricto sensu*, to the daughters of his daughters: 'I am your grandfather who engendered your mothers, I am the pouch of eggs from which all the caterpillars emerged. Now give me another granddaughter so that I can marry her and engender from her other children, just as I engendered your mothers.'[30] It is hard to see how such a formula could legitimately be applied to the daughter of sons. This time the violence with which the ideology is enforced is patent. Furthermore, it is particularly in a case such as this that a grandfather may be seen to resort to the practice of seizing a hostage, usually a close relative of the desired woman, to get what he wants, whereas to obtain the daughter of a uterine nephew in marriage (case 1), he usually needs to do no more than send a messenger to him.[31] We should note, in this connection, that a neighbouring people, the Mbum, systematically favour marriage with the daughter's daughter, denying the same value to union with the son's daughter, while apparently not going so far as to forbid it.[32]

The enigma of marriage with the son's daughter is illuminated if we consider that this granddaughter is also, by virtue of the canonical patrilateral marriage, the sister's daughter's daughter. L. de Sousberghe notes that certain chiefdoms of the former province of Leopoldville allow union with this great-niece despite the fact that it is in violation of the principle of lineage exogamy.[33] Now this marriage is simply a variant of the incestuous union with the daughter of a sister that most of the Pende regard with horror because it is connected with sorcery. Nevertheless, a certain Mayamvuna, an orator of renown, had married a sister's daughter, as had his father and grandfather before him.[34] Now we can put our finger on the explanation. Intellectual gifts, like magical powers, are transmitted from father to son.[35] By systematically marrying their sister's daughter, men of great talent, braving all accusations of sorcery, transmit their exceptional psychic gifts patrilineally even within their matrilineal lineage, since their son also happens to be their great-nephew. The paternal grandfather's claim over his granddaughter, that is to say over his sister's daughter's daughter, is simply a more easily tolerated transformation of this union characterised as incestuous. They both constitute a threat to the matrilineal system. As we shall see later on, union with a sister's daughter can only become canonical in a patrilineal society (see p. 44). Among the Pende, the incestuous nature of this marriage deliberately places it on the periphery of the social organisation. The union with a great-niece or a granddaughter that derives from it must be seen as a violent act brought off by a powerful and feared grandfather. As such, it does not account for the formula of canonical marriage with a patrilateral cross cousin, as, once again rashly, L. de Sousberghe suggests.

The conclusion that can be drawn from this body of data is that, among the Pende of the former province of Leopoldville, three preferential marriages are privileged structurally and should be placed in diachronic order: patrilateral marriage, the keystone of the entire construction, effects an exchange of sisters over two generations, between two clans; then, according to rules clearly described by de Sousberghe (which we have examined in detail), there follow two marriages which set up a direct reciprocity between alternate generations: union of the maternal grandfather with his daughter's daughter is matched by marriage of his grandson with a matrilateral cross cousin which, in these circumstances, is allowed. But marriage with a daughter's daughter may also be compensated for by marriage with the daughter of a uterine nephew.

So it seems as though the cycle of alliances unfolds over three generations, alternate generations being identified. But far from marriage in the third generation reproducing marriage in the first (as is the case with the Pende of the Kasai, who, accidents excepted, strictly apply marriage with the patrilateral cross cousin), the Pende of the former province of Leopoldville seem to strive to annul the debts by any means, through direct exchanges between alternate generations.

What happens in the fourth generation? Unfortunately, de Sousberghe provides no answers to this question. However, we have seen that a short cycle usually ends in a series of marriages with a matrilateral cross cousin, the sequence of which reproduces the circulation of women as it took place in the preceding generations (see Fig. 1.1b), rather than reversing it (Fig. 1.1a). This model only has to be repeated a third time for the entire system to swing to generalised exchange, that is to say a model in which clan A constantly gives its sisters to clan B, while clan B gives its sisters to clan C and so on. Such a development appears to be emerging in certain regions of the Pende area, according to de Sousberghe. However, his meticulous analyses provide no evidence for this. The fact is that, both according to the terminology and in matrimonial practice, marriage with the daughter of a paternal aunt appears, either on its own or in combination with other forms, as the canonical form to which priority is given.

In a more recent publication (1963), L. de Sousberghe suggests a new hypothesis: that the development of marriage with a matrilateral female cross cousin might, in some regions, have accompanied a spread of domestic slavery. The clan segment that is the issue of the woman purchased from far away is in a permanent relationship of filial dependence with respect to the purchasing clan; the former is obliged to provide a wife for the latter in each generation.[36] Alternating reciprocity, which characterises patrilateral marriage, is clearly incompatible with this hierarchisation of matrimonial exchange where givers of women are inferior to their partners. But if marriage with the daughter of the maternal uncle is frequently the mark of the servile origin of the line, which remains fixed in a position of 'sons' in relation to a line of 'fathers', then clearly this preferential

40

marriage cannot be placed on the same footing as canonical union with the daughter of a paternal aunt, real or classificatory.[37] Eventually this link of vassaldom is weakened when the servile line multiplies and prospers. Its members are then regarded as 'grandsons'.

There is evidence that, from every point of view, marriage with a matrilateral female cross cousin occupies a special position among the Pende. For the most part it concerns women of inferior status who enter into hypergamous marriage. As such it is impossible for it to become general throughout the society, so it was to be expected that L. de Sousberghe would not discover chains of matrimonial alliance that are characteristic of generalised exchange. It is clear that men from the servile lineage cannot in their turn marry into an inferior line whose masters they would thereby become. But the fact is that we know nothing about their matrimonial status.

The daughter of a free man can also, but this time with the agreement of her maternal uncles, remain in her father's village, 'there giving birth to a house which continues to bear the name of the maternal clan but which recognises that from the point of view of its locality it is a vassal of the fathers' clan'.[38] We do not, however, know if this dependent line is permanently linked with a line of 'fathers' through matrilateral marriage, in the same way as lines that are the issue of a slave woman. It nevertheless seems reasonable to suppose that this phenomenon, together with slavery, of which it appears to be a faithful reflection, contributes towards the 'process of disintegration which tends to encourage the disappearance of union with a patrilateral female cross cousin, or at least makes this much more common' in some regions of the Pende area.[39] But L. de Sousberghe admits that he has only incomplete or confused data on this subject.

Patrilateral marriage and its group of transformations

The fundamental structural problem posed by societies in which several rules of preferential marriage coexist seems to me to lie in the hierarchical order that is the context for their concrete emergence. We shall shortly be returning to this subject in connection with another society of Zaïre in which the empirical facts seem even more complicated: the Yombe. In both cases, patrilateral marriage is the basis for the social construction. First, however, I shall be attempting to place the classic marriage with a patrilateral cross cousin within a group of transformations. For once history comes to the aid of logic, since the Pende of the Kasai declare that their present matrimonial system is derived from a more ancient form, marriage with a paternal aunt. They also think that their strict fidelity to marriage with the daughter of a paternal aunt conforms with the ancestral custom of patrilateral union with the father's sister.[40]

According to corroboratory evidence collected by de Sousberghe, the Pende used to marry their father's sister.[41] If we reconstruct this ancient model, which was abolished in favour of marriage with the daughter of a paternal aunt, we notice that it implies a direct exchange of women, limited to two lines, each of which alternately, every other generation, finds itself in the position of either giver or receiver.

It is easy to see that this oblique patrilateral marriage can be combined perfectly well with matrilateral marriage: *2* is for *1* both a paternal aunt and a daughter of a maternal uncle. The same applies to *4* for *3*, *6* for *5* and *8* for *7*. A bilateral system as closed as this is hardly viable, so it is understandable that the Pende had to widen the network of alliances by adopting marriage with the daughter of the paternal aunt. The formula of marriage with a paternal aunt was probably never an exclusive one.

Fig. 1.3a demonstrates something else too. It looks as if a patrilineal line links together the two matrilineal lines which are the partners in the exchange. I shall have more to say about the spiritual links which continue to unite men, from father to son, in present-day Pende society (see p. 65). The entire ideology of marriage with a patrilateral female cross cousin can be related to the need to make the father's face live once again in his clan. For the moment I shall limit myself to pointing out that a patrilineal line firmly ties matrilineal clans together in pairs in the present-day canonical Pende system (Fig. 1.1a), just as it used to intertwine the two matrilineal lines that sufficed for matrimonial exchange in the days when the Pende practised marriage with a paternal aunt. Before carrying the analysis any further we must broaden the field of investigation concerning patrilateral marriage.

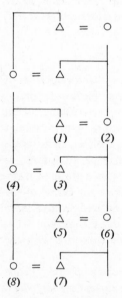

Fig. 1.3a Theoretical model of marriage with the father's sister

42

It is worth making a comparison between on the one hand oblique patrilateral marriage which, even within living memory, was the point of departure for the Pende system and, on the other, a form which is its strict symmetrical converse: marriage with a sister's daughter.

It is clear that the old preferential marriage with a paternal aunt could develop among the Pende only in a matrilineal society. In a patrilineal system marriage with the father's sister would be incestuous. On the other hand, the converse oblique form is only compatible with a patrilineal system: in a matrilineal system a sister's daughter would be an incestuous wife. I have already discussed this problem (see p. 39).

In *The Elementary Structures of Kinship*, Lévi-Strauss quickly deals with this problem. He writes: 'There exists, in fact, a still more simple structure of reciprocity than that found between two cross cousins, viz. that which results from the claim that a man who has given his sister can make on the sister's daughter.'[42] Jean Carter Lane must take the credit for being the first to distinguish clearly the theoretical model that follows from a systematic application of marriage with a sister's daughter.[43] Peter Rivière, for his part, accepts the general validity of the model suggested by Carter Lane, but questions the 'empirical probability' of such a system.[44] On the basis of his profound knowledge of an Amazonian tribe, the Trio, he points out that marriage with a sister's daughter is only one of a number of preferential unions and that the society as a whole would not be able to conform with the ideal schema that we reproduce in Fig. 1.4. Let us consider this extremely interesting debate. We shall begin by continuing the theoretical analysis started by Carter Lane and Rivière, showing that the models that can be constructed starting with, on the one hand, marriage with the father's sister and, on the other, marriage with a sister's daughter stem from the same set of circumstances.

On comparing this structure with that given by marriage with the father's sister (Fig. 1.3a), it becomes clear that it constitutes a mirror image of the latter, with the sexes reversed. In both cases an oblique patrilateral marriage (with a woman belonging to the previous or following generation) produces an original form of restricted alternating exchange: the circulation of women between these two lines is in effect reversed every generation. The expression 'oblique discontinuous exchange' that Rivière applies to marriage with a sister's daughter can be applied equally well to marriage with the father's sister. Furthermore, in both cases the oblique preferential wife is confused with the matrilateral female cross cousin. We have already verified this in Fig. 1.3a as applied to Pende society in the past. When we consult Fig. 1.4, we notice an analogous situation: by marrying b, the sister's daughter, a is also marrying his maternal uncle's daughter; the same goes for c with regard to d and for e with regard to f. This bilateral marriage introduces a direct exchange between two patrilineal lines, just as marriage with the father's sister introduces a direct exchange between two matrilineal lines in the old Pende system.

43

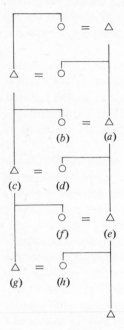

Fig. 1.4   Theoretical schema of marriage with a sister's daughter
(after Rivière, 1966b)

A simplified form of each of these two models (Figs. 1.5 and 1.6) reveals a new underlying structural fact. The arrows indicate the preferential marriages. In both cases we are presented with exchanges of sisters between consecutive generations. Marriage with the father's sister, which accompanies a matrilineal system, is related to an implicit patrilineal axis, and conversely marriage with a sister's daughter, which implies a patrilineal system, is developed on a matrilineal axis.

It seems that, in the first case, the men constitute a patrilineal line while the women who are exchanged are distributed into two matrilineal lines, one to the right, the other to the left of this central vertical axis: these matrilineal lines are indicated by dotted lines in Fig. 1.5. In the second case, the women appear to constitute a central matrilineal line and the men who exchange them seem to be distributed along two adjacent patrilineal lines (indicated by dotted lines in Fig. 1.6). Thus what can be detected beneath the surface is an exceptional formula of sex affiliation.

Now let us see to what extent the hypothesis can be applied in the Trio society, which practises oblique patrilateral marriage with a sister's daughter. Rivière, who has provided a masterly description of this Amerindian society, sets us on our guard: the theoretical model of Fig. 1.4 is far from being strictly

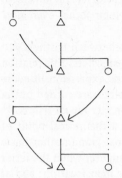

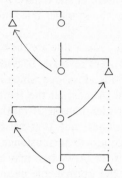

Fig. 1.5   Marriage with the
father's sister

Fig. 1.6   Marriage with the
sister's daughter

applicable to the extremely diversified matrimonial system of the Trio.[45] He starts by questioning the patrilineal character of their system of descent. But one is mindful of Lévi-Strauss's warning: 'The marriage privilege of the mother's brother over the sister's daughter is conceivable only in a regime of patrilineal descent *or in a regime which does not yet admit of systematic descent.*'[46] The second alternative clearly corresponds more closely with the Trio situation. Nevertheless, as we shall see, Rivière's own analysis suggests that, latently, there exist two patrilineal exchanging lines distributed on either side of a matrilineal axis, as is suggested by Fig. 1.6.

Rivière tells us that the concept of unilinearity in the strict sense of the term is absent from the Trio representations.[47] The ideology of the transmission of the soul (*amore*) and body down a patrilineal line is not adhered to by all informants.[48] Some claim that the child's soul comes from both the father and the mother, while others say that a boy possesses the soul of his father and a girl that of her mother. The latter belief clearly illustrates the thesis of sex affiliation suggested by our theoretical study. Not everyone, however, is aware of it. Rivière writes that most of the Trio are unconcerned with the problem.[49] Neither the kinship terminology nor the system of attitudes allows us clearly to distinguish two distinct patrilineal lines. All the same, there are a number of significant nuances. The term *itipime*, which in essence designates membership of a group of descent, is applied to a man's own children and to those of his brother but it is not so clear that it also applies to the children of his sister.[50] The concept of *itipime* must nevertheless be understood to be relative. A sister's children will be considered *itipime* as compared with those of a person not related at all.[51]

To be sure, it is impossible to make a radical opposition between the relationship between, on the one hand, father and son and, on the other, maternal uncle and nephew; both are characterised by a certain reserve. However, the link with a father is clearly the stronger one, since sons hunt with their father even after they are married.[52]

Certainly more remarkable are the extremely close links between mothers and daughters that Rivière reveals: 'Together with that between sisters, this relation is the most obvious close one, since it receives continuous expression in economic cooperation. Almost all the female subsistence activities are carried out in working parties which consist of mother and daughters or a group of sisters.'[53] The pivotal matrilineal line that we have detected from a theoretical point of view seems to acquire some substance in fact. The maternal grandmother has a place in this picture: 'A woman may substitute for her daughter when the latter is unable to fill her normal role because of pregnancy or menstruation; and as she becomes older the grandmother will take on the duty of minding the grandchildren while the mother is working.'[54] It should be added that marriage is normally matrilocal.[55]

Rivière himself arrives at the following conclusion: the opposition between men and women is fundamental in Trio society: 'Unisexual relations are characterised by cooperation and differentiated by an inequality based on age difference, although the former is more obvious among women and the latter among men.'[56] Rivière also notes: 'the father–daughter and mother–son relationships suffer from the double restraint of different sex and generation'.[57]

So it does seem that the hypothesis of a double dichotomy based on sex affiliation is not simply an intellectual theory. In view of this it is easier to understand Rivière's hesitation faced with a society where the patrilineal principle manifestly does not suffice to account for the extremely complex data.

We must now consider Rivière's major question: the theoretical model represented by Fig. 1.4 cannot be applied to the Trio, since they also allow marriage with a patrilateral female cross cousin, which ought theoretically to be prohibited. He notes, however, that the kinship terminology is strictly in conformity with marriage with a sister's daughter. Indeed, we find the following equations: the mother's brother (MB) = the father's sister's son (FZS); the mother (M) = the father's sister's daughter (FZD); the mother's brother's son (MBS) = the sister's son (ZS).[58] All these equations can easily be checked in Fig. 1.4.

As in the case of the Pende, I shall use the term 'canonical' for the preferential marriage which clearly holds first place in the structural hierarchy suggested by the kinship terminology. This is, of course, marriage with a sister's daughter who is also the daughter of a maternal uncle. But how are we to account for the apparent contradiction between the existence of this canonical marriage and the frequent practice of marriage with a patrilateral female cross cousin referred to as 'mother'?

One important fact becomes immediately clear. The canonical marriage always takes place with the daughter of an elder sister (*wei*); the daughter of a younger sister (*akemi*) is theoretically forbidden. On the other hand, there is no reserve in the relationship with the daughter of a *wei*.[59] The kinship terminology reflects this important nuance, since the wife of a maternal uncle, who is canonically *ego*'s sister, is in fact referred to as *wei*, elder sister.[60]

This rule, all the consequences of which are not drawn by Rivière, immediately suggests that only elder sisters and their daughters have a place in Fig. 1.4 and that the marriages of younger sisters and of their daughters follow different channels. Rivière shows clearly that most of these marginal marriages (which are nevertheless statistically the most numerous) take place, depending on contingencies, according to one or another form of direct exchange: 'a man can give in marriage either a daughter or a sister, or even a sister's daughter, and receives back a woman related in any of these ways to the recipient', the authority of the adult men over the young women being extremely diffuse.[61] Rivière immediately goes on to say: 'For the Trio, the important thing is the replacement of a sister who has been lost, and there is a definite obligation on the husband to do this.' In a brief but penetrating analysis Lévi-Strauss some time ago suggested the possibility that marriage with a sister's daughter and likewise the exchange of sisters are combined with other forms of direct exchange, 'a man not being restricted to only one daughter or to only one sister, but being able to have several of them with nothing to prevent them from being exchanged according to different modalities'.[62]

The limitation of the canonical marriage to the daughter of the elder sister in fact opens up other types of direct exchange among the Trio, and so it is no surprise that in this series the incidence of bilateral marriage with one or other cross cousin is very high. In the order of the expressed preferences, a man will marry either the daughter of a paternal aunt or the daughter of a maternal uncle, with, Rivière notes, a possible slight bias towards the first of these two options.[63] Only some of the informants went on to say that a man should marry the daughter of an elder sister (*wei*).[64] In reality, marriage between cross cousins is the most popular matrimonial form.[65] However, the female patrilateral cross cousins are called 'mothers' (*imama*) in conformity with the canonical marriage, which implies that the mother and the mother's sisters (who are clearly forbidden) fall into this class. Rivière admits it freely: 'this usage derives from the practice of marriage with the sister's daughter, and is a logical adaptation of the relationship terminology to it'.[66]

There is no intrinsic contradiction between marriage with a sister's daughter and marriage with a patrilateral cross cousin, as Lévi-Strauss showed clearly in the case of the Korava of southern India. A man generally claims his sister's daughter for his son. 'In this tribe, as in a number of other tribes in southern India, a man has the option of marrying his niece, always provided that she is the daughter of his *elder* sister; the daughter of his *younger* sister he may not take to wife.'[67] Lévi-Strauss also notes that this preference for the niece sometimes takes precedence over that for the cross cousin. He emphasises one fact upon which we shall be insisting throughout this study: in several groups in this region the various types of marriage can be seen to follow an order of preference: first, the elder sister's daughter; only then the patrilateral cross cousin, and in her absence the matrilateral cross cousin; finally, and in the absence of the first three types, the younger sister's daughter. He concludes that there is no doubt that in India as in South America marriages between cross cousins and marriages between uncles and nieces 'are closely associated'.[68]

The essential characteristics enumerated by Lévi-Strauss are to be found among the Trio: the structural predominance of marriage with the daughter of an elder sister is attested by the terminology and, in practice, marriage with either cross cousin is frequently introduced into the system.

Rivière himself raises the specific historical problem posed by the Trio situation. Attempting to account for it, he proposes two opposed hypotheses between which we will not attempt to choose. On the one hand, he thinks that the present system 'has grown out of and superseded a preference for marriage with the ZD. Although there is no factual evidence for this, there is considerable circumstantial evidence and, if the assumption is right, the ZD marriage has exerted great influence on the social organisation of the Trio.'[69] On the other hand, he writes that the present state of things is 'a development (or degeneration) of bilateral cross cousin marriage which, indeed, is how the Trio conceive their own system'.[70]

I will limit myself to observing that marriage with a sister's daughter is the basis for an original form of bilateralism in which the oblique preferential wife is confused with the matrilateral cross cousin but not with the patrilateral cross cousin, who is forbidden. Naturally, it is not possible to know whether the Trio have always restricted the field of application of this canonical union to the daughter of the elder sister or whether, on the contrary, this was a later development. In any event, the introduction of the possibility of marriage with the daughter of a paternal aunt does not have the same structural significance among the Trio as among the Pende of the Kasai. Through the concomitant effect of marriage with the two cross cousins, the Trio develop in a fluid form the principle of direct bilateral exchange which is already to be found in oblique patrilateral marriage, whereas the Pende, by abolishing oblique patrilateral marriage, have also abolished the direct reciprocity that this implied, only to re-establish it in new forms but this time between alternate generations.

Even though it seems impossible to foresee their contingent historical evolution, the two forms of oblique patrilateral marriage — the one the converse of the other — that we have compared clearly stem from the same overall structural situation. Into this a third form can be integrated: union with the daughter of the paternal aunt's daughter, which I shall describe in a matrilineal African society which, like the Pende, belongs to the cultural zone of the central Bantu in Western Africa: the Yombe of Zaïre.

The patrilateral formula of marriage among the Yombe

The Yombe practise several types of preferential marriage, but, once again, in order to discover the architecture of the overall system it is important to establish the hierarchy that governs them and also the relationships of interdependence by which they are linked. The Yombe society of Lower Zaïre was described in 1967 by A. Doutreloux. The complex fresco of matrimonial exchange is dominated by one preferential union: marriage with the paternal aunt's daughter's daughter.[71] Even before we embark on this new analysis it will be noted that this decision represents the third patrilateral option possible within a group of transformations where the other two formulae are represented by the preferential unions adopted successively, in the course of their history, by the Pende.

I shall show that the two contrary oblique formulae, marriage with the father's sister as formerly practised by the Pende, and marriage with the daughter of the daughter of the father's sister (Yombe), restore the conditions for restricted exchange, whereas marriage with the daughter of the father's sister (contemporary Pende) to some extent moves away from it, in accordance with the classic formula established by Lévi-Strauss.

There is no doubt that marriage with the paternal aunt's daughter's daughter belongs to the same historical field as marriage with a patrilateral cross cousin in the cultural group using the Kongo language to which the Yombe belong: both the southern Yaka[72] and the Mbata[73] practise the second type of union; the Yombe, the first. The father's sister's daughter's daughter is, in their eyes, the partner of the 'ideal marriage'; such a marriage is indissoluble. During the period when Doutreloux was carrying out his enquiry (1961–3), it was almost obligatory; it was impossible to avoid it 'without falling under the curses of the paternal aunts'.[74] But the Yombe also allow another type of oblique marriage:

Pende (the old form of preferential marriage)   Pende (the existing form of preferential marriage)   Yombe (the principal form of preferential marriage)

Fig. 1.7

49

with the maternal uncle's daughter's daughter. Although she is theoretically prohibited, the daughter of an uncle can sometimes be married. It cannot, however, be said that such a marriage has any preferential status. On the contrary, it is brought about by a violent act in both the literal and the metaphorical sense: 'Marriages with these women (matrilateral cross cousins) were effected more or less by force. In the old days especially they were usually engineered by the Mantadu, the leader of the henchmen of an invested chief.'[75] This matrilateral union is only licit if the maternal uncle is the leader of a lineage, Ngwa Kazi.[76] This latitude — or laxity — might lead one to believe, with F. Korn, that the structural theory of kinship is altogether derisory. I have just refuted such an accusation in connection with a problem that is not so complicated: the hierarchy of patrilateral and matrilateral marriages among the Pende. It is clear that marriage with the daughter of the maternal uncle is a part of the political horizon and that the second marriage in the usual order of preferences is a union with the maternal uncle's daughter's daughter.

But to complicate the situation further, a number of marriages also take place between certain second-degree cross cousins.[77] We shall study them carefully presently. It seems most unlikely that all these forms of marriage are independent of each other.

One wonders whether the interplay between them does not in effect constitute the structure of Yombe kinship. If we are to believe the Yombe themselves, absolute priority must clearly be given to marriage with the paternal aunt's daughter's daughter. I shall begin this analysis with three remarks borrowed from Doutreloux and will quote directly from him.

1. 'Regular marriages with the daughter of the daughter of the maternal uncle rapidly end up in generation gaps that are unacceptable between married couples.'[78]

2. 'One cannot, in fact, help applying these formulae of marriage concurrently, especially in the case of second-degree cross cousins.'[79]

3. 'A simple form of a model of restricted exchange sometimes comes into being. It allows the brothers and sisters of one group to marry the brothers and sisters of the other group ... This form of continuous alliance between two groups is explained or justified by the following proverb ... : the stems of [climbing] beans intertwine in order to fertilise each other abundantly.'[80]

Can these apparent fantasies be translated into a nuclear model? As we have just seen, there is a proverb that invokes restricted exchange, whereas the oblique forms of marriage are respectively patrilateral and matrilateral: the former is in some ways considered sacred and the latter cannot operate on its own. So the most satisfactory model that can be devised must incorporate both an exchange of sisters and union with the paternal aunt's daughter's daughter.

Following an initial exchange of sisters between the matrilineal lines A and B, let us apply the quasi-obligatory marriage with the daughter of the daughter of the paternal aunt: *1* marries *4* and *2* marries *3*. But it is immediately noticeable

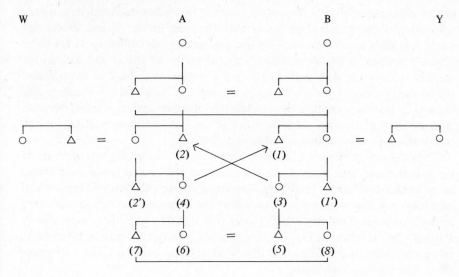

Fig. 1.8

that *3* and *4* are also, in respect to *2* and *1*, the daughter of a daughter of a maternal uncle (which is equally a preferential union). These then are oblique cousins doubly crossed. In the second generation *1* and *2* find themselves exchanging their respective uterine nieces (*3* and *4*), while in the preceding generation their maternal uncles had exchanged sisters. But then, in the fourth generation, an exchange of sisters can again take place, through a new application of the canonical rule. Indeed, it can be seen that *6* is the paternal aunt's daughter's daughter of *5*, as *8* is as regards *7*. But in virtue of the bilateral aspect of the system, these two complementary marriages can be interpreted from another point of view: *6* is also the mother's mother's brother's daughter of *5*, as *8* is as regards *7*. This preferential union is explicitly allowed for in the Yombe matrimonial code. The gap between generations disappears and the application of the canonical rule thus favours a new exchange of sisters between *5* and *7*. The suggestion that such an exchange could immediately be followed by marriage with a double cross cousin[81] must be viewed with caution, since it is in contradiction with the canonical rule, namely the quasi-obligatory union with the daughter of the daughter of the paternal aunt. In practice, women of the second generation are excluded from this direct exchange between lines A and B (see Fig. 1.8).

But how can the four preferential marriages with cross cousins of the second generation be integrated into this analysis? In practice, 'a man may equally take a wife from the four groups to which he is related through his grandparents'.[82]

First let us examine the possibility of marrying 'the daughter of the daughter of one's maternal great-uncle'. In Fig. 1.8 this rule implies that *1'* can marry *4*, just as symmetrically *2'* is allowed to marry *3*. Obviously, such unions can only take place if the maternal uncles of the interested parties (*1* and *2*) did not marry according to the canonical oblique preferential rule (unless there are other available women in this generation). I should point out that *4* and *3* also have another relationship with regard to *1'* and *2'* respectively: each of them is also the mother's father's sister's daughter's daughter. Now, such a union is also allowed.[83] In other words, a direct exchange of sisters is then effected between cross cousins of the second generation (*1'* and *2'*) without waiting for the succeeding generation as in our earlier hypothesis.

Thus the two preferential unions brought about through the intermediary of the two maternal grandparents are assimilated in the general model inaugurated by an exchange of sisters (Fig. 1.8). Now let us examine the last two preferential formulae: marriage with a cousin to whom one is related through one or other of one's paternal grandparents. It is clear that this time other lines must also be involved. Let us return to Fig. 1.8. The sister of *1* necessarily marries into line Y, just as the sister of *2* marries into line W, since cross cousins of the first generation cannot marry each other.

Let us construct this expanded model (Fig. 1.9) – which introduces the paternal grandparents of *1'* and *2'* – bearing in mind that these two new adjacent lines are themselves linked respectively to lines X and Z through a direct exchange: it is this in fact that is the basis for the exchange of sisters as well as for the bilateral oblique marriage.

Let us take *1'* and *2'* as our points of reference. Suppose that as a matter of priority each marries the daughter of the daughter of his paternal aunt, that is to say, respectively *y'* and *w'*, as is indicated by the arrows in Fig. 1.9. But *1'* can also marry *z* as *2'* can marry *x*: in effect, *z* and *x* are respectively for *1'* and *2'* female cross cousins of the second generation through their two paternal grandparents. (It can easily be seen from Fig. 1.9 that *z* is both the father's mother's brother's daughter's daughter of *1'* and his father's father's sister's daughter's daughter. The same goes for *x* with regard to *2'*.)

We have thus integrated into a model originally based on the exchange of sisters and oblique bilateral marriage the four preferential unions between cross cousins of the second generation, the formulae for which are summarised in Fig. 1.10.

On the question of the last two cases, which are unquestionably the most difficult to interpret, Doutreloux expresses himself in somewhat obscure terms. According to him, the matrimonial relationship established through the paternal grandmother can be explained by 'an assimilation of the son to the father' and the complementary relationship with the line of the paternal grandfather by an 'extension' of the patrilateral rules to the father's father's lineage (*kiyaya*).[84] But it is quite clear that it is really a matter of something quite different. All the rules of preference concerning unions between cross cousins in the second degree can be explained coherently if one introduces a series of lines that are linked in

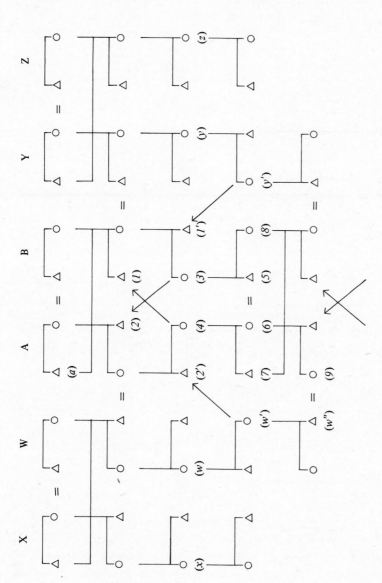

Fig. 1.9   The arrows indicate the canonical patrilateral unions with a daughter of the paternal aunt's daughter

I. Crossed union established by the maternal grandmother

II. Crossed union established by the maternal grandfather

III. Crossed union established by the paternal grandmother

IV. Crossed union established by the paternal grandfather

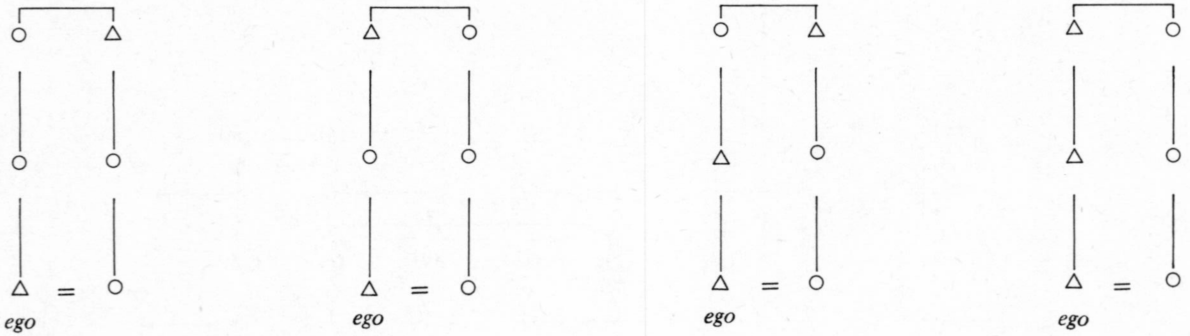

Fig. 1.10

pairs by restricted exchanges, in effect intertwined like climbing beans, as the Yombe themselves put it.

The canonical marriage with the paternal aunt's daughter's daughter necessarily leaves the marriages of the sisters of *1* and *2* open to partners from outside system A and B (i.e. partners belonging to Y and W in Fig. 1.9). In these circumstances one of two things happens in the next generation. Either *1'* or *2'* can exchange sisters if they are available: in this case rules I and II in Fig. 1.10 are applied; or *1'* and *2'*, who are each without a wife, can operate in their favour a preferential right in one of the two adjacent lines. There are two possibilities: either the canonical patrilateral marriage is applied (*1'* marries *y'* and *2'* marries *w'*, as indicated in Fig. 1.9); or rules III and IV of Fig. 1.10 are applied and *1'* marries *z* while *2'* marries *x*. In any event it is not possible to marry two sisters 'as they only have one sex'.[85]

Within the framework of these extended restricted exchanges, then, each man has a number of possibilities open to him. I will try to formalise them, placing myself in the position of *2'*, that is from the point of view of line A:

(*a*) If *2'* enters into an exchange of sisters with a man of his generation from B group, direct reciprocity between A and B continues. However, taking into account oblique marriages of the preceding generations, it is more probable that this direct exchange will occur in the next generation, between *7* and *5*, as indicated in Fig. 1.9.

(*b*) The most likely hypothesis is then that *2'* himself will effect the canonical union with the paternal aunt's daughter's daughter by marrying *w'*. A restricted exchange is then settled between A and W. As a matter of fact, in this case, *2* has given his sister to a partner from the W lineage, and *2'* receives a great-niece from the latter.

(*c*) In the hypothesis where the choice of *2'* falls on *x*, a new alliance is created between A and X. Here again, the exchange between the two lines could be balanced later on by a canonical marriage (see Fig. 1.11b).

This system has the advantage of multiplying forms of restricted exchange by bringing into play three pairs of exchanging units: A–B, A–W, A–X. By virtue of the fundamental structural demands (the exchange of sisters, the canonical marriage with the daughter of the paternal aunt, and subsequent union between cross cousins in the second generation), every line necessarily finds itself associated with three others through a completely original formula of restricted exchange. Restricted exchange is in some measure extended within the limits of a wider circle, without, however, in any way taking the form of generalised exchange. The reality of these four principal lines is attested by the terminology. The term *tata* (father) also covers the matrilineal descendants of paternal aunts 'for at least two generations'.[86] This, as we have seen, is *par excellence* the line from which to take a wife. The Yombe justify this first preferential marriage by an ideology that is close to that of the Pende: the 'need to return the male principle or, as the free translation of informants themselves has it, to return the progeniture. The father has taken a wife from *ego*'s group and engenders for this group. It is fitting that in return *ego* should take a wife from the paternal group and engender for it.'[87] A crucial position in the system is thus held by the father's line. The descendants of the father's paternal aunts (the line of the paternal grandfather) belong to the category of grandparents (*kiyaya*).[88] On the maternal side, 'the descent of the line of the mother's paternal aunts (the line of the maternal grandfather) also falls within the category of *kiyaya*.'[89] The maternal grandmother's line is clearly *ego*'s own.

We thus find, expressly designated either by a father—son or by a grandfather—grandson relationship, the three lines in which $2'$ can take a wife in accordance with Fig. 1.9. It should, however, be noted that the system also includes local terminological variants.[90]

The care taken to establish emotional links with these three adjacent lines, which constitute the overall matrimonial network, is manifest in how people are named. Each individual has two names. 'The second is always the father's first name, in the case of all children. The first name is in general determined in accordance with the following norms:

— whether a boy or a girl, the first-born takes the name of the father's father.
— if the second child is a boy he takes the name of his mother's father; if she is a girl, that of her mother's mother.
— if the third child is a girl, she takes the name of her father's mother. If he is a boy there is no norm.'[91]

Can this matrimonial network be maintained indefinitely? Let us see what happens in the fourth generation in Fig. 1.9. Where are the three lines of grand-parents from which 7 can, in principle, take a wife when it comes his turn?

The father's father's line is not included because it is none other than that to which 7 himself belongs (A). Only two possibilities remain: on the one hand, the father's line (B) where 7 finds in 8 a wife of the same generation and qualified from the canonical point of view; on the other hand, the maternal grandfather's line (W), where 7 can marry his mother's father's sister's daughter's daughter. This case is illustrated by Fig. 1.11a, which shows that the exchange of sisters is theoretically possible by virtue of the preferential rules. The probability of direct exchange between A and W is, however, slight. Indeed, in the hypothesis where 7 would marry a woman of line W, as his maternal uncle $2'$ did according to the canonical marriage, the two men would find themselves married to two sisters (true or classificatory). Such a situation risks creating some tension, since the nephew must maintain a respectful distance in his relationship with his uncle's wives.[92]

One may well now wonder if direct exchanges can go on between A and X in the hypothesis envisaged above where $2'$ married x. Let us place 7, our reference point, in a new figure (1.11b). First let us apply the canonical marriage: x' marries his paternal aunt's daughter's daughter. This time 7 can bring into play, to his advantage, another type of oblique marriage, i.e. with the mother's

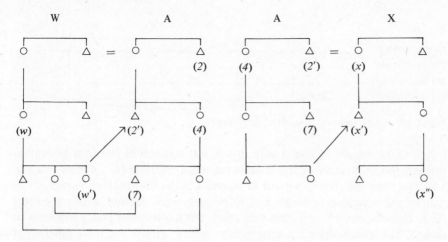

Fig. 1.11a   Fig. 1.11b

brother's daughter's daughter (x''). Thus 7 and x' would exchange directly their uterine niece. But there still remains an initial imbalance that is hardly compatible with the bilateral logic so dear to the Yombe: in this perspective, the marriage of $2'$ with x appears arbitrary, since it is never really compensated for. On the other hand, a short cycle is clinched between A and X if the initial marriage of $2'$ is followed only by the canonical union of x' with a woman of the line A.

The strongest hypothesis thus seems to be that the matrimonial exchanges of A with X as with W fade away in the fourth generation (that of our point of reference, 7) for the benefit of the exchange of sisters between A and B. So the immediate reciprocity of the first generation is repeated in the most harmonious manner possible. In analysing Fig. 1.8, we saw that the two matrilateral oblique forms of marriage (with MBDD and with MMBD) result from the canonical patrilateral oblique marriage which assures the system's vigorous bilateralism (see p. 51). In the best of cases, the latter leads to an exchange of sisters within the fourth generation, as we have supposed from the very beginning.

We may therefore conclude that the oblique marriages and the preferential marriages between cross cousins of the second generations necessarily imply first two lines (A and B) and then two adjacent lines (W and X or Y and Z). It is important to realise that the successive generations do not all find themselves faced with the same matrimonial options. The field of options broadens at the second and third generations (when the relationships A–W, A–X, B–Y, B–Z come into play). Then they shrink, perhaps in order to limit themselves again to the initial direct exchange between A and B. Fig. 1.12 attempts to illustrate the diachronic pattern.

Is it possible for this cycle to be reproduced with the same partners? The

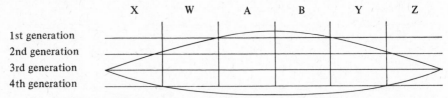

Fig. 1.12   The field of restricted exchanges

restricted exchanges of line A with line W will reappear in the fifth generation through the application of the oblique canonical marriage (*w"* marries *9* in Fig. 1.9). But then the overall pattern of alliances in the fifth generation reproduces that of the second generation, and so marriages can develop within the same field. There is, nevertheless, one indication that matrimonial policy will soon be revised. The Yombe have a precise term to refer to each of the three generations that follow that of the great-nephews. The fourth generation is called *tsafudi'la*, the fifth *tleludelwa* and the sixth *tuvi twa nzimbu*.[93] This last expression is particularly interesting. According to Doutreloux, it means 'the rubbish that a man cannot hope to know'. On consulting Bittremieux's lexicon, however, it is possible to suggest a more precise translation. *Tuvi* means 'excrement' and *nzimbu* refers to the liana *Panicum brizanthum* 'which intertwines beautifully'.[94] The expression *Tuvi twa nzimbu* may thus be translated as 'the excrement of the Nzimbu liana'. This is a metaphor close to that used by Doutreloux's informants to describe the consequences of an exchange of sisters: there is an intertwining of beanstalks. We should also point out in this connection that, among the peoples of the former kingdom of Kongo, the word *nzimbu* also designates the traditional shell currency.[95] Now among the Yombe marriage is accompanied by a transfer of goods.[96] We must surely conclude that the sixth generation marks the splitting of the lineage and the end of its network of alliances.

The segmentation of lineages is in fact a dominant aspect in the Yombe social structure. Examining matrimonial policy, which is intimately linked with power relationships, Doutreloux notes that 'the sphere of exchanges shrinks . . . to a few allied groups, groups whose contours are constantly being reformed'.[97] He correctly notices that the relationships between fathers and sons are regularly reversed from one group to another and thinks that 'the combined use of different forms of marriage gives rise to new segmentations'.[98] What he does not notice, however, is that the internal regularity of a process that balances exchanges within a few generations subsequently makes it possible to revise matrimonial policy completely.

This reveals the power and originality of oblique patrilateral marriage with the paternal aunt's daughter's daughter. It makes it possible to intertwine the beanstalks of several lines linked in pairs by restricted exchange.

One more observation remains to be made. The aim of this analysis was to set out all the elements in the interplay of Yombe marriage, without prejudging the frequency with which the various options appear. We have reconstructed the model to which the empirical reality conforms, although we regret the lack of more precise information about how it actually works. We would simply point out that this theoretical structure involves no contradictions.

Conclusions

Let us summarise the structural implications of the three patrilateral marriages that we have compared (see Fig. 1.7). The classic marriage with the father's sister's daughter (Pende) conforms with the principle of the alternation of generations: every other generation A, B and C are alternately givers and receivers of women in relation to the adjacent lineages (see Fig. 1.1a). This formula lies midway between restricted exchange and generalised exchange, since a direct reciprocity operates in the space of two generations between A and B, B and C etc. On the other hand, oblique patrilateral marriage, whether with the father's sister (the old Pende system) or with the paternal aunt's daughter's daughter (Yombe), purely and simply restores the conditions for restricted exchange. But whereas the first oblique union (with a woman from the previous generation) limits the general field of exchange to two lines, the second (with a woman from the next generation) implies an indefinite number of lines, as does marriage with a patrilateral cross cousin. It is not a simple variant, however; it constitutes a true transformation. In fact it implies the adoption of an exchange of sisters, without which this system could not function. The advantage of this transformation is that it succeeds in combining bilateralism with a multiplicity of lines in a formula that is infinitely more supple — even sinuous — than marriage with the daughter of the paternal aunt.

There is reason to believe that marriage with the paternal aunt's daughter's daughter cannot, by itself, answer all the matrimonial needs of any society that adopts it as the canonical form, whereas it is at least theoretically possible for marriage with the father's sister (the old Pende system) and marriage with the daughter of the father's sister (the Pende of the Kasai) to do so. However that may be, the multiplicity of complementary preferential unions among the Yombe is not arbitrary, nor are the new types of marriage possible following a canonical marriage with the daughter of a paternal aunt in the case of the Pende of the former province of Léopoldville. It is important to discover this internal hierarchy if we are to reach a structural understanding of a preferential system which allows a number of types of marriage in an apparently chaotic manner. Despite the complexity of these options, we shall remain within the domain of the elementary structures.

As we have noted, the canonical oblique patrilateral forms that we have been comparing (marriage with the father's sister and marriage with the paternal aunt's daughter's daughter) keep the overall system firmly within the limit of restricted exchange. Only marriage with the daughter of the paternal aunt has the structural power to operate a transition from restricted to generalised exchange. But we have also seen that the canonical marriage with the paternal aunt's daughter's daughter has a remarkable feature in common with marriage with the daughter of the paternal aunt: it makes it possible to establish restricted exchange in a continuous chain of partners associated in pairs.

Descent, residence and preferential marriages

It is well known that the problem of residence is crucial in the evaluation of matrilineal systems. The Anglo-Saxon literature on the subject rightly devotes much consideration to it. But, more often than not, the investigators proceed in an empirical fashion, without taking into account the fact that this decisive factor might in some way be linked with the various preferential marriages that one so often finds associated with this system. I should now like to tackle one aspect of the theory of kinship which seems to have progressed hardly at all since Lévi-Strauss established its bases. Lévi-Strauss starts off by pointing out that one cannot 'treat patrilineal and matrilineal descent and patrilocal and matrilocal residence as abstract elements in chance pairings'.[99] At the end of *The Elementary Structures* he ponders on the structural laws that might govern the association of these factors, and he makes a clear opposition between disharmonic and harmonic regimes. The former are those 'in which residence and descent separately follow the father's and the mother's lines';[100] it is only this dichotomy that makes possible the development of restricted exchange, that is to say the transition from a system of two moities to one of four sections or eight sub-sections. Harmonic systems, on the other hand, which are much more common, are those in which 'descent and residence are at once paternal and patrilocal, or maternal and matrilocal respectively'; it is in these regimes that indirect (or asymmetrical) exchange 'arises, as the only possible mode of integration of groups'.[101] Whereas disharmonic regimes are stable, harmonic ones are unstable 'and can acquire an autonomous structure only when they reach the stage of systems of generalised exchange with "*n*" sections'.[102]

To be more precise: 'the development of restricted exchange goes hand in hand with the admission of an even greater number of local groups participating in the exchange, e.g. two in a Kariera system and four or eight in an Aranda system. Organic development (i.e. development in the degree of integration) goes hand in hand with a mechanical development (i.e. the numerical increase in the number of participants). Conversely, generalised exchange, while relatively unproductive in the matter of systems (since it can engender only one single pure system) is very fruitful as a regulating principle: the group remaining unchanged in extent and composition, generalised exchange allows the realisation of a more supple and effective solidarity within this mechanically stable group.'[103]

But Lévi-Strauss also notes that 'the number of matrilineal systems which are also matrilocal is extremely small'.[104] There is no doubt that the Bemba of Zambia, in the conditions foreseen by Lévi-Strauss, offer us an example of generalised exchange associated with a harmonic matrilineal regime, that is to say one that is both matrilineal and at the same time matrilocal. In his recent remarkable study, Tardits tried to interpret from a structuralist point of view the data earlier collected by A.I. Richards.[105]

The Bemba belong to the 'matrilineal belt' that crosses central Africa from west to east, to the south of the great forests. Tardits tries to discover a model, while taking into account the large number of preferential unions with the daughter of a maternal uncle which Richards indicated — although on uncertain statistical bases. At all events, marriage is uxorilocal. If these two factors are taken together it can be seen that the preferential marriage with a matrilateral cross cousin implies, for the men who practise it, two successive residential status. As a child he first lives in a matrilineal group consisting of his mother and his maternal grandmother but under the authority of the husband of the latter.[106] Subsequently he lives with the maternal uncle whose daughter he has married. As Tardits points out, in this case 'the husbands whose residence was both uxorilocal and avunculocal and whose destiny was to succeed their maternal uncles who had become their fathers-in-law did not in their lifetimes have to change their residence again'.[107] The system presents one remarkable feature which Tardits pointed out clearly: it can also be interpreted as a circulation of men between residential units: 'When the young people, boys and girls, in a village were of an age to marry, uxorilocal residence provoked an exodus of sons and brothers and an influx of husbands and sons-in-law.'[108] I should like to develop this analysis a little further.

The women, who do not move away, constitute the permanent nucleus of the local segments of the matrilineage. Each man follows the path taken by his maternal uncle and great-uncle before him if, like them, he has indeed married his matrilateral cross cousin: the men of the matrilineage find themselves all together, in the same place, but separated from their sisters, mothers and maternal grandmothers with whom they spent the first part of their existence. Fig. 1.13 illustrates this ideal territorial split in the lineage on the basis of sex.

The men are torn from their initial matrilocal bonds and, after childhood, move from locality 1 to locality 2. Fig. 1.13 illustrates the structural model of residence where matrilateral unions are effected in the regular way. The empirical reality is much more complicated, since there are several other residential possibilities open to the Bemba. This residential model can clearly not be applied to the whole population. Men who do not marry their cross cousins introduce a factor of instability into the system. After living for a number of years with their fathers-in-law, by virtue of the uxorilocal nature of marriage, they move for a third time to the village of a maternal uncle or to install themselves with a village chief not of their kin.[109]

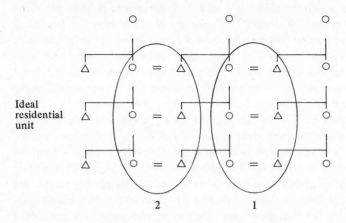

Fig. 1.13   (residential units are grouped into a single whole)

In an interesting discussion following the publication of Tardits's article, A.I. Richards emphasised the fact that Bemba matrisegments do not have great genealogical depth, exercise no collective rights and do not, as such, play any part in the arrangement of marriages. Tardits is in agreement with her and recognises that 'the analysis of exchange between matrisegments does not imply that matrimonial relations involving the same groups perpetuate themselves in time'.[110] In this connection he underlines the difference that exists in Africa between patrilineal and matrilineal societies, and he wonders whether the latter do not attempt, 'on the basis of fixed matrimonial rules, to ensure a temporary stability for groups that are destined to split periodically'.[111] One element in this discussion seems to me particularly important. Tardits acknowledges that he has provisionally excluded from his analysis the preferential marriage with a patrilateral cross cousin that A.I. Richards claims is also practised by the Bemba.

Clearly the pure model distinguished by Tardits does no more than indicate a general tendency in the Bemba matrimonial structure, and the very existence of a preferential union with the other cross cousin introduces a certain coefficient of bilateral exchange that it is difficult to evaluate, given the state of the information we actually possess. We must nevertheless examine the question of this apparent incapacity on the part of a matrilineal matrilocal society to set up generalised exchange in an exclusive organic system. The model of generalised exchange remains a fragile one among the Bemba; the matrisegments do not really constitute themselves into giving and receiving groups. The complementary preferential right of a man over the daughter of his son short-circuits the lines, as Tardits correctly saw. What is more, the possibility of marriage with a patrilateral cross cousin also bedevils the system, preventing it from truly constituting itself on the basis of generalised exchange. The fact is that the harmonic regime places matrilineal societies in a situation that is the converse of that experienced by patrilineal ones. It is the men, rather than the women, who have to move. The harmonic character of the system requires that masculine residence should be first matrilocal and subsequently avuncular. A man lives first with the closest female relatives of his lineage, and then with his closest male ones. At the end of this process descent and residence are, it is true, in agreement, but the unity of the matrilineal group is far from assured. A.I. Richards remarks: 'The practice of matrilocal marriage disperses brothers into different villages and there are no groups of closely related men who can exert moral influence as there are among the Bantu people who practise patrilocal marriage.'[112]

This is the nub of the whole discussion. I shall be defending the following propositions:

1. As Lévi-Strauss rightly saw, the systematising of marriage with a matrilateral cross cousin implies a harmonic regime, that is to say, in the case of a matrilineal society, uxorico-avunculocal residence; but this is a precarious situation.

2. On the other hand — still in the case of a matrilineal society — marriage with a patrilateral cross cousin usually goes hand in hand with a hybrid residential system, the various modalities of which we shall be examining.

3. Despite their apparent fragility, it is the societies of the second type, not those of the first, that have the greater chance of establishing themselves in accordance with a stable structural model.

We will begin by once again examining Pende society, where marriage with a patrilateral cross cousin holds a dominant position. Lévi-Strauss does not consider patrilateral systems in his theory of harmonic and disharmonic regimes. But we shall see that, from this point of view, they occupy a specific and remarkable position. Marriage with the daughter of a paternal aunt sets up an original regime that is neither harmonic nor disharmonic. Now it is this hybrid character that assures it of a greater viability than the generalised exchange to which the Bemba incline, without however truly achieving it.

If we consider the destiny of an individual in Pende society we find an apparently paradoxical situation. The Pende insist upon a change of residence both for the men and for the women. Marriage is virilocal. To start with, the men live patrilocally with their fathers. Mothers are constantly reminding their sons that they are, to some extent, living in an alien place: 'We are not at home here, we are only here through marriage' (that is to say temporarily).[113] Although a number of men elect to establish themselves in their father's house, the norm on reaching adulthood is avunculocal residence. As for the women, they find themselves in a much stranger situation. The matrilineal lineage of which they are the root is, so far as they are concerned, an empty space. Let us examine Fig. 1.14. By virtue of the virilocal marriage of her mother, *b* is born into an alien lineage, that of her father (*c*); when she in her turn marries, according to the patrilateral model (from the men's point of view), she goes to join her cross cousin in lineage A, which is equally alien to her. Fig. 1.14 shows how, from a

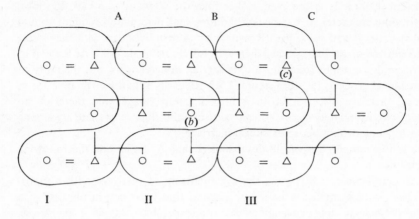

Fig. 1.14

residential point of view, the women to some extent overstep their own local lineage segment, with which they maintain episodic relations; they return 'home' to the villages of their maternal uncles in times of sickness or to give birth to children. They may settle there eventually when they have 'finished producing children'.[114] To tell the truth, they do not move very far away from this ideal location for social rooting for which they, so to speak, constitute the original root, since marriage with a female patrilateral cross cousin establishes alliances between neighbouring villages. This is why a woman is held to marry 'on the spot'.

From a residential point of view, women from lineage B are alternately born into groups III and I, and in accordance with the same alternation, they marry into I and III.

What is the situation with regard to the circulation of men? The consequence of patrilocal residence is that the young men of lineage B are alternately born into III and I. But their subsequent avunculocal residence ultimately brings them all back to II, where the lineage is rooted and where they live with their wives, who have come from elsewhere. Harmony between matrilineal descent and residence is thus finally achieved but at the price of the men being provisionally torn from the location of their social rooting. As for the women, until their old age they always live 'somewhere else'. Such a society turns the men initially into aliens in that they live with their fathers, while the women have no proper place at all of their own. Only maternal grandmothers and their granddaughters live in the same place: alternate generations are brought together while succeeding generations are separated (see Fig. 1.14). This hybrid regime truly exists, since it corresponds to empirical reality for the Pende. Although a number of men elect to remain in their father's house upon reaching adulthood,[115] the matrilineal lineage divides into local segments (*jigo*), grouping together the male descendants

64

of a common female ancestor for four generations at least.[116] In the Kasai, the *jigo* constitutes a village; in the former province of Leopoldville the colonial authorities regrouped these small dispersed units, but each *jigo* has its own neighbourhood. The groupings of neighbouring villages between which matrimonial alliances are made are referred to as *mujiba*, so that a virilocal marriage with a patrilateral cross cousin constitutes a marriage 'on the spot', within the *mujiba*.[117]

We will now isolate from this regime a characteristic that is more or less latent and that we cannot fail to find surprising. Despite matrilineal descent, the Pende transmit immaterial rights, for instance that of singing a particular song or dancing a particular dance (as they do magic knowledge and dietary prohibitions), from father to son.[118] On these grounds de Sousberghe believed that marriage between cross cousins should be interpreted as a formula to reunite the vital principle transmitted by mother and father.[119] My own opinion is, on the contrary, that the theory of matrimonial exchange made perfect sense of the overall system of preferential formulae put into operation by the Pende. The spiritual links of solidarity that unite the men – and apparently only the men – from father to son demand another type of explanation.

The fact that the Pende consider the function of marriage with a patrilateral cross cousin to be to restore 'the father's face' within his clan furthermore suggests that there is a mystic affinity that is transmitted through the same patrilineal channels, from father to son but not from father to daughter. But we would then find ourselves in the presence of a complementary mode of descent known in anthropology as sex affiliation. In such a system, symmetrical rights should be transmitted through the female line, from mother to daughter. De Sousberghe tells us nothing on this subject, but, as we shall see, the overall conditions in which marriage with a patrilateral cross cousin takes place among the Pende – and in general in matrilineal societies that practise this preferential union as well as the virilocal rule – strongly favour the emergence of the principle of sex affiliation.

Let us refer once again to Fig. 1.14, which illustrates the residential regime of the Pende. The men live with their sons, at least until the latter marry, and expect to receive into their households the sons of their sons, in the person of their uterine great-nephews. Patrilineal continuity is thus an empirical reality by virtue of virilocal marriage together with patrilocal residence of the children. The same residential group includes grandmothers and granddaughters, but daughters live with their mothers until they marry. Thus a purely female matrilineal line can also be seen to be a concrete reality even when consecutive female generations may subsequently be separated through marriage. To be more precise, each residential group includes two female lines of this type, since the men receive their wives alternately from two different clans. The fact that the male and the female lines can be defined in opposition to each other stems from a structural factor: maternal grandmothers and their granddaughters belong to the same clan; their husbands, who stand in the relationship of paternal grandfathers to grandsons, belong to a different one. The Pende are well aware of the symmetry that obtains between the female and the male lines, since 'the first name given to a daughter is regularly that of her maternal grandmother', whereas a boy will receive that of his paternal grandfather or that of his maternal great-uncle (but, as we know, the latter is confused with his paternal grandfather).[120] The different matrimonial destiny of brothers and sisters and the territorial split affecting matrilineal lineages which results from this favour the appearance of the complementary phenomenon of sex affiliation.

Lévi-Strauss has on several occasions stressed the importance of this mode of affiliation, which is capable of taking on a systematic autonomous form. This is, for example, the case with the Apinaye of Brazil[121] and also with certain peoples in New Guinea, where F.E. Williams has described the phenomenon, being the first to suggest that it should be described as 'sex affiliation'.[122] I shall be developing this important topic following Chapter 2. Let us for the moment limit ourselves to noting that this type of affiliation is perfectly compatible with patrilateral marriage, as can be seen from Fig. 1.15.

Of course such a model in no way defines the overall social structure of the Pende. They are content to sketch out the phenomenon, although meanwhile, in the case of the men, they firmly maintain the principle of belonging to the matrilineal clan. However, one cannot rule out the possibility that it was more rigidly adhered to in former times, when the Pende, according to their own account, used systematically to marry their paternal aunt (see p. 44).

Let me now put forward contradictory hypotheses in order to control the propositions we have been discussing. First let us imagine a system in which marriage with a patrilateral cross cousin might go hand in hand with the converse regime of uxorilocality. Next, let us construct a model of a society in which marriage with a matrilateral cross cousin would be associated with a virilocal regime. I shall begin with the first hypothesis.

The residential group would include the women from line B and the alternate

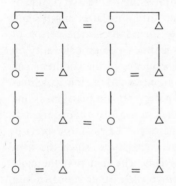

Fig. 1.15

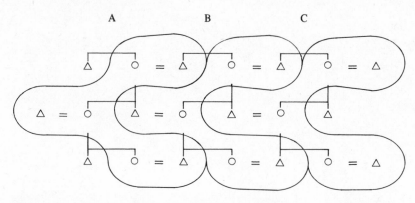

Fig. 1.16   First hypothesis: patrilateral marriage and an uxorilocal
matrilineal regime

male generations stemming from the two adjacent lines A and C. This time the
men would live in a 'harmonic regime' only during their childhood. On attaining
adulthood they would join a wife in another residential group where they would
find only part of their lineage segment, namely their maternal great-uncles. The
situation would thus be the strict converse of that which obtains in the case of
the Pende, where the residential group includes the alternate female generations
of two allied lineages and the consecutive masculine generations of the lineage
that owns the land. But such a hypothesis is unlikely to be verified empirically.
The fact is that it is difficult to see how the authority of the maternal uncle
could be brought to bear when he is always absent from the life of his nephew.
Brought up close to their father and mother, the children would only occasionally meet their mother's brother. Furthermore, the maternal great-uncle whom
the great-nephews are supposed to join when they marry also happens to be their
paternal grandfather. There is a strong likelihood that, thus drained of its substance, the matrilineal regime will accentuate the phenomenon of sex affiliation
which we have seen to be latent in the last regime we considered, where patrilateral marriage was accompanied by virilocal residence (Pende). The result
would be a system composed this time of a continuous matrilineal female line
(B) whose members would live with the men belonging to two discontinuous
patrilineal lines (A and C). As the sons of these men live with their fathers until
they marry, the gaps in the consecutive male generations would in effect be
filled up and the patrilineal line would become even more unavoidable for the
men. The situation which would then begin to emerge and which is illustrated in
Fig. 1.16a would at this point almost necessarily be transformed into a regime of
sex affiliation.

It goes without saying that these difficulties would cease to exist if all the
allied lineages constituted a residential unit, but then the endogamy of the

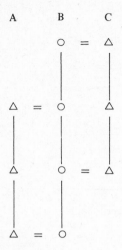

Fig. 1.16a

village would considerably weaken the very notion of uxorilocal marriage that I have retained as part of my hypothesis.

A look at the Ashanti

The extreme complexity of the Ashanti kinship system is a good illustration of the difficulties facing a matrilineal society in finding a satisfactory solution to the dialectic between descent and residence. We know that the Ashanti transmit rank and rights connected with the land through maternal descent (*abusua*), while children inherit a spiritual principle (*ntoro*) from their fathers.[123] They appear to practise marriage with both cross cousins indifferently and have a wide variety of residential models. In view of this, would it not be pointless to attempt to apply to them the structural principles we have isolated in connection with other matrilineal societies?

Let us try to get a clearer view by examining first marriage and then residence.

1. For a male *ego*, matrilateral marriage aims for 'the daughter of a man of his mother's generation belonging to the lineage segment descended from her great-grandmother'.[124] No such classificatory extension is indicated with regard to the patrilateral cross cousin. On the contrary, the Ashanti system of double descent and the identification of alternate generations to some extent favours marriage with the daughter of a paternal aunt. Rattray thought it possible to explain the marriage of cross cousins by the need to bring the *ntoro* back into the matrilineal clan every other generation.[125] But, following Seligman, Lévi-Strauss has quite clearly shown that this dialectic between alternate generations is only compatible with patrilateral marriage.[126] It is in fact then, and only then, that

68

the grandson reproduces the status of his paternal grandfather — whom he is supposed to reincarnate from the point of view of the *ntoro* and *abusua*.

It is to marriage with a patrilateral cross cousin that the Ashanti are explicitly referring when they tackle the question as follows: 'if my niece does not marry my son, but marries a man not of my *ntoro*, then I cannot call any of her children after myself or my ancestors'.[127] Marriage with the daughter of a maternal uncle, on the other hand, is justified quite differently: 'because it will keep my daughter in my house'.[128]

2. Residential status varies considerably. One of the most remarkable features of the domestic organisation described by Meyer Fortes is that frequently husband and wife do not live together.[129] 'For a man to live in his wife's house is considered to be contemptible.'[130] It does not necessarily follow that a sister and a brother find themselves in the same place. The residential model is often constituted by 'an effective minimal matrilineage or part of it as a woman and her sister or daughter, or a man and his sister or sister's son'.[131] Other domestic units based on the elementary family also exist, as do yet others that are a combination of these formulae: for example, a man, his wife, his children and his sister's children. Faced with such great variety, Meyer Fortes believes, not without reason, that the use of words such as 'matrilocality' or 'patrilocality' is futile.[132] I should point out, however, that the men's aversion to permanent cohabitation with their wives, which Fortes himself calls 'the most striking feature of Ashanti domestic life', breaks up the conjugal cell, since, as Robin Fox observes, the husband becomes no more than a 'visitor'.[133] The system seems to oscillate between the disjunction of husband and wife and that of the siblings, just as it oscillates between patrilateral and matrilateral marriage. However, these two preferential marriages stem from two different ideologies and can certainly not be put on the same footing. The fact is that they are practised on different social levels. A precious piece of information provided by Marc Augé tells us that the practice of marriage with a patrilateral cross cousin 'occurs among princely families seeking to reproduce in the person of the [eldest] grandson the total psychic formula of the paternal grandfather', thereby strengthening their power.[134] In that case the practice of marriage with a matrilateral cross cousin, real or classificatory, is likely to be followed by ordinary folk. Fortes does indeed believe that this union is more common than the other.[135] He also declares that beliefs relating to the *ntoro* 'are rapidly disappearing except among the older men and among the lineages in which chiefships of superior rank are vested'.[136]

If the transmission of the *ntoro* is indeed associated with patrilateral marriage and with it alone, the analyses that we have carried out will perhaps make it possible for us to throw new light on the ideology itself. It seems to me that the patrilineal line implied by the *ntoro* stems not so much from 'double descent', as is usually claimed, but rather from the regime of masculine sex affiliation. To put it another way, the Ashanti are simply systematising one of the principles

69

that we have seen to be at work in Pende society, where intelligence and magic knowledge are transmitted exclusively from father to son (see p. 65). The patrilineal continuity of the vital principle of *ntoro* concerns only the men. Women cannot transmit it to their descendants. Patrilateral marriage allows the men, but not the women, to combine matrilineal clan descent and masculine sex affiliation. The principle of sex affiliation seems to have been more widespread in the past if we are to believe an early piece of information given by Bosman, describing Ashanti society at the end of the eighteenth century. Lévi-Strauss, who was the first to draw attention to the phenomenon, reports it through Herskovits: the son used to follow the dietary prohibitions that applied to his father, the daughter those that applied to her mother.[137]

We should perhaps relate this complex situation to the Ashanti's fluctuating residential regime that hesitates between virilocality and uxorilocality. Have we not seen that, from a theoretical point of view, uxorilocal marriage would simply accentuate the natural tendency of any patrilateral system to produce, in a more or less developed form, a regime of sex affiliation?

At all events, the theory of the *ntoro* is quite alien to the second preferential union practised by the Ashanti, namely marriage with a matrilateral cross cousin, real or classificatory. This definitely calls for uxorilocal residence or at the very least the regime of the 'visiting' husband, as Rattray's informant reminded us; I quoted him above as saying, 'because it will keep my daughter in my house'. A harmonic regime is, in effect, the only one compatible with this union. Now we will consolidate this statement by considering our second counter-hypothesis: can matrilateral marriage exist in a matrilineal society which adopts virilocal residence? In other words, is generalised exchange possible in a disharmonic regime? As we shall see, the answer is negative.

Let us put this second counter-hypothesis to the test. Let us suppose the existence of a matrilineal society practising marriage with the daughter of a maternal uncle and imposing virilocal residence. The children's residence would necessarily be patrilocal. The sisters and daughters would, however, have to leave their brothers and father and go and live with their husbands. Two alternatives are possible here: either the husband continues to live with his father or he goes to join his maternal uncle (avunculocal residence). The second alternative is in contradiction with the departure of the daughters, since they would have to leave their father at the very moment when their future husband's would be joining him in order to marry a matrilateral cross cousin who is not there! So let us suppose that the husband lives with his father and that his maternal uncle's daughter joins him. The marriage would be virilocal for the wife, and residence firmly patrilocal for the men. But in this case the sons, grandsons and great-grandsons would form a patrilineal residential line from which only the sisters and daughters would be detached at the moment of marriage, and the system would in effect be converted into a harmonic patrilineal system. In any case, given such a hypothesis, it is quite impossible to see what role and significance matrilineal descent could have (see Fig. 1.17).

This model is all the more improbable given that the patrilineal line thus formed in the village would find that, each generation, its wives came from a different matrilineal line. Thus in matrilineal societies Lévi-Strauss's thesis is confirmed: generalised exchange (systematic marriage with the daughter of the maternal uncle) implies a harmonic, matrilocal or, to be more precise, uxorico-avunculocal regime.

Patrilateral marriage and disharmonic regime

We must now ask ourselves whether the disharmonic regime pure and simple (virilocal and patrilocal), which is incompatible with matrilateral marriage, can sometimes be associated with patrilateral marriage in matrilineal societies. The answer is, emphatically, that it can. However, this regime calls for a number of new observations. Kopytoff describes it among the Suku of Zaïre without, unfortunately, insisting upon the implications of preferential union with the daughter of the paternal aunt.[138] Here the sons often remain living with their father until he dies; they may even establish themselves definitively in their father's village after his death rather than opt for an avunculocal residence. Kopytoff interprets this situation in functionalist terms: by opting for patrilocal residence mature men are able to escape the control of the elders of the matrilineal lineage.[139] However, one may well wonder whether, by making this choice a general one, Suku society may not be in the process of constituting a new residential model, moving away from the hybrid regime which accompanies marriage with a patrilateral cross cousin in the regions we have so far considered. Here, a patrilineal line starts to make its appearance on the scene, as a residential unit, in the place of the matrilineal lineage that theoretically holds the rights over women, so that a zone of patrilocal allegiances is established in opposition to the 'avunculocal zone'.

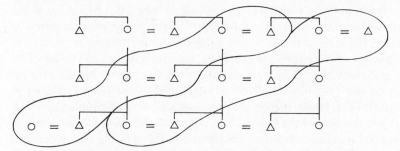

Fig. 1.17   Matrilateral marriage with a matrilineal virilocal regime (second theoretical hypothesis)

A regime of double descent stemming from the contradiction that exists between patrilocal residence and matrilocal descent, in fact if not in theory, becomes established. In such a situation, therefore, if a woman marries a long way away, the men of the lineage are in danger of losing control over her and her descent.[140] This point of rupture is reached by two matrilineal societies from the People's Republic of Congo, the Punu and the Kuni. Here a transition to a system of double descent occurs, thanks to the frequency of marriage with women from distant villages. Even if the patrilineal line is not explicitly named, it exercises a decisive function in the controlling of economic activities. J.-P. Rey develops this idea at length in his book.[141] This time there is total disharmony between matrilineal descent and residence, which is deliberately patrilocal. The local groups establish themselves around segments composed of the sons and grandsons of the chief, and these are joined by numerous descendants of domestic slaves who are integrated with a status close to that of the sons and grandsons.[142] According to Rey, this patrilocality has an essentially economic function, 'the exploitation of the land controlled by the father's or grandfather's lineage by the sons and grandsons in the paternal line'.[143] Thus the disharmonic regime of the Punu and the Kuni could be interpreted as 'a process of production'.

First of all we should note that the model thus obtained differs considerably from the matrilineal and virilocal regime which, among the Pende, is associated with matrimonial exchanges between matrisegments which really do constitute residential units. Rey himself points out that the matrilineal lineage that has been dispersed has no 'synchronic reality' among the Punu and the Kuni.[144] Unfortunately, he does not undertake any systematic study of the matrimonial network nor of kinship relations as a whole. There are, however, a number of indications that suggest that in the past marriage used to be systematically patrilateral: 'the father chose for his son a woman from his own clan but from a different lineage and *nzo* (sub-clan)'.[145] In the strictly patrilateral system of the Pende, sons leave their fathers on reaching adulthood. If they decide to remain with him, far from being exploited, for the rest of their lives they enjoy all the communal wealth of the paternal matrilineage.[146] The specific problem raised by the Punu and the Kuni is therefore the following: what is the more or less perverse mechanism which allows the chief of a matrilineal lineage to dispose of his sons and grandsons as if they were dependants with a status hardly different from that of the descendants of slaves established in the same community?

In the traditional system, preferential marriage was not accompanied by bride-wealth (this is also true of the Pende). But, before colonisation, the introduction of marriage 'by purchase' disturbed the situation. This growing phenomenon is linked directly to the intervention of fathers, to the detriment of maternal uncles: 'the first marriage was generally decided by the fathers of the two parties: the young man's father paid the girl's father a large part of the bride-wealth (sometimes as much as half) even before telling his son of the choice he had made. It was only after these payments that the uncles from both sides were consulted to discover whether the two clans already had previous matrimonial ties ... and whether they might not have been broken by some unsettled affairs.'[147] It will be noted that this first development was undoubtedly favoured by the particular character of patrilateral marriage among the Punu and the Kuni. The preferential wife is not the true patrilateral cross cousin. She indeed belongs to the young man's father's matrilineal clan, but to a different line or sub-clan: that is to say the father does not surrender to his son his own uterine niece, as among the Pende. The young man's father then finds himself in competition with the young girl's maternal uncle. He bypasses the uncle by applying directly to the girl's father. Structurally, matrimonial exchange to a large extent escapes the control of the matrilineal lineages, which thereby lose some degree of their *raison d'être*. But even nowadays when marriage obeys this particular patrilateral rule, less bride-wealth is demanded.[148]

The growing intervention of bride-wealth appears as the decisive factor in the disruption of the structure of the matrilineal lineage. This phenomenon, linked to the slave-trade, appears early in the region; it explains the system's evolution towards patrilocality pure and simple. In the past, 'most marriages were effected within a limited matrimonial zone which bound all the lineages in a network of multiple ties constantly renewed. However, as a result in particular of the slave-trade, it sometimes happened that a man took a wife from a distant group ... In that case the bride-wealth was paid in the normal fashion and the wife was in no way considered to be a slave; however, once she was installed with her husband, she found herself a long way from her kin, was unable to visit it and gradually became cut off from it.' The descendants of her children 'were no longer considered part of their distant lineage of origin ... the marriage of the daughters did not entail bride-wealth being paid to distant uncles' and 'these descendants found themselves definitively integrated within the lineage of their father or grandfather'.[149] On these lines Rey gives a perfectly coherent description of the process of disintegration in a virilocal matrilineal system founded upon preferential unions of a patrilateral type.

Once again the Pende can provide us with a field of comparison. We have seen that, despite the existence of local matrilineal lineages, the Pende also take account of patrilineal descent. This is the channel through which dietary prohibitions are transmitted, as are immaterial property rights and magical knowledge (see p. 65). But this secondary line does not constitute a residential unit. Only paternal grandfathers and grandsons find themselves reunited by virtue of marriage with a patrilateral cross cousin. Meanwhile the Pende also practise a type of marriage by purchase which does not obey this canonical rule.

In the past Pende chiefs and rich men used to seek extra wives among the patrilineal Luba. This marriage 'by purchase' was assimilated to the acquisition of a slave, and the descendants of the wife belonged to the master: they were integrated into his clan, forming new stock there. The initial relationship of descent which linked the sons and daughters of the slave woman to their father was subsequently prolonged following exogamous marriages between the paternal line and the line issuing from the slave woman. For several generations her descendants were considered the 'sons' of the lineage which had bought her. The stock of servile origin installed itself in a hamlet close to the line that owned the land.[150] This clearly does not mean that a patrilocal and patrilineal line is established, as it is among the Punu and the Kuni. Among the Pende, the vassal matrilineal line was supposed to provide its daughters, each generation, for the master clan. Slavery makes no difference to descent but does affect marriage. Where slavery is present the preferential union with a matrilateral cross cousin is widely substituted for the preferential union with a patrilateral cross cousin. In the eyes of the Pende, this new situation is 'an intermediary form between "marriage on the spot" (with the daughter of a paternal aunt) and "marriage away, with a stranger" '.[151] But children who are free and those who are slaves are 'associated with their "father" in exactly the same way'. They stand in the same situation of dependence, with no voice in decisions affecting the life of the community 'although, unlike the slaves, the free children cannot be sold'.[152] At this point de Sousberghe slightly forces the issue, since, in a different study, he declared that the children participated in rights to the common *jigo* matrilineage wealth: 'hunting rights, rights in the palm-wine harvest and in that of the kola nut etc.' He even went on to say: 'If they want to go on living in their father's *jigo* ... these rights will be acknowledged to them in so far as they are "children of the clan". They belong to the same economic community or, as the Pende put it, "to the same chest".'[153]

The effects of slavery on the matrimonial structure of the Punu and the Kuni are quite different. Here the patrilateral system is in danger of breaking up and we find the more definite form of the disharmonic regime established, descent and residence having become definitively divorced. Only in exceptional circumstances does a nephew go to live with his maternal uncle.

A complex historical process is the explanation for the formation of this regime, which is close to the system known in Africa as that of double unilineal, or double, descent. The matrilineal clan continues to determine access to power and, to some extent, controls matrimonial exchange: the maternal uncle shares the bride-wealth with the father;[154] the local segment, which is patrilineal and patrilocal, constitutes the territorial group. But the right to the land is, by virtue of matrilineal descent, theoretically held by the chief of this group, and the phenomenon of exploitation of the residents — sons, grandsons and slaves — may arise. On this point I will not argue with Rey's analysis: 'as a result, more prestations in goods and in labour are made to the father or even to the paternal uncles than to the maternal uncles'.[155]

However, to explain the lineage organisation that slavery helps to upset by the development of slavery itself would be to beg the question and would be in defiance of the historical logic that Marxism claims to follow. Despite this, Rey has no hesitation in declaring that 'the reintegration of slaves into local groups as the social "sons" or "grandsons" of the lineage chief clearly reveals the fundamentally economic role of kinship relations'.[156]

Rey also opposes this regime[157] to the matrilineal virilocal system of the Kongo and the Yombe (without suspecting the complexity of the latter, which I analysed above) and to the matrilineal uxorilocal system of the Bemba, which I have also described. But his analysis is radically different from mine because it does not take the matrimonial forms of these societies into consideration, despite the fact that they are so clearly delineated. He is more concerned to discover who is practising 'extortion'; and never fails to find a guilty party.

From the general point of view that I have adopted throughout this study, I would conclude that the patrilateral system cannot survive in its rigid form (marriage with the daughter of a paternal aunt) unless it maintains a hybrid residential regime (virilocal for the women, and for the men first patrilocal and subsequently avunculocal). When the disharmonic regime appears in its pure form and patrilocality becomes accentuated, the patrilateral system is forced to adopt, more or less consciously, the principle of double unilineal descent, since residence demands the constitution of a patrilineal group. To me it seems significant that the Punu and the Kuni transform the classic preferential patrilateral union into a more distant marriage in the paternal clan, at the same time renouncing avunculocal residence. On the other hand, I have shown that a matrilineal society that combines the practice of marriage with a patrilateral cross cousin with a harmonic regime (uxorilocal) would, either in fact or in theory, find itself committed to sex affiliation (see p. 67). In no way do I claim that these theoretical and practical observations explain the historical emergence of all systems characterised by either double descent or sex affiliation.

None of the existing societies formed by the dialectic between alliance and descent can be studied from an economic point of view until their matrimonial structure has been clearly defined. Meillassoux, for his part, notices that 'matrimonial mobility ... has immediate effects upon residence and descent'.[158] But obviously I cannot follow him when he declares, despite evidence to the contrary indicated by the human geography of Africa, that there is a correlation between matrilineal organisation and an agricultural system of planting and propagation by cuttings. Is it really necessary to point out that most of the matrilineal Bantu of central Africa live outside the forest zone where this agriculture is practised? It is altogether arbitrary to claim that these groups 'can only sustain alliances with no future' and to reduce the diversity of formulae that I have described to what he calls 'gynecostatism'.[159]

General conclusions

Descent, marriage and residence constitute the empirical factors in any kinship system. It is impossible to decide, *a priori*, whether or not matrimonial rules and the choice of a principle of descent are more decisive than demands of residence in historical transformations. I have at least shown that in matrilineal societies these three factors are linked by structural relations of compatibility or incompatibility. Finally I shall show that this structural field is not the same for societies that opt for patrilineal descent.

Matrilineal African societies, principally located in a vast zone of central Africa stretching southwards from the great forests, present an extraordinarily wide range of matrimonial models based on preferential unions. The position held by restricted exchange is by no means negligible: we find it in an original form among the Yombe and in the former Pende society; kinship terminology is clear evidence of its existence among the Yao, despite the transformations it has undergone under the pressure of political factors.[160] Generalised exchange appears as an exceptional but no doubt not unique solution among the Bemba. On the other hand, patrilateral marriage and its transformations do demand our attention: the transformations define a structural locus where a difficult synthesis between restricted and generalised exchange is attempted. On analysing the dialectic between descent and residence associated with these various models, it has seemed to me that, as predicted by Lévi-Strauss, generalised exchange implies a harmonic regime that is uxorilocal and avunculocal. To this I would add a new conclusion: marriage with a patrilateral cross cousin can only be maintained in a relatively stable form in a specific hybrid regime that is virilocal for the woman and initially patrilocal and subsequently avunculocal for the man. I have described this in its paradigmatic form among the Pende. The adoption of the harmonic regime (uxorilocal) could only contribute to the development of a tendency, which always exists in a more or less embryonic form, within a patrilateral system, namely sex affiliation. The Ashanti, whose residential regime is uncertain, may illustrate this from the masculine point of view. It also appears among the Pende. We have found a hybrid regime to be remarkably viable, despite the encroachment of matrilateral marriage, in certain regions of the Pende area. I have shown that this new matrimonial model is linked either with an internal transformation of the patrilateral system or with an external factor, the development of domestic slavery. It is definitely this last element that also explains the widespread appearance, among the Punu and the Kuni, of the disharmonic (virilocal and patrilocal) regime. In all these cases patrilateral marriage is found to be seriously threatened; it seems no more than a vestige of the past, and a system of double descent emerges, in fact if not in theory. The patrilocal groups in effect establish themselves as patrilineal lineages, constantly acquiring more slaves, and the matrilineal lineages find they have surrendered their primary social function to an aristocracy constituted by their chiefs, who are masters of the land by virtue of ancient rights. But such an evolution cannot be considered to be a universal historical law, since the Suku, who also tend systematically to adopt patrilocal residence, seem on the contrary to believe that by establishing themselves definitively in their father's house men escape the influence of the elders of their matrilineal lineage. Thus comparable concrete situations may be explained by opposite strategies. However that may be, there are limits to the structural transformations of matrilineal societies practising patrilateral marriage.

Now we must try to understand the overwhelming success of the patrilineal system in Africa. I shall show that the limitations imposed by matrilineal descent in the field of structural transformations cease to exist for societies that have opted for patrilineal descent. I will start by pointing out that, as is not the case in matrilineal societies, in such a hypothesis in these societies the harmonic regime imposes itself upon patrilateral systems as well as matrilateral ones. Let us consider Fig. 1.18. It shows that marriage with the daughter of the paternal aunt can perfectly well constitute itself around patrilineal lineages that are patrilocal and virilocal, which the daughters and sisters leave as the wives enter them.

On the other hand, adoption of the disharmonic regime (uxorilocal in this instance) would cause the dissolution of the patrilineal system into a series of matrilineal residential units where the husbands would belong alternately to two different patrilineal lineages, as can be seen from Fig. 1.19.

The conclusion that must be drawn, then, is indeed that the harmonic regime, in the sense defined by Lévi-Strauss, imposes itself on patrilineal societies that practise marriage with a patrilateral cross cousin as well as upon those which opt for the matrilateral formula. On the other hand, when descent is matrilineal, the harmonic regime imposes itself only on societies which adopt marriage with a matrilateral cross cousin; it is not reconcilable with marriage with a patrilateral cross cousin.

This absence of absolute symmetry between patrilineal and matrilineal societies could well explain a number of historical facts.

We have noticed that patrilineal societies are much more numerous than matrilineal ones. If the historical fate of the latter has been manifestly less happy than that of the former, could it not be because their capacity to adopt generalised exchange, whether in a simple or a complex form, remains limited? By

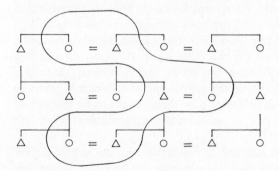

Fig. 1.18

77

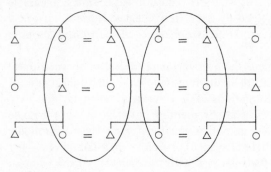

Fig. 1.19

opting for marriage with a patrilateral cross cousin, matrilineal societies remain the prisoners of a hybrid regime unless they embrace double descent or sex affiliation. They could only accede to generalised exchange by modifying both their matrimonial rule (the matrilateral cross cousin instead of the patrilateral cross cousin) and their residential rule (which would have to become uxorilocal rather than virilocal). Such a profound change is unlikely to occur all at once, whereas a virilocal patrilineal society can easily make the transition from a patrilateral regime to a matrilateral one or vice versa, without changing its masculine residential structure. Furthermore, when generalised exchange tends to establish itself, as in the case of the Bemba, the matrilineal lines, where the men fluctuate given that they are dispersed at the moment of their uxorilocal marriages among a number of villages, are fragile; and this makes it almost impossible to constitute lasting segments between which continuous exchanges over long periods can be established, as often happens in patrilineal societies. This is the explanation for the occasional strategic resorting to patrilateral marriage among the Bemba. Conversely, some Pende groups adopt marriage with the matrilateral cross cousin in their relations with servile lines, without, however, giving up patrilateral marriage (see p. 40).

So it is understandable that the matrilineal Bantu societies of central Africa should in the main be constructed on the basis of patrilateral marriage and its transformations. This is remarkably evident in the western zone of the region where the ethnographic evidence is the most consistent. However, the fact that (with the exception of the few excellent studies we have considered) there have been no detailed analyses of kinship in the central and eastern part of the same cultural zone, and the peculiar indifference of anthropologists to the distinction between the two types of cross cousins, makes it as yet impossible to apply this conclusion generally.

The fragmentary results that we have obtained bear out an incisive remark made by Lévi-Strauss. Countering the unacceptable psychological theory put forward by Homans and Schneider, he restates his principal theory, namely that there is 'no necessary connection between matrilateral or patrilateral marriage on the one hand, and the type of descent — patrilineal or matrilineal — on the other'.[161] He admits, notwithstanding, that if a statistical correlation could be established, the explanation for the greater frequency of patrilateral marriage in matrilineal systems should be sought 'in the instability characteristic of matrilineal societies . . . which would make it more difficult for them to adopt long cycles of reciprocity, while the extremely short cycles of patrilateral marriage would be less affected by the conflicts always found in matrilineal societies'.

What I have attempted to show is that a detailed analysis of the residential regime gives us a better understanding of the structural reasons for this correlation. If so many matrilineal societies of central Africa have been forced to adopt other models than that of generalised exchange, it is because for the most part they live according to a hybrid regime which is virilocal and avuncular. This is an extremely fertile model, however, since it is capable of giving rise to a number of matrimonial formulae. It may also, as we shall presently see, engender an original form of generalised exchange: that which the Lele of the Kasai are successful in constructing even though they forbid marriage between cross cousins (see Chapter 2).

The inventory of preferential unions is far from being complete in central Africa. Nevertheless, one conclusion does emerge from these initial comparative forays: it does not seem likely that marriage with a matrilateral cross cousin is dominant.

I will not broaden the field of this study beyond the 'matrimonial belt' of central Africa. We should, however, bear in mind that matrilateral marriage comes into competition with marriage to the daughter of a paternal aunt among the Ashanti (see p. 68). The patrilateral alternative to the Ashanti system confirms the general impression that generalised exchange is far from constituting itself in a systematic form in matrilineal African societies. L. de Sousberghe drew the overhasty conclusion that this model did not exist. What I, by contrast, am attempting to understand are the reasons for its comparative rarity when marriage with the daughter of a maternal uncle has been adopted with such success in a large number of patrilineal societies. I have not moved far from the conclusions put forward by Lévi-Strauss in the closing pages of *Elementary Structures*. I have simply proposed new developments to the theory of harmonic and disharmonic regimes, the importance of which appears to have been only rarely appreciated.

The Anglo-Saxon school, for its part, has admirably shown that it is not possible to have a valid discussion on the subject of a kinship system without taking account of residence. If I have deliberately adopted a theoretical position, it has been the better to show that empirical analysis cannot be dissociated from a search for models, even when some may be purely imaginary, as they are in a number of the schemata that I have felt no hesitation in putting forward, despite the fact that they have no doubt irritated a number of my readers. What I have tried to establish in my own circuitous way is that a number of different patri-lateral systems, established, at the cost of much imaginative effort by those concerned, in the matrilineal societies of central Africa, have undergone a series of structural transformations which are seldom successful in breaking away from restricted exchange. I have demonstrated this in the case of the Pende and the Yombe. And the underlying cause for this limitation seems to me to be that a matrilineal society finds it so very difficult to emerge from a more or less dis-harmonic system so as to introduce generalised exchange, which, as Lévi-Strauss clearly saw, can only tolerate a harmonic regime. True developments of the harmonic regime are necessarily associated with patrilineal systems.

But then Africa appears to present us with a new paradox. The brief com-parative general study which Tardits, to his credit, was the first to undertake, shows that marriage between cross cousins is more usually associated there with matrilineal rather than patrilineal descent. His observation is assuredly correct, but it is necessary to distinguish carefully between all the different kinds of patrilateral unions — an exhaustive catalogue of which is far from being com-pleted — and unions that are strictly matrilateral, bearing in mind that they may come into competition, as in the cases of the Ashanti and the Bemba. It should also be remembered that there are societies, such as the Lele, which forbid marriage between cross cousins of the first generation and construct original forms of matrimonial exchange which can be interpreted from the point of view sometimes of restricted and sometimes of generalised exchange (see Chapter 2). Nor, finally, should we forget societies such as the Kuba, which have set up one of the most impressive kingdoms in central Africa by strictly prohibiting marriage of any kind in the clans of the eight great-grandparents.[162]

Having said which, it is clear that all forms of preferential unions are either forbidden or in the process of disappearing over vast patrilineal areas of Africa. Southern Bantu Africa seems to be, *par excellence*, the area in which they have survived.[163] Innumerable patrilineal African societies have entered into complex forms of generalised exchange. Recent studies have shown that the Omaha system is particularly widespread in patrilineal Africa. It is to be found among the Samo of the Upper Volta,[164] the Nyoro of Uganda,[165] the Lega of Zaïre[166] and also the Tsonga of southern Africa.[167] In connection with the last-named, I would confirm Lévi-Strauss's point of view, namely that the so-called Omaha system truly constitutes an autonomous structure based on the articulations between the elementary and the complex structures of kinship (see Chapter 3). Two provisional conclusions may be drawn from all this:

1. Patrilineal societies are infinitely more capable than matrilineal ones of developing generalised exchange. There are not many African examples to illus-trate this point, but other areas in the world support this thesis, which I have attempted to establish upon theoretical grounds.

2. The patrilineal African societies display their historical dynamism in a

different way: most of them have elaborate models of matrimonial exchange which firmly turn their backs on elementary structures of kinship.[168]

Thus, in Africa, the distance is accentuated between patrilineal societies for the most part engaged in complex forms of matrimonial exchange, and matrilineal societies which are seldom successful in disengaging themselves from the patrilateral system or even restricted exchange. I have tried to show that it is the very structural constraints of matrilineal societies that account for their being unable to escape from the elementary structures of kinship. It would, however, be unjust not to note that the eminently diversified preferential unions that they bring into play are particularly successful in conferring upon them, within the field of elementary structures, a coherence that patrilineal societies are more prone to do without. If these conclusions are not entirely fictitious, choice of descent should be considered to be not entirely indifferent to the theory of kinship and its appreciation within a diachronic perspective. The earliest anthropologists were aware of this, but the reasons they put forward were far from convincing.

2

Social structure and praxis among the Lele of the Kasai[1]

The Lele of the Kasai by Mary Douglas is a fascinating book which cries out irresistibly for a structuralist reading. It is the most important monograph ever devoted to a Bantu society of Zaïre. Mary Douglas lived among the Lele, on the southern boundary of the great forest, in 1949—50 and then again in 1953. Her book combines the qualities of precise documentation, elegant style and strong analysis. Mary Douglas is not only an extremely talented observer, faithful to the slightest nuances in Bantu thought, but is furthermore gifted with that socio-logical second sight capable of revealing latent structures.

While the author remains attached to the empirical procedures of the British tradition in social anthropology, the scope of her description prompts us to attempt a more radical formulation on the basis of the fruitful perspectives opened up by her analysis. I shall attempt, in particular, to reveal the subtle interaction of praxis and the structural order which is occasioned among the Lele by an ideology at times explicit and at others implicit.

The economic infrastructure and the circulation of wealth

Mary Douglas wisely devotes the first chapters of her book to the economy of the Lele. A man's work is distinct from that of a woman. This fundamental opposition — which is also a complementary relationship — is a common one in Bantu Africa, but the Lele appear to have made it even more radical, as they have other contradictions that are similarly less apparent in other societies. The most exciting work is hunting and the forest is, *par excellence*, a male world. Food production is for the most part the responsibility of the women; the savanna where they cultivate groundnuts is their exclusive domain. A man collaborates only occasionally with his wives in agricultural work, in the forest which he clears for maize cultivation. Already in an earlier publication Mary Douglas had clearly picked out this 'basic theme' in Lele society, namely the rigid separation and interdependence of the sexes in all socio-economic and ritual contexts.[2] We shall see as we proceed that the general dualism which

82

characterises the overall social structure of the Lele is rooted in this primary opposition.

It is upon hunting that the cohesion of the village, seen as a productive unit, depends ('In one sense we can even say that the village was a hunting unit', p. 39). This observation is all the more interesting given that the village, as an independent residential group comprising many functions, is opposed on every level to the dispersed matrilinear clan which controls matrimonial debts and credits and, in the first instance, ensures the distribution and circulation of wealth (raffia tissues and items of equivalent value). Marriage implies bride-wealth. In order to marry, a man must possess large quantities of bands of raffia. True, this currency is also involved in other 'formal prestations', but one may consider its primary function to be to ensure the circulation of women between the exogamous matrilinear clans.

The correlation between what Sartre would term 'sparse material goods' and social organisation has seldom been so marked in an African society. The intense need for raffia and its concentration in the hands of the older men is the salient characteristic of the Lele economy. It could be said that Lele gerontocracy is explained by the accumulation of raffia and women (through polygamy) by the senior generation. Through the clan structure, as through the village structure based on the antinomy between the generations, the older men who hold the wealth impose a temporary but long-lasting state of socio-economic dependence upon the younger generation.

The result, in Mary Douglas's own words, is 'an inflationist pressure': there is too little raffia circulating to settle too many debts or to cover too many obligations. it is a remark worth developing from the point of view of monetary theory. The author tells us that the unit known as an *iboka* is a roll of nine *or* ten bands of cloth; similarly, the accountancy unit of the *lutuku* (the body, i.e. one slave) is made up of ninety *or* 100. This latitude of 10 per cent was not tolerated when a debt was repaid using a currency other than raffia (p. 56). I myself noticed a similar phenomenon in 1954 among the Songo-Meno of the Kasai, who also give this special value to raffia: four rolled bands represented the monetary unit (*okupfa*) estimated at one Congolese franc; the unit made up of nine *okupfa* rolls, referred to by the number expressing one hundred (*nkama*), was valued at ten Congolese francs. The number one thousand (*ladji*) applied to ten times nine *okupfa* rolls, the total of which was worth one hundred Congolese francs. If 9 equals 10 in these remarkable calculations, this is because the Songo-Meno decided to deduct one roll from each unit of ten in order to facilitate circulation.[3] In this case at least, it was a matter of taking deliberate action aimed at increasing the volume of the means of payment. Elsewhere Mary Douglas gives a most subtle analysis of the reasons for the Lele society resisting the substitution of Congolese money for raffia in the traditional circuits of exchange: the privileges of the older men would collapse, since only the younger generations are in a position to earn money. If money had supplanted raffia 'another society would have been shaped' (p. 63).

Social structure

The village, which is an autonomous political unit, is a collection of age groups. Its nominal chief is the oldest man from the founding clan or clans. But it is only outside the male assembly that he acts as the village representative. However informal it may be, the political organisation itself seems to conform with the age dualism which we shall find determines the shape of the village. The chief, the super-elder, is to some extent matched by a village orator (or spokesman) chosen for his personal qualities by his predecessor, from amongst the young men. He is the village treasurer.

The whole of the male population is divided into quarters representing as many age groups. These form a system of oppositions visible on the ground. Fig. 2.1 is a plan of a number of Lele villages as it is presented (p. 78) by Mary Douglas. It should be noted that more complex schemas also exist.

The village is cut in two by an imaginary diagonal. The first moiety (or 'hand') contains the huts of the oldest men (1) along one side and those of the first generation of young men (3) along the other side. The second 'hand' contains the second generation of old men (2) and the youngest generation of all (4). Thus the hierarchy of age groups, from the oldest down to the youngest, follows a numerical order. The avowed function of this system is to establish a respectful

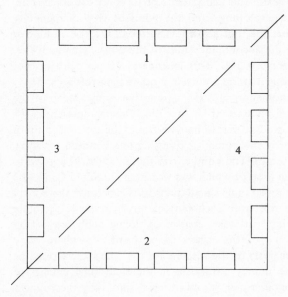

Fig. 2.1

distance 'between successive generations which are considered to be natural rivals and so likely to fight one another' (p. 80). In contrast, the alternate generations grouped together in the same 'hand' are expected to collaborate. In a way they are considered as one and the same generation. They are united by a network of reciprocal relationships. It is significant that the two alternate groups in the same 'hand' go hunting together.

In effect, we find ourselves in the presence of a double dualist structure. The rigid opposition of the two 'hands' expresses tension. It makes a radical separation between successive generations. But within each 'hand' the institutional desire for collaboration between alternate generations is aimed at reducing a much more violent socio-economic contradiction, by masking it. Beneath an unbalanced network of reciprocity this secondary dualism cunningly conceals the opposition between on the one hand the old men as a whole (groups 1 and 2) who own the women, the credits in women and the wealth and, on the other, the young men as a whole (groups 3 and 4). It is a glaring paradox: although the differences in wealth are in fact greater between alternate than between successive generations, in praxis it is precisely at the point where the gap is largest that the social structure attempts to reduce it and even to deny it by identifying opposing groups.

We find evidence of the same process where kinship groups are concerned. The general adoption of the principle of identifying alternate generations is, at least in part, a mystification set up to the advantage of the old men. True, certain concessions are made. Mary Douglas has much to say on this subject in her study in depth of a quite remarkable institution for sexual compensation, namely polyandry in the village. When the young men reach the age of about eighteen, their elders provide them with a collective wife, of particularly high social status, until such time as each of them can procure a private wife for himself. But even in this concession, and despite the possible sociological virtues of the institution, which Mary Douglas recognises most subtly, the long arm of the older generations again appears. The fact is that, at least in the southern sector of the Lele region, the village men as a whole reserve the right to have sexual relations in the forest with these permanent wives who, in the village itself, are the exclusive property of a younger age group (p. 81). No doubt the 'village wives' also, as we shall see, symbolise the village seen as a synchronic residential group, as opposed to the clan, which is non-residential and diachronic. What is important, at this point, is to situate this curious institution at the point where praxis and the structure of the age groups hinge together.

One of Mary Douglas's observations directs our attention to another aspect of the dualism of the age groups: 'It is very important to understand that every village was composed of a younger generation, which was expected to go away, and an older generation which was in permanent residence' (p. 95). This phenomenon is simply an accentuated form of the classic opposition that prevails in a society whose clans are matrilinear but which practises virilocal marriage. This time the contrast operates in favour of the younger generation. When the Lele boast of the merits of their freedom of movement they point out that all able-bodied men are allowed the choice of any local section of their matrilinear clan, in whichever village this may be, when it comes to a place to marry, have children, obtain wealth and die. Ideally, a man lives for as long as possible in his native village, near his father. He does not have to leave him to go to some maternal uncle. It is more likely that he will be drawn away by a maternal great-uncle, whether a real or a classificatory one. In effect, the Lele give the older men a preferential marriage right over a daughter of their own daughter. Grandfathers make free use of this matrimonial credit. They can either marry their granddaughter or give her in marriage to a 'clan brother'. But more frequently they will give her to a junior member of their local clan section, that is, to the sister's daughter's son (ZDS). This privilege makes it possible for the older men to draw to them young men of their clan who are enticed by the prospect of at last being able to marry.

This poses the whole problem of the structure of the clan. Although it is a social unit radically distinct from the village, the clan is nevertheless based on the same principle: namely, the identification of alternate generations and the avoidance and opposition of successive generations. Mary Douglas gives a skilful explanation of this significant homology. Within a local section of a clan no account is taken of genealogical kinship. The author is therefore quite right not to describe as lineages these loosely structured groups without authority which tend to form in the villages which their ancestors helped to found. If the structure of the village is based upon the age groups, its uncertain history is connected with clan affinities. All wealth and credits in women derived from the marriage of a female member of the clan belong to these fluctuating groups of co-residents united by their feeling of belonging to the same kin. The management of this wealth and these credits falls to the senior generations, who are free to choose whether to let the junior generations benefit from them or not.

Age groups and kinship

However, the Lele conceive the clan and age-group systems as irreducible. Mary Douglas makes an illuminating remark which explains this peculiar aspect of Lele society. The concepts of *mbai* (the term by which members of the same age group refer to one another) and of 'brothers' are antithetical (p. 73). Children born at the same time (ideally in the same month) are *mbai* to each other. They owe each other affection and loyalty. The greatest familiarity exists between them. In contrast, relations between brothers are governed by a strict formality. They are always respectively the older and the younger and, theoretically, it would be impossible for them to be *mbai*, since several years elapse between the successive pregnancies of a woman. The Lele draw the most extreme conclusions from this opposition. Twins, who combine the qualities of *mbai* and brotherhood, are considered monstrous, for they embody the fusion of contraries. But elsewhere Mary Douglas tells us that the parents of twins find themselves excellently placed to mediate between the human and the animal world (the latter being characterised in particular by its extreme and remarkable fertility). The parents of twins become diviners and carry out special rituals concerning hunting and fertility. My suggestion is that the Lele see in every birth of twins an excessive, outrageous presence of animal nature in human nature. They attempt to deny or neutralise this abnormal, disturbing invasion of nature into culture by means of a cultural excess which is its reverse: although they always use distinctive names for men and women, the Lele invariably give twins the same names, taking no account of the difference in sex which is so crucial in all other social contexts. The first-born twin is called Ihaku, the second Mboyu (p. 73). The particular interpretation suggested by Mary Douglas coincides with my own view. She writes: 'Thus, by the distinctive naming, seniority was introduced into their relations and the social anomaly in their situation reduced' (that is to say, the confusion of the antagonistic qualities of *mbai* and brother).

It is important to realise that the incompatibility between the quality of *mbai* (implying friendship and a high degree of familiarity within a single age group) and that of brother (implying reserve) is an ideological one. It shows significantly that the structures of age groups and of kinship groups are antithetical, as the rest of this analysis will show. On a practical level, however, as Mary Douglas engagingly confirms, brothers are sometimes to be found within the same group, as are even twins.

Nevertheless, from a structural point of view, the antithetical pair *mbai*– brother refers us to two radically distinct types of sociability. The first term implies the egalitarian society without age or kinship distinctions partially realised within each quarter of the village; the second implies the reserved, difficult relationships within the local clan sections where age differences play a determining role. Mary Douglas writes: 'A man could not be at ease or speak freely or intimately with any of his own clansmen as they were all older or younger than he' (p. 103). Generally speaking, within a clan section there can only exist relationships of 'brotherhood' in the sense defined (p. 96). For the time being we will put off examining one difficult problem, namely why, in the age-group as in the kinship system, alternate male generations refer to each other using the term *mbai*. We shall be able to answer this question only when we have a deeper understanding of the structure of marriage. For the moment let us limit ourselves to testing an interpretation suggested by the Lele themselves, and to trying to connect it with the great dualist schema that they put forward on a religious level. Here we shall have to refer to earlier studies published by Mary Douglas.[4]

Human beings possess characteristics radically different from those of animals. Man's essential quality is *buhonyi* (shame, reserve, modesty); animals are devoid of this. In contrast to the animal, man feels an immediate repulsion from anything that is *hama* (dirty, impure, spoilt, rotten). But the Lele are aware that this antithesis is too absolute. Within the human world itself the woman is less sensitive than the man to *buhonyi*. Even the man comes into contact, through his left hand, with what is *hama*. Already a series of oppositions becomes discernible in which the gap between the two terms progressively decreases.

Humanity	Animality
Man	Woman
Right	Left

Similarly, within the animal world, certain creatures present difficult problems of classification because they have certain important characteristics which bring them closer to the human race: for example, the pangolin, which is anomalous within the category of mammals, since it both has scales like a fish and gives birth to its young one by one as human beings do. In this respect the pangolin is the reverse homologue of the parents of twins (see above). It is through the intermediary of mixed creatures such as this that mediation between the animal world (hunting and fertility) and the human world is made possible.

It can be seen that the *mbai*—brother pair, which refers us to the structural opposition between the age group and the matrilinear clan, might fall into place in this perspective, which we shall do no more than indicate briefly. At the extreme limit, this opposition suggests the ontological dualism between nature and culture which is perhaps the basis of the classificatory logic of all 'savage thought'.[5] The age group, characterised by the *mbai* relationship, is exclusively male; it has no biological, natural, female root; it is purely cultural. The matrilineal clan, in contrast, which is partly biological, is rooted in the woman. Mary Douglas tells us that the nature of comradeship is illuminated by a fable in which the eagle and the tortoise conclude a pact of friendship of the *mbai* type (p. 74). These two animals exchange their most precious possessions. The eagle gives his feathers; the tortoise, his shell. The feathers of the eagle soon grow again, but the shell of the tortoise does not, so the tortoise has sacrificed his life. The story illustrates the great generosity that prevails between age-group companions (*mbai*). Let us analyse the symbolism in greater depth. For the Lele, the tortoise is an animal that eludes classification. Its shell distinguishes it clearly from other reptiles; it is equipped with four feet like mammals and yet it lays eggs. It could be said that the fable attempts to resolve these contradictions by projecting the tortoise into the category of airborne ovipara, since, all in all, that of the earthbound creatures (reptiles, mammals) is ill suited to it. The tortoise and the eagle exchange their specific characteristics as oviparous creatures. The story relieves the tortoise of its ambiguous natural condition; using an entirely cultural procedure, the tortoise and the eagle exchange their respective natures so as to become associated socially. The story expressly glorifies the ideal of age companions who are brought together in the most intimate manner on the social plane although they are different by birth, i.e. in their kinship groups. If the tortoise dies, this is because total negation of links of kinship (the chimerical ideal of the age groups) is too absolute an undertaking. Only the eagle, which is a sovereign animal, is successful in doing so, like *Nyimi*, the chief of the aristocratic clan who is torn from his kinship relations by ritual incest at the moment of his enthronement (see below). The Lele are obliged to take account of the local matrilinear sections; the age groups (who stand for an ideal, unconstrained way of life) must in the village come to terms with the demands and the reality of the kinship groups. They have to live in a contradictory way with their feathers and shells. But it is always going to be difficult because the kinship and the age groups, which, as we shall see, the Lele distinguish as carefully as they do the oviparous creatures of the air and those of the earth, are in competition when it comes to possessing women. This praxis is something that must not be forgotten when we attempt to integrate these two types of structure in the dualist thought of the Lele.

The difference between the age and the kinship groups can be connected with two different types of rights over women. There are two different matrimonial status for men and for women (p. 133): on the one hand *numande njua mbulu* (her house husband) and reciprocally *ngalande njua mbulu* (his house wife) and, on the other, *ba bola* (village husbands) and reciprocally *ngal a ba bola* (village wives). The first status gives a man, in his capacity as the member of a local clan section, one or several wives (polygamy) for his own private and exclusive use; the second gives a woman several husbands who are members of the same age group (polyandry). A woman is always either a village wife or a private one. But the two status are not mutually exclusive in the case of men. Every man can have one or several private wives and also share a village wife with his age-group companions. As we have seen, polyandry is closely connected with the institution of age groups with its residential rather than family structure. The junior group of a moiety (or 'hand') waits for the senior group of the same moiety to provide it with a collective wife who will be considered a 'village wife'. Similarly and inversely, private wives are ideally provided by the older men for the younger ones in the same clan section (p. 81). In both cases the position as givers of women of the senior generation in relation to the junior generation stems from the principle of the preferential right of the mother's father over the daughter's daughter.

Mary Douglas correctly emphasises the perfect homology of the two matrimonial systems: in the matrilinear kinship groups the junior generation hopes that the alternate senior generation will allow it to benefit from the matrimonial credit the older group enjoys where their daughters' daughters are concerned. Similarly, each junior age group waits for the alternate age group in its own moiety ('hand') to offer it the daughter of the daughter of its own village wife as a polyandrous wife. But the organisation of the age groups and that of the clans function as autonomous systems opposed to and separated from each other. So true is this that a clan section never gives one of its daughters or sisters to an age group as a village wife. This at least is what we may deduce from Mary Douglas's analysis. There are, in fact, only two ways in which to acquire a village wife: either a junior group asks its alternate senior group to give it the daughter of the daughter of the latter's own village wife, or else the young men go and carry off a girl from a neighbouring village (p. 130). Marriage by elopement is the sign of the deliberate refusal to reconcile – or the impossibility of reconciling – the polyandrous system of marriage which is the prerogative of the age groups with the regular marriage alliance that implies recognition of the exogamous matri-linear clans and respect for their rights.

By taking further the analysis of the ideological antinomy between *mbai* and brother we have uncovered a new aspect to Lele dualism: the opposition between two homologous social systems (the age groups and the clans) which are comple-mentary but antithetical within the society as a whole. We must now tackle a difficulty which does not appear to have attracted the attention of Mary Douglas. Why is it that, within the kinship system, one finds behaviour of the *mbai* type which is the fundamental characteristic of the extremely warm relations between companions from the same age group? It is easy enough to grasp the starting point of our analysis: in both systems the alternate generations are identified together. So it is normal that the alternate senior and junior groups in the same village moiety should also consider one another *mbai*. But it is less easy to under-stand how it is that this relationship is to be found again within the kinship system where one would expect, rather, to see the alternate generations call one another brothers (the elder and the younger). The fact is that three categories of male relatives are *mbai* to one another:

1. the son's son and the father's father;
2. the daughter's son and the mother's father;
3. the sister's daughter's son and the mother's mother's brother.

The last case is particularly ambiguous, since the mother's mother's brother belongs to the same matrilinear clan as his great-nephew whom he may equally well call *mbai* (age-group companion) or younger brother. This case is extremely upsetting, since the quality of *mbai* (which in principle excludes any age differ-ence) and the antagonistic quality of brother (which necessarily supposes an age difference in Lele thought) are found to be confused.

Mary Douglas, who in her book does not seem to attach much importance to the *mbai*–brother opposition, has been good enough to provide me with some complementary information which resolves the problem I have posed. Clearly, we cannot be satisfied with the extreme (but revealing) position which served as our starting point. If true *mbai* are those men born at approximately the same time outside the links of kinship, it nevertheless remains a fact that this definition is far from being rigorously applicable to all the members of the same age group. Furthermore, analogous friendly relationships can be entered into through a pact, regardless of age, between commercial partners and even between different tribes. Everything seems to indicate that, to explain the structural opposition between age groups and kinship, the Lele refer to a model with which they themselves do not conform in practice. It is worth underlining this discrepancy between the structure and the lived reality of Lele society. A number of similar examples could be found in Africa, involving either an extension or a limitation of an original meaning. Be that as it may, the application of the term *mbai* to alternate generations within a kinship system poses a problem which must be resolved in structural terms, for we are dealing here with an overall system.

Our attention is immediately attracted by another of Mary Douglas's remarks. The term *mbai* is also used by a man's co-wives and the brothers-in-law — provided that the age differences which imply mutual respect are not too striking — even though a specific term (*ngahang*) exists to refer to this joking relationship. There is reason to believe that the underlying meaning of *mbai* should be sought at the point where these manifest and different elements intersect. We are first led to examine whether alternate generations (grandfathers—grandsons; maternal great-uncles—maternal great-nephews) are not, like brothers-in-law, united by links of matrimonial alliance. And after that there will be occasion to seek for the analogy between co-wives and the companions within an age group.

Mbai, brothers-in-law and alternate generations

A grandson and each of his grandfathers reciprocally call each other *mbai*.[6] Clearly, neither of these two grandfathers (the mother's father or the father's father) belongs to the matrilinear clan of the grandson. We shall see that each of the two grandfathers, for various reasons, takes a wife from the clan of his grandson. The mother's father is the potential brother-in-law of his daughter's son, since the Lele confirm the excellence of a preferential marriage between a man and the daughter of his daughter, even if in practice the grandfather hands on this matrimonial credit to a junior member of his clan section.

There exists among the Lele a secondary type of preferential marriage which could explain why the same reciprocal term *mbai* can equally be used by the father's father and the son's son. Unfortunately, Mary Douglas does not tell us much about this second type of preferential marriage, which to some extent competes with the first. She simply tells us that in practice the right of the mother's father to dispose of his daughter's daughter is limited by the similar right held by the father over his daughter. The final result is a compromise: the clan of the mother's father takes one of the daughters, the father takes another of them for his own father's clan (p. 116). What does this mean? I believe we should understand that the two grandfathers, the paternal and the maternal, are in competition for the sisters of their grandson, who thus finds himself to be their *mbai*. In this context then, *mbai* refers to the matrimonial alliance between clans which is realised through grandsons and grandfathers.

Let us examine the third type of *mbai* relations between alternate generations (the mother's mother's brother—the sister's daughter's son). The status of these two *mbai* is somewhat different from the matrimonial point of view. The second man (the younger one) expects the first (the older one) to pass on to him the granddaughter whom he has received through his rights of preferential marriage. If we attempt to establish a relation between the first case analysed and this one, we notice that a woman given by a *mbai* grandson eventually ends up with a *mbai* great-nephew. The result of the operation is that two men (*1* and *2*) both find themselves in *mbai* positions, one as the giver of the woman (*1*), the other as the receiver (*2*) in relation to the third (*3*) who is for one of them the mother's father and for the other the mother's mother's brother. What we have here is an exchange between the sons of cross cousins through the mediation of the alternate generation, which holds the matrimonial riches and credits. This mediation in some way annuls the reserve that normally exists between members of the same clan section; this explains the ambiguity (and even contradiction) in the terminology which simultaneously assimilates the mother's mother's brother to both an elder brother and an age-group companion (*mbai*). The great-nephew does not have to avoid his maternal great-uncle, since the *mbai* relationship obliterates the elder-brother one (p. 104).

So, applied to alternate generations, the term *mbai* denotes relations between the giver and the receiver of a woman. It now becomes easier to understand that it can be extended to apply to commercial partners.

Mbai, co-wives and co-husbands

The extension of this same term to the co-wives of a man is easy to understand: the situation is the reverse homologue of the marital status of authentic *mbai*, members of the same age group who are the co-husbands of a polyandrous wife. The *mbai* relationship is thus at every level connected with wives. The authentic *mbai* share the same wife, whom they receive from their alternate age group in the same village moiety, the members of which are also considered to be *mbai*. Within the kinship system alternate generations are *mbai*, whether within the clan or outside it, to the extent that one generation is the receiver of a woman and the other the giver. The *mbai* relationship always implies either a gift (of a

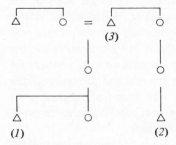

Fig. 2.2

92

sister to the senior alternate generation or of a granddaughter to the junior alternate generation) or a sharing (of one wife between several companions in an age group).

The brother–*mbai* antinomy thus appears to be reinforced by all these situations. The status of *mbai* is close to that of brothers-in-law. It refers to matrimonial alliances between exogamous clans through the mediation of preferential marriages with granddaughters. The intrusion into the clan system of this relationship (between the mother's mother's brother and the sister's daughter's son) constitutes the only ambiguity: in this case the 'elder brother' is the giver of the woman, acting as a kind of intermediary.

The structural opposition between age and kinship groups can be formulated in even more general terms. The age groups belong wholly to the village. In a sense they are the village. The polyandrous wives of an age group are, more generally, 'village wives' excluded from the matrimonial circuit established between exogamous clans. The age groups are part of a residential structure, localised in space. Clans exist only in the dimension of time. They break up haphazardly into a series of local sections whose composition is always unstable. The life of the village is synchronic; that of the clan, diachronic. The matrimonial ideal of the former is polyandry; that of the latter, polygamy.

The autonomy of the two homologous structures (age groups and clans) strikes one yet again in the following observation made by Mary Douglas: the idea of coordinating age-group and kinship relationships is quite foreign to the preoccupations of the Lele. The author on more than one occasion noticed a case where a father and a son were situated in different groups but ones that belonged to the same moiety of the village (p. 80). Apparently the contradiction between the attitudes required (familiarity where *mbai* was concerned and reserve between son and father) was resolved in favour of the kinship system. The son in fact continued to avoid his father carefully. Ideally, he should have adopted the same behaviour towards his father's age companions (p. 80). So the two systems do not 'fit'. But no doubt statistically one could predict that fathers are more often separated from their sons, each living in a different moiety ('hand') in the same way as nephews and maternal uncles.

A structural analysis of marriage will now show us how the endogamous tendency of the village is both opposed to and comes to terms with the rigorous exogamy of the matrilinear clans.

Matrimonial structure and contingency

Before embarking upon these new investigations I must sound some notes of caution. The Lele's preferential marriage with the daughter's daughter comes into competition with other matrimonial circuits that are entirely dependent on contingency. In all cases, whether preferential or not, marriage is characterised by a substantial transfer of wealth. The possession of riches is always decisive; it explains how it is that there is an accumulation of women (polygamy) in the hands of the older men.

Another aspect of the matrimonial system of the Lele is that it is complicated by a remarkable legal institution which Mary Douglas situates right at the centre of Lele society. This is *bukolomo*, the pawnship of a woman and all her matri-linear descent. It is an institution worth examining as a matter of priority, for at first sight its very existence appears to compromise the validity of any struc-turalist schema.

The clans, like the villages, have at their disposal a substantial number of women who have been designated to them as compensation for 'blood debts'. These debts arise from various injuries suffered by a group, in particular when the death of one of its members has been attributed to an act of criminal sorcery or sexual pollution. This legal system seems to be founded on both the principle of 'a life for a life' and a refusal to allow the law of retaliation pure and simple to take over social life. A woman is ceded to the injured group to repair the damage, as a pawn (*kolomo*). A *kolomo* woman is in no way assimilated to a slave. She remains under the protection of her own clan. But the receiving group has full powers over her marriage and over the marriage of women descended from her. These women may also be used to settle 'blood debts' of the receiving group. It would even seem that this last function is considered the most obvious by the Lele, who reckon that 'the advantage of owning pawns is that if you incur a blood debt you can settle it by paying one of your pawns, and your own sisters remain free' (p. 144). The male as well as the female descendants of a *kolomo* woman remain *kolomo* indefinitely for the receiving group. But this state of dependence in no way sets up a feudal system of clientship. Mary Douglas is insistent on this point: any man exercising a pawn right over a section of clan X may himself be the *kolomo* of a man from clan Y. The status of *kolomo* is always relative. This legal status in no way impairs the freedom that the pawn-man retains to insist upon and in his turn receive, if it be his due, a pawn-woman and to exercise his control over her descendants. A circuit of reciprocal obli-gations is set up between the 'master' and the *kolomo*: the former must protect the latter, who, for his part, owes his master certain services. It may seem audacious to attempt an interpretation of this institution given that Mary Douglas herself warns us to be circumspect about it. She writes: 'The ramifi-cations of the system were so complex that it is difficult to isolate its effects' (p. 144). Nevertheless, it seems to me that this institution should be considered first of all from a matrimonial point of view. The crucial problem faced by the Lele society is, as we have seen, the shortage of women, aggravated by the short-age of the riches (raffia) that are needed to obtain them. The pawning of a num-ber of women may be interpreted in the economic context of the currency crisis in raffia (see above). The social consequences of the institution are of secondary importance compared to this primary fact: it is always a woman, initially, who is pawned, which is to say that she is withdrawn from the normal matrimonial circuit. The demand for women is such in this society in its perpetual state of imbalance, of crisis, that neither raffia nor rights of preferential marriage suffice to answer demand. It seems as if the legal system (compensation for injuries) had itself been contaminated by this economic factor. Deaths attributed to some injury demand compensation in the form of matrimonial credit. Even if the Lele assert that the essential function of the institution is to cover the total damages and interests inextricably intertwined at the heart of the society, this view is logically derived from one fundamental factor: every woman pawned, whatever her eventual use, is first and foremost removed from the various matrimonial networks (preferential unions and others). Although it is affected by historical fluctuations and unforeseeable legal tensions, the institution of *bukolomo*, contrary to what might be expected, in no way invalidates every structuralist interpretation of Lele marriage. The intrusion of *bukolomo* simply shows that certain events put pressure upon the ideal model of matrimonial exchange imagined by the Lele on the basis of the harmonious relations that ought to prevail between the exogamous clans and the villages. The 'blood debts' are a constant drain upon the reserves of women available within the clans. But conversely they are also a source of enrichment by introducing new pawn-women under the jurisdiction of the group. Overall, then, this institution tends to restore the equilibrium compromised by each individual injury done. In the end it helps to intensify the circulation of women just as, as we have seen, the re-evaluation of raffia fulfilled a similar function on another level.

There is therefore no reason to see the purely legal function of the institution of *bukolomo* as fundamental to the society. Logically and historically this could not in itself represent the sole basis of Lele society. No human society can stake everything on chance. *Bukolomo* postulates that the women belong to the clans; now, the clans can only coexist through exogamy. So *bukolomo* implies a pre-existing matrimonial structure on which it is parasitic without, however, succeeding in destroying it altogether. This precise example could be used to verify the heuristic value of the opposition between structure and events to which Claude Lévi-Strauss has drawn attention. The fact that a certain number of women are pawned in perpetuity together with their female descendants tends here to change the event (the legal incident) into a structure and to use history, or contingency, to establish a new right. The institution of *bukolomo* emphasises the role praxis can play in creating structures. The institution of pawn-women appears to proliferate rather like a cancer within the fabric of matrimonial exchange. Thus the adultery of a pawn-woman gives her husband the right to claim a new pawn-woman, whereas reparation for the same transgression on the part of a wife with the normal status consists in raffia cloths (p. 144). As Mary Douglas points out, the Lele will exploit any opportunity of claiming a woman by *bukolomo* (p. 169).

The antinomy between village and clan is again emphasised by *bukolomo*. Faced with this institution, the village and the clan appear as groups in competition. Each has its own blood debts, which means that each has its autonomous legal personality. Similarly, as we have seen, each is supplied by its own separate circuit of women (village wives–private wives). *Bukolomo* reinforces the structure of the clan as well as that of the village. Mary Douglas emphasises that it represents the only institution that transcends the separate units that make up the local clan sections: whether or not they live together, all the members of the clan have joint blood debts and credits (p. 140). In this sphere, the village at last enters into a relationship with the clan, as an established rival unit: it may insist on payment of a blood debt on the part of a clan just as it may on the part of another village.

I cannot delay here to comment upon this complex institution that I have attempted to reduce to its primary socio-economic significance. Whatever the complications that it introduces, an analysis of the initial schema that it upsets in various ways is indispensable. In other words, what is the structural schema for preferential marriage among the Lele?

In order to make it quite clear, let us point out once again that this schema is far from reflecting the total shape of Lele society. This is affected by the interaction of several different structural levels (preferential marriage, marriage with bride-wealth, polyandrous marriage), all of which are upset by the institution of *bukolomo*. As we have indicated, the Lele in effect practise two types of preferential marriage: in every family the first daughter (x) is given to the clan of her mother's father; the second (y), to the clan of her father's father. The first option is the first step in a system of generalised exchange according to which clan A alternately (every two generations) provides a certain number of wives for B and B'.[7] Here we shall consider the most usual hypothesis, which is that the father of the mother, who is the receiver of the woman, passes his granddaughter on to his sister's daughter's son. Thus the preferential marriage is reduced to a union between the son and the daughter of cross cousins.

The secondary preferential marriage of a second daughter (y) of, for example, clan A with a member of the clan of her father's father (*1*) creates an extra bond of alliance, this time between clan A and clan C'. It helps to widen the circle of asymmetrical generalised exchange. For y' in the next generation, the clan of the paternal grandfather (*2*) is C. The juxtaposition of the two types of preferential marriage thus results in every clan permanently having the status of giver of women in relation to four others which are grouped in pairs according to alternate generations: for A these clans will be now B and C' (the generation of x and y), now B' and C (the generation of x' and y'). In effect, the maternal grandfathers belong alternately to B and B' and the paternal grandfathers to C' and C, as can be seen in Fig. 2.3.

The system can only operate if the men marry neither their patrilateral cross cousin nor her descendants. It is therefore understandable that marriage should be forbidden in the clan of the father as well as in the clan of the mother (p. 111). Lele ideology maintains that every man is indebted to his father: each clan is

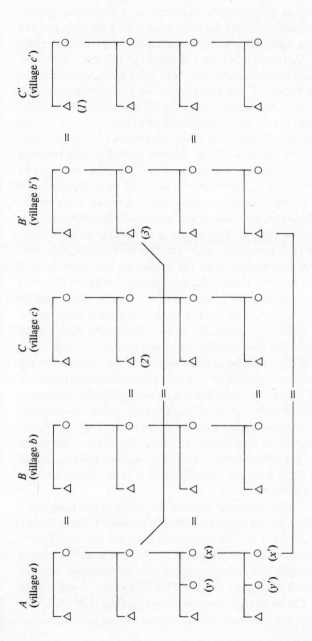

Fig. 2.3   First type of preferential marriage: the mother's father gives his daughter's daughter to his sister's daughter's son

under the perpetual obligation to give women in marriage to the clans which engendered its members. In spite of the dispersion of the clans, the Lele deliberately manifest their desire to preserve the stability of their mutual relationships by means of this system.[8] Thus our schema is not the gratuitous view of a scientific structuralist mind; it is simply the synthesis of a conscious system.

However, it must be remembered that the clans are not very strongly marked sociological units among the Lele. They hardly manifest themselves at all except as local sections. We must therefore bring the full weight of our analysis to bear upon the residential groups. In a note she has been kind enough to send me, Mary Douglas defines the nature of the second type of preferential marriage: when a man (*3*) claims one of his daughters (*y*) for the matrilinear clan of his own father (*1*), he can give her to any member of this clan (which is not his own). But he will for preference choose a son-in-law who lives in the same village as himself (marriage, remember, is virilocal). In this way he will benefit from his son-in-law's services. We must therefore emphasise the endogamous tendency of the village. In this type of union the father of *y* in effect intervenes not as a representative of clan *C'*, to which he does not belong, but rather as an inhabitant of the village benefiting from the advantages of patrilocality. He seeks out for his daughter a member of clan *C'* who is also a co-resident in the village. However, this contingency (the Lele enjoy great freedom as to where they live) throws into relief a quasi-structural feature of the village: its endogamous ideal stands in strong opposition to the exogamy of the clan. In this second type of preferential marriage the village imposes its own law on interclan exchanges. Its synchronic dimension (it is composed of people living in the same place at the same time) overrides the diachronic dimension of the clan, whose matrimonial alliances are forged in time. Thus this second type of preferential marriage is not so much in the interest of the clans but rather reinforces the cohesion of the villages. The women themselves hope not to have to leave their native village and thus of their own accord favour the endogamous tendency of the residential group. It could even be said that the rights of the father to control the marriage of one of his daughters and half the bride-wealth of all the others is an expression of the intrusion of the village (seen as a distinct sociological unit) into the matrimonial circuit governed by the clans. It is as if the village did not want to lose all the advantages that it can draw from patrilocality, that is from the presence at close hand of the daughters of its members.

The first type of preferential marriage reflects the desire for a generalised exchange between the clans; the second emphasises the village's desire for endogamy. But the first type can itself also be interpreted from the point of view of the fathers, that is from the point of view of the village. A most revealing schema of Mary Douglas's, illustrating the relationships between residence and the mother's father's right over his daughter's daughter, has helped me to understand this phenomenon (p. 92). Let us examine my own diagram (Fig. 2.3). Adopting a female point of view, Mary Douglas notes that a woman *x* from clan *A*, born in the paternal village b' (where there is a local section of clan B') marries into village b (where there is a local section of clan B); there she gives birth to a daughter x' who will marry into village b'. The daughter of this daughter, born in b', will marry into b like her maternal grandmother, and so on. A certain number of women (a limited number, it is true) thus circulate — first mother, then daughter — within a residential network limited to two villages. In each family at least one granddaughter marries into the village where her maternal grandmother was married. If we now interpret this structural situation from a male point of view, we notice that every other generation a man from village b' gives one of his daughters (whom he has fathered for clan A) to a man from village b, who in the next generation will repay village b' with one of the daughters whom he has fathered for the same clan A.

The system of generalised exchange by which clan A gives women alternately to clans B and B' is thus also a restricted exchange between the two villages b and b' whose men are the preferential fathers for clan A. It seems as though, as fathers, the men use at least two of their daughters to set up an endogamous residential structure restricted to one or two villages. The marriage takes place within the same village when the father exercises his right to dispose of his daughter by giving her to a member of his clan who is also a co-resident in the village. It takes the form of an exchange between two villages, from one father to another, through the normal system of preferential marriage of the first type (the right of the maternal grandfather). The first case results purely from contingency: it is, simply, probable that a man will be able to find in his own village a possible son-in-law who belongs to the clan of his father. The second results from the structural order; it is a part of the system of generalised exchange based on the right of each man to dispose of a daughter of his daughter. The first case results as much from the exogamous law as from a major intervention on the part of the village as such in the matrimonial structure governed essentially by clan organisation. The two types of preferential marriages are in competition. Once again, behind this partition or conflict, we find the opposition between the village and the clan.

The theoretical antinomy between *mbai* and brothers led us to a first opposition, to wit, between age group and kinship, and then to a second, between village and clan. Even the duality of preferential marriages refers back to it, just as does the duality of village and private wives. The father's secondary right over one of his daughters is exercised in favour of the village, which tends to confirm its closed structure, its socio-economic unity and its political sovereignty. In a society where women are particularly scarce, this right favours the rooting of young men within the village; it counters demographic haemorrhage. It confirms the endogamy (never fully realised) of a coherent residential group which already possesses its own polyandrous wives who are constantly renewed within the village itself through autonomous matrilinear channels. It will be remembered that the daughter of a daughter of a village wife is expected to take the place of her grandmother, in the same role, for the benefit of a new age group.

Although irreducible on a structural level, the village and the clan are obliged to come to terms with one another, since the dispersed clans which have no religious or political unity only exist as local sections implanted serially and contingently in the village. In accordance with the matrimonial law of the clans, we can see a residential structure of marriage take shape: endogamy within the village or restricted exchanges between two villages. So it is that the two antinomous structures of Lele society (the village and the clan) contrive the master stroke of finding within a single institution the means to reconcile their contradictory tendencies (endogamy, exogamy). In practice, naturally, the territorial dispersion of the women of a particular clan is much more complex. But although this schema is no doubt too rigid, it may have the merit of illuminating the fundamental principles to which the Lele refer either explicitly or implicitly when they declare that they desire to 'give an appearance of antiquity to the existing relations between clans',[9] whatever upsets history may have inflicted upon the structural model.

In a way, the village can be seen, in opposition to the matrilinear kinship groups, as the collective father of the children born to the village wives; it is also a collection of individual fathers (patrilocality) who are concerned to place their daughters, who do not belong to their own clan. Furthermore, the village has its own separate legal personality. As the holder of pawn-men and -women, it is in competition with the clan. It is the collective debtor or creditor of other villages, and even of clans. From all these points of view, the village, which is a synchronic unit, also appears to possess a diachronic role quite distinct from kinship. Mary Douglas stresses the privileged position of the village, as compared to the clan, in the *bukolomo* system; it is never possible for an entire village to fall into a state of pawnship, whereas a clan section descended from a *kolomo* woman will be placed collectively under the domination of another clan (p. 169). The historical event (the injury which leads to a blood debt) therefore presents a greater threat to the clan than to the village. By means of *bukolomo* the village tends to absorb clan sections, whereas normally it has to come to terms with them. The fact is that the village has the backing of force. It alone is capable of enforcing respect for a blood debt by force of arms. This is why one sometimes finds a clan selling to a village a blood debt that another clan has contracted towards it (p. 171). This legal institution founded on praxis highlights a new facet to the structural opposition between village and clan.

Structures of reciprocity and structures of subordination

Although, as Mary Douglas has stressed, it does not create a true system of clientship, *bukolomo* nevertheless introduces the principle of subordination into structures based on reciprocity. The links that it forges should not, strictly speaking, be described as 'contractual', which is the way Mary Douglas describes them. In his review of Mary Douglas's work, Vansina has pointed out that the term *kumu* by which the pawn-man or -woman refers to his or her 'master' is derived from the common Bantu root meaning chief.[10] The same word appears in the expression *kum a bola* (village chief). Furthermore, despite the *de facto* independence of the villages, there is among the Lele an aristocratic clan (the Tundu) all of whose members are called *kumu* (chief) by people belonging to other clans. I should like to point out that in all three cases the notion of 'chief' is based on praxis, not on the structural order. *Bukolomo* appears at the point where events may cause a breakdown in the structures of reciprocity (see above). The appointment of a village chief (*kum a bola*) also operates according to historical criteria: the chief is the oldest man in the founding clan of the village (p. 68). The privileges of the aristocratic Tundu clan are clearly also historical in origin. What is remarkable is that the subordination (more theoretical than real) of the non-Tundu clans (collectively known as Wongo) never establishes itself as a class system any more than *bukolomo* appears as a system of clientship. When the chief of a Tundu village pays a visit to a Wongo village, he receives a tribute of raffia. Later on, however, the Wongo village receives one of the Tundu chief's daughters as 'village wife'. From that moment on, the historical links of subordination between the Wongo and the Tundu are transformed into a relation of reciprocity between a collective son-in-law (the village) and an individual father-in-law. The son-in-law village renders services and makes presents to the parents of the young woman. In accordance with the system of preferential marriage, the daughter of this village wife will be sent to her mother's father; now the Tundu aristocrat becomes the village's son-in-law, and Mary Douglas quite rightly points out that the relationship of subordination has been reversed: it is now the village that receives gifts in its capacity as father-in-law (p. 195).

One may conclude that the structure of matrimonial reciprocity among the Lele is of sufficient strength effectively to resist the intrusion of a praxis which threatens the equality of the clans. The Lele have been successful in neutralising the historical dualism of the Tundu and the Wongo and in preventing the formation of a stratified society. The dualism has been reabsorbed at the level of the village because the Tundu clan is no more capable of imposing domination through force of arms than any of the Wongo clans. The weakness of the clan organisation has preserved the *de facto* independence of the strongly structured residential groups.

What we have here, posed in a concrete fashion, is the problem of the transition from clan to State. Moreover, it is delineated all the more clearly given that the Tundu do have a chief who appears to have all the embryonic characteristics of a sacred king. The chief of the Tundu clan bears the same name (*Nyimi*) as the sovereign of a neighbouring tribe, the Kuba, who are culturally and linguistically related to the Lele. The Kuba kingdom (an excellent study of which has been produced by Vansina) is a federation of chiefdoms subjected (initially by force of arms) to the central authority of the chief of the dominant tribe, the Bushong. A chiefdom, which is the principal political unit, may include an entire tribe, a part of a tribe or even sometimes a single village. The 'noble' clans control a large number of voices in the various chiefdom councils, and the function of chief is the prerogative of one of these clans. The king (*Nyim*) is also the chief of the Bushong chiefdom and his residence is the centre of the State. Vansina writes: 'The rights and duties of the king towards the chiefdoms constitute the whole structure of the State.'[11]

Now, the Lele *Nyimi*, the chief of the Tundu aristocracy, and the *Nyim*, the Kuba sovereign, share a number of common fundamental characteristics – a fact which emphasises the contrast between their distinctive features. It is clear that these can be explained by the different histories of the two societies. We are not particularly concerned here with whether the Lele borrowed the royal institution from the Kuba, as Mary Douglas suggests, or whether, as I believe to be the case, the two societies evolved along different lines starting from a common ancient tradition. Whatever the case may be, the diachronic dimension of an African structure of subordination is clearly detectable: two neighbouring societies, speaking dialects of the same language, are characterised by in one case a deflected (or debased) royalty and, in the other, fully developed royalty.

Among the Kuba, as among the Lele, the *Nyim(i)* forgoes all kinship links at the moment of his enthronement; he is projected out of the clan, to the summit of society, in an incestuous solitude. The chief of the Tundu clan is ritually married to a classificatory sister; from that time onwards he can no longer look the members of his own clan in the face and lives in royal seclusion until his death (Douglas, p. 199). The Kuba king, who has sexual intercourse with a sister and who marries a niece within his clan, belongs to the category of beings and things that are impure: sorcerers, excrement etc.[12] Vansina states, in a personal communication, that this incestuous marriage is 'more or less secret and at all events it is unseemly to talk about it'. The same significant ritual action on which royalty is founded differs, depending on which point of view is adopted: whereas the Lele *Nyimi*, isolated and shut away, must no longer bring any children into the world, the Kuba *Nyim* is a great polygamist; far from being a recluse, he is the very centre of political life. From the point of view of succession, seniority has an absolute value among the Lele but only a relative one among the Kuba. The Lele *Nyimi* is the oldest man in the Tundu clan; the successor to the Kuba *Nyim* may be the eldest of his brothers or of his maternal nephews. In short, the fully developed type of royal power is hereditary and automatic within a well-defined matrilinear line. The tribute due to the Kuba sovereign involves no reciprocity, and this stands in strong contrast to the situation we described above in connection with the Tundu: the Kuba king receives a wife from each circle (group of chiefdoms); a Tundu village chief who has received the homage of a Wongo village gives a wife, whose daughter will later return to him. Among the Lele, the nascent structure of subordination has been neutralised by its insertion into the structure of matrimonial reciprocity. Among the Kuba the structure of subordination successfully imposed by the chief of the Bushong takes advantage of a pseudo-structure of asymmetrical reciprocity: the *Nyim* grants his military protection to the various chiefdoms which acknowledge allegiance to the central power. The only political privilege the chief of the Tundu seems to have managed to arrogate for himself is ultimate control over all human lives: in theory, nobody could be put to death in the whole Lele country without his permission. But Mary Douglas's own view is that this claim, which perhaps reflects some ancient form of domination, must be treated with some caution. The military force of the Tundu is imposed only in ritual circumstances. At the funeral of the *Nyimi* the Tundu used to capture two Wongo and sacrifice them (p. 200). The fact is that the Tundu appear never to have been able to impose a centralised power over the Wongo. The Tundu clan itself comprised three branches in the eastern sector of the Lele country studied by Mary Douglas, and each one installed its own *Nyimi*.

Structure and praxis are mutually illuminating. Ritual incest reveals a structural dimension to African royalty;[13] it is the basis for its magic sacral character and a symbolical expression of the bypassing of the clan structures, founding a new order on the (partial) negation of an older one. But when the Kuba assimilate the sovereign to the sorcerer and the Lele declare that the origin of sorcery lies in the aristocratic Tundu clan, they are both surely saying the same thing, namely that this bold and dangerous denial of the egalitarian clan order governed by exogamy and the exchange of riches is a threat to the society. There is a glimmering of a feeling of alienation in this theory. It now becomes easier to understand how it is that the failed king of the Lele is destined to seclusion and (social) sterility once the dominating will of his own clan has torn him from the ancient family order. The audacity of the ritual of incest is short-circuited, since the Tundu are not successful in establishing an effective royalty by force. All it can offer is the doubtful prestige of sorcery to the Tundu clan as a whole and shame to its chief: he can no longer meet face to face with the members of his clan, whose fundamental law he has transgressed — to no avail. The praxis can be deciphered from the structures of the ritual. In the case of the Kuba (where royalty is triumphant), the same act of incest is freed from the weight of the curse which it nevertheless continues to assume. In one case we have an institution devoid of continuity, invested with shame, marginal and misbegotten; in the other, royalty is fully hereditary, magico-religious, central. The reason is that, unlike the Tundu, the Bushong were successful in setting up a State framework, a structure of subordination. The Kuba king is a synthesis of shadow and light, of evil sorcery and beneficent magic, and he symbolises both protection and alienation. Even if each chiefdom, governed by its own councils, remains autonomous within the federation, the tribute that is paid to the king is in this instance real tribute, that is to say an unequivocal recognition of political sovereignty. In the context of this study it is beside the point that the Kuba should have so skilfully combined the old and the new orders, namely democracy and State rule, without falling as the Lele did into the traps of the economically sterile institutions of gerontocracy and polygamy.[14] However, I feel it is a reservation I should make, since, in another historical perspective, a comparison between the Lele and the Kuba societies has prompted me to hail the Kuba society as one of the most astonishing successes of traditional Africa.[15]

Social structure and religion

The Lele village is not only a political unit but also the centre of religious life, the seat of the cults responsible for ensuring the fertility of women and successful hunting. The weakness of the clan's role as opposed to that of the village is evident at every level. The matrilinear clan is negatively characterised by the absence of any ancestor cult. To put it another way, its diachronic dimension is reduced, to the advantage of the synchrony of the local sections, which are residential units. The village, in contrast, is in contact with the spirits of the forest. Its various cult groups place the accent on paternity, which is a qualification with no meaning within the matrilinear clan. The first cult grouping associates those men who have fathered a child (Begetters), the second − the cult of the Pangolin Men − includes those who have fathered a boy and a girl (Douglas, ch. XI). The association of the Pangolin Men, however, bridges the gap between the synchronic structural level (the village) and the diachronic level (the clan). The fact is that paternity *per se* is not enough; it is further necessary that the two children brought into the world by the candidate should be born from the same woman and that she should belong to one of the founding clans of the village. And not only the candidate himself but his father too must fulfil these conditions. The result of this odd system is that the Pangolin cult to some extent encourages intermarriages between the local sections of different clans within the same village, favouring those individuals who combine the qualities of being co-residents and members of a founding clan. At this extremely abstract level, the cult of the Pangolin Men would appear as a final attempt to synthesise the two antinomous and complementary structural levels. In formulating the problem in this way I am very close to Mary Douglas's own interpretation: 'The implicit intention in these regulations was to honour the members of the founding clans, to encourage their inter-marriage and thus to sustain the continuity of the clan population in the villages' (p. 209). To put it another way, it is a matter of harmonising the synchrony and the diachrony which arises from the different structures.

Let us integrate these factors in a diagram of matrimonial alliances as it is determined by the first preferential marriage, the right of the maternal grandfather to dispose of the daughter's daughter to a great-nephew (Fig. 2.3a).

Assume three founding clans, *A*, *B* and *C*. If (*1*) is a Pangolin Man, his great-nephew (*2*) is eligible to be one too, since he fulfils the necessary sociological

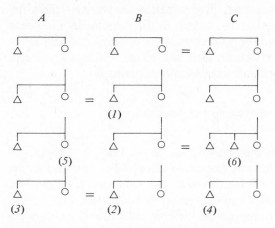

Fig. 2.3a   The first preferential marriage and the Pangolin Men

conditions. On the other hand, (*3*) and (*4*) can be Pangolin Men only provided that their fathers and their wives are also members of a founding clan. It is immediately apparent that there must exist in each village one lineage which is dominant from a religious point of view (*B*), which will try to keep close to it, by means of the first preferential marriage, the male members of the two others (*A* and *C*). This pattern is further facilitated by the application of the second preferential marriage, which allows *1*, who belongs to lineage *B*, to claim his daughter (*5*) who belongs to lineage *A*, for a member of lineage *C* who is also a co-resident (*6*). From a socio-religious point of view the two preferential marriages are thus perfectly in harmony: they both work towards the same end.[16]

One might wonder why this socio-religious synthesis should appear under the sign of the pangolin. On this point I would refer the reader back to p. 88. The pangolin is the mediator *par excellence* between the human and animal worlds. Within the human world the significant gap that opposes the matrilinear clan (a tense world of 'brotherhood') to the age group (an agreeable world of companionship and the focus of the village) reflects, on a smaller scale, the primordial gap which, in the eyes of the Lele, separates nature from culture. From this point of view the Pangolin Men in the village and the pangolins in the forest occupy homologous positions. One of the conditions for initiation is to have killed a pangolin in the forest; the ritual implies that some of the animal's flesh should be eaten. Thus a close association is established between the Pangolin Men and the pangolins. The Pangolin Men are mediators on the one hand between two antagonistic components of society and on the other between men and women; the animals are mediators, in a more general sense, between nature and culture. The rituals of the Pangolin Men concern both hunting (a male activity) and the fertility of women, despite the fact that the respective socio-economic spheres of the two sexes are kept rigorously separate. It is notable that the Begetters have no ritual function; their initiation simply gives them full rights as hunters. Thus the Begetters, in contrast to the Pangolin Men, are only connected with a male activity. Their ontological status lacks the richness of those through whom man and woman, clan and village, diachrony and synchrony achieve a harmonious, difficult and exceptional synthesis.

Postscript: horizontal and vertical exchanges (a discussion with Claude Lévi-Strauss)[17]

Lévi-Strauss has undertaken his own examination of the Lele matrimonial system, in connection with the criticisms that I have elsewhere put forward on the subject of the *atome de parenté*.[18] On this latter point the answer he provides seems to me totally convincing, and I will not return to the subject. I should like instead to make a number of comments on the new and extremely interesting model for Lele society that he proposes. Lévi-Strauss notices that generalised exchange, producing unions between the sons and daughters of cross cousins on the horizontal axis (see Fig. 2.3), can also be deciphered as a vertical exchange between generations: the Lele themselves hold, in fact, that 'a man who fathers a daughter and then gives her to the clan of his wife has the right to demand in return the daughter born to this daughter'.[19] Thus, the Lele model may be interpreted as direct exchange of a daughter for a granddaughter with the understanding that the latter will not be kept by her grandfather but will be passed on to a man of the same generation as herself.

Fig. 2.4 is the schema proposed by Lévi-Strauss. I have myself shown how the

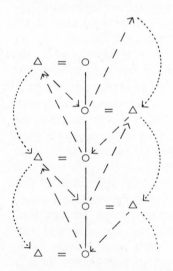

Fig. 2.4   Vertical exchange among the Lele, according to Lévi-Strauss, 1973, p. 130

preferential right of every man over the daughter of his own daughter results in an alternate exchange of daughters, carried out by the two fathers, between two villages (see p. 99). The residential model is thus consistent with Lévi-Strauss's analysis in terms of vertical exchange. It should be added that the right of the father over the daughter is also expressed in the fact that, whatever the nature of the marriage, it is he who has the last word;[20] furthermore, the father receives the greater part of the matrimonial wealth brought by the husband of his daughter.[21]

The new viewpoint suggested by Lévi-Strauss prompts me to examine neighbouring societies which also, in one way or another, maintain the right of the grandfather over his daughter's daughter, in the hope that this will make it possible to discover to which group of transformations Lele marriage belongs. There are two comparatively close peoples, the Pende and the Yanzi, who insist on the right of the maternal grandfather. Like the Lele, the Yanzi declare that a man has the right to claim for his clan the daughter of his daughter, his *ketyul*.[22] He passes her on either to a nephew or a great-nephew. But every man may equally marry either the daughter or granddaughter of his paternal aunt (FZD or FZDD). This group of options stems from a restricted exchange broadened to include three generations, as is shown in Fig. 2.5.

The Yanzi situation clearly reveals a crisis in the patrilateral system. The keystone of the system is, as among the Lele, the right of the maternal grandfather over his granddaughter; the transfer of this credit to the alternate generation, which is a fundamental characteristic of the Lele matrimonial structure, can already be detected. The Pende of the former province of Leopoldville, for their part, react to the crisis in the patrilateral system — to which the Pende of the Kasai remain unswervingly faithful — with a similar strategy. They insist emphatically that the grandfather himself has the right to marry the daughter of his daughter (see p. 35). This marriage takes place only following a union with the patrilateral cross cousin, and no more than in the case of the Yanzi does the system open out into generalised exchange: in fact, as we have seen, the right of the grandfather over his daughter's daughter is compensated for by the symmetrical preferential marriage of his grandson (DS) with one of his great-nieces (ZDD). This grandson thus marries his matrilateral female cross cousin (see p. 36). In this last case the maternal grandfather (*1*) gives a great-nephew to his grandson (*2*), who is expected to give him his own sister (Fig. 2.7).

It is by making the right of the maternal grandfather over his granddaughter the very basis of the matrimonial system and by forbidding any union between cross cousins of the first generation that the Lele — and only the Lele — are successful in making the transition from restricted to generalised exchange. But the remarkable thing is that a restricted exchange (a daughter in exchange for a granddaughter) continues to operate on a vertical axis, as Lévi-Strauss has revealed: the Lele in theory base their system of alliance on this direct reciprocity, even though 'in practice, they develop it from a system of horizontal

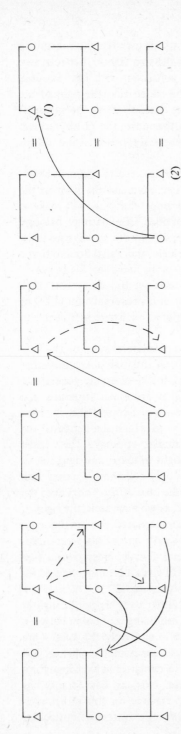

Fig. 2.5   The right of the maternal grandfather among the Yanzi

Fig. 2.6   The right of the maternal grandfather among the Lele

Fig. 2.7   The marriage of the maternal grandfather and of his granddaughter among the Pende of the former province of Leopoldville

exchange: the maternal grandfather in most cases hands on his conjugal right over his granddaughter to his sister's daughter's son, that is to say to a man who belongs to the same generation as the granddaughter'.[23] I have, above, already described the peculiarities of this generalised exchange.

This remarkable situation is worth examining in the light of the two preceding cases where emphasis is laid on the same conjugal right. The Lele model (Fig. 2.6) is obtained from the Yanzi model (Fig. 2.5) and the Pende model (Fig. 2.7) by a simple transformation: the suppression of patrilateral marriage in both its direct and its oblique forms. In effect the Lele preferential marriage introduces a generalised exchange between alternate generations, as does the patrilateral system; but it eliminates the periodic return of restricted exchange that the patrilateral system implies. The Yanzi, for their part, assert the pre-eminence of the maternal grandfather's right over his granddaughter; ideology does in fact bring to the fore the marriage with the *ketyul*.[24] However, this does not mean that the Yanzi have renounced marriage within 'the house of the father', which in one form or another (FZD or FZDD) is dominant throughout the area. The Lele have simply made the Yanzi option more radical; they have drawn the extreme consequences from the right of the maternal grandfather to dispose of his granddaughter, by excluding any return to patrilateral union.

Seen in this perspective, it will be possible for us to understand more fully why it is that the Lele ideology of preferential marriage finds its inspiration in a 'vertical' logic of restricted exchange even though its practice introduces generalised exchange. As we have seen, matrilinear societies which practise marriage with the patrilateral female cross cousin are bound to be virilocal. I would refer at this point to the earlier discussion of the residential system of the Pende, and in particular to Fig. 1.14 on page 64. In the analysis of the circulation of women between residential groups we noticed that these groups exchange daughters in pairs: a man from the first group gives his daughter to a partner from the second group who will subsequently reciprocate by giving his own daughter to the first group. In this respect the patrilateral system is in practice in the same situation as the Lele system, in which marriage is similarly virilocal. But such a phenomenon is not merely a matter of fact. In both cases it is part of the very structure of marriage.

Let us pursue our examination of the similarities and differences in the relations between alternate generations. Among the Lele as among the Pende, grandfathers and grandsons are linked by familiar relationships which abolish all age differences. In both societies they refer to each other by the term *mbai*, implying comradeship. But significant nuances can be detected.

Among the Lele one does not find the element of aggressiveness that characterises the behaviour of the grandson among the Pende of the former province of Leopoldville, where the grandfather's right over his daughter's daughter disturbs the patrilateral system. In certain Pende groups the grandfather can even claim his son's daughter for himself, although in a coherent patrilateral system this union is considered incestuous. It is clear that the matrimonial formulae that appear among the Pende of the former province of Leopoldville present themselves as a transformational state which is close to the Lele system. If marriage with the daughter of the paternal aunt (FZD) were abolished, this would be enough for the right of the grandfather over both his granddaughters to introduce a matrimonial system similar to that of the former state of Lele society. Mary Douglas in fact shows that in the old days grandfathers kept their granddaughters for themselves and for the men of their own generation so that a young man often had to wait for the death of his maternal great-uncle before he could inherit one of his widows.[25] It will furthermore be remembered that even today the Lele reserve the theoretical possibility of marrying the daughter of their own daughter or of giving her to a younger brother.[26] Inevitably, such a system has to be unstable and provisional. The example of the Pende shows clearly that the right of the grandfather over his granddaughter calls for some compensation in favour of the alternate generation. Passing on the grandfather's matrimonial credit to a great-nephew is at the very basis of Lele as it is of Yanzi society. But the Yanzi have no more given up marriage with the patrilateral female cross cousin than have the Pende; both societies nevertheless imperfectly prefigure the original Lele solution.

There are other indications that suggest that a similar set of problems beset the region as a whole, resulting more or less everywhere in a crisis in the patrilateral system.

It will be remembered that the Pende patrilateral system presents a clear example of a male patrilinear line of descent down which dietary prohibitions, magic knowledge and immaterial property rights are transmitted (see p. 65). Now, Lévi-Strauss has convincingly shown that a similar phenomenon exists among the Lele. However, the line here is not as systematised as in the case of the Pende: it is a matter, rather, of personal feelings. Furthermore, there also appears to be a corresponding matrilinear female line of descent of the same kind. Lévi-Strauss concludes: 'It is as if the Lele, who conceived their rule of descent in a matrilinear mode, were in fact living it in a different mode: from the point of view of their feelings for one another, son and father are united in one line and daughter and mother in another.'[27] So the Lele are familiar with the phenomenon of sex affiliation at least in a latent or embryonic form.

But the Lele system is also based on the identification of alternate generations, and Lévi-Strauss wonders if there is not a correlation between this phenomenon and sex affiliation. He then undertakes a very complex analysis, via the Mundugumor of New Guinea, the Apinaye of Brazil and the Ashanti of Ghana, in order to show that these societies, like the Lele but from various points of view, are based on a mode of transmission of certain elements of personal status separating brother and sister and binding each of them, in an elective way, to one or the other of their ascendants.[28] Finally, he notes that the system of alternate generations can also find its origin either in a double dichotomy of moities, respectively patrilinear and matrilinear, or in marriage with the patrilateral cross cousin.[29] He considers that these three formulae belong to a group of transformations where patrilateral marriage might mark a precarious null position between the two other states.

This last remark will hold our attention as far as the Lele are concerned. Does not the analysis just undertaken show precisely that the matrimonial exchange relations operating among the Lele through alternate generations can be described as a transformation of the patrilateral system? I have also shown that there is no incompatibility between patrilateral marriage and sex affiliation in the region under consideration. This phenomenon appears, in a form even more distinct than among the Lele, in the Pende society. Matrilinear and virilocal, the Pende practise canonical marriage with the daughter of the paternal aunt. We have also seen that a radical transformation in the direction of the Lele system (affirmation of the grandfather's matrimonial right to his granddaughter) operates within certain Pende groups. In this continual field of structural variations, patrilateral marriage, identity of alternate generations and secondary sex affiliation belong to one historico-cultural ensemble.

In *The Elementary Structures of Kinship*, Lévi-Strauss is perfectly aware that, on the other hand, marriage with the matrilateral female cross cousin 'is an absolute barrier to the reproduction of alternate generations'.[30] I shall, then, finish with a prudent query. Societies that set up a true regime of sex affiliation forbid — like the Lele — any marriage between cross cousins of the first generation. This is the case with the Apinaye of Brazil as well as with the New Guinean societies, where this social structure seems largely widespread.[31]

Could we not then, imagine that in these diverse American and Oceanic cases sex affiliation and the matrimonial regime that is associated with it might proceed from the historical transformation of matrilinear and virilocal societies practising marriage with the patrilateral female cross cousin?

The reply assuredly belongs to the specialists of these civilisations. We have seen, however, that from a general theoretical point of view matrilinear societies suffer from structural difficulties in opening up to generalised exchange (Chapter 1). If the Lele succeed in this, it is by transposing, on a vertical axis, the principle of restricted exchange: a man who has given a daughter expects in return a daughter born from this daughter; he will dispose of her within his own group.

Now, Lévi-Strauss notes the following concerning Melanesia: 'The study of sexual affiliation without cross-cousin marriage thus allows the definition, throughout the whole Melanesian world, of a sort of "fault" of generalized exchange, the significance of which seems even greater when it is noted that it borders that wide zone of breakdown of kinship structures which is the Polynesian world. The whole eastern area, the "Oceanic—America" area as it might be called, thus forms a sort of theatre in which restricted and generalized exchange meet each other, sometimes in conflict, sometimes in harmony.'[32]

In my opinion, the original solution of the Lele achieves precisely such an harmonious combination within the African world.

3

The debt of the maternal uncle: contribution to the study of complex structures of kinship

If there is one favourite theoretical question which British and French anthropologists have never stopped discussing, it is: why in many patrilineal lineage societies has the uterine nephew free *entrée* into the house of the maternal uncle? Why does he do all he can to push about a man who shows him the greatest affection, looting the goods of his uncle, casting daring jokes, even insults, towards his wife; in brief, setting about in many ways to 'diminish' him while also acting at times to 'purify' him, as is the case among the Dogon? Goody (1959) has aptly defined as 'privileged aggression' this eccentric behaviour, which, in his first and celebrated analysis of 1924, Radcliffe-Brown likened too simply to an affectionate joking relationship. There is no opportunity to review here the weaknesses of that first attempt at sociological interpretation, which was truly pioneer work; neither shall I be able to retrace the long polemic that this attempt led to and in which the late Evans-Pritchard, Lévi-Strauss, Goody, Adler and Cartry, among others, took part. For my part, I proposed in 1958, in my book on royal incest in Africa, an interpretation that I now find too summary. I shall here try to reformulate it, while at the same time indicating some new extensions.

Most of the authors who have dealt with this question share the conviction that the avuncular relationship is a particularly significant fragment of a vast sociological pattern, and the keystone of kinship. Two French authors, moreover, Adler and Cartry (1971), have asserted that in order to understand this institution, it would be necessary to hold rigorously to the ideology of the interested parties in its occurrence among the Dogon. Although these two authors analyse with much lucidity the 'internal logic', as they call it, of Dogon cosmology, I will say first why their theoretical position seems to me difficult to accept. They recall that the Dogon ideology associates the singular behaviour of the uterine nephew with nostalgia for the twin sister. The union of twins of opposite sex is the ideal marriage; realised at the beginning of the world, it has since that time been unrealisable. Adler and Cartry think that in this loss of twin-like harmony they can discern the basic reason for the paradoxical status of the uterine nephew in numerous societies of West Africa. I am persuaded, like these two

112

authors, that there is a need for the anthropologist 'to enter more deeply into the universe of ideas'. But, notwithstanding that, nothing guarantees that these categories and these schemata offered by the Dogon myth, or any other myth, provide the ultimate and universal explanation for the avuncular relationship. In the field of comparative analysis, no particular ideology can be given a favoured treatment. We should rather ask ourselves whether the totality of the conceptual systems that claims to account for the singularity of the avuncular relationship in a certain number of societies (all patrilineal) does not rest in its turn on a type of 'external logic' which would be consistent with a general phenomenon, that is to say, a structural one, appropriate to a certain type of kinship organisation.

I

Among the Dan of the Ivory Coast as among the Tetela of Zaïre, the sister's son merely pilfers with impunity the goods of his maternal uncle, with no implication of any ultimate metaphysical plan. And yet there is an essential similarity between the conduct of the Dan—Tetela and that of the Dogon: in both cases the nephew makes reference to his mother, relies upon her to put forward a claim, the nature of which is not yet clear to us. The Tetela used in front of me almost the same words as those that Marie puts in the mouth of the Dan: 'My uncle has given my mother to other men, and he has consumed the marriage wealth; that which he has is therefore mine.'[1] As for the Dogon, they liken the behaviour of the uterine nephew towards his maternal uncle to an incestuous search for the forbidden mother.

The Dan and the Tetela see the situation in terms of marriage exchange. Among both of them, the circulation of marriage wealth is particularly important. Among the Tetela, these substantial goods, that have from time to time been thought of as bride-price, formerly comprised iron and copper 'money', but also chickens and goats; money of European origin was largely substituted for these traditional valuables in the Colonial period. As among the Dan, the son-in-law is in perpetual debt to his father-in-law and to his wife's older brothers. In any case, it is these matrimonial valuables accruing from the marriage of their sisters which allow the group of brothers to honour their own perpetual debts towards their affines.

Now, a remarkable change of direction is found in the following generation. The son of the perpetually in-debt brother-in-law presents himself this time to the affines of his father as a creditor: the uterine nephew is entitled to demand the matrimonial goods of his maternal uncle. The behaviour of the nephew is aggressive and unpleasing. Not only is he the perpetual scrounger, but in addition he can take possession of at least part of the goods of his uncle in the latter's absence. He can even steal the goat of a neighbour of the uncle, who feels bound to compensate the victim. Among the Tetela, as among many other African patrilineal peoples, the permanent claim of the uterine nephew is curiously

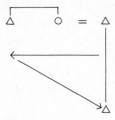

Fig. 3.1   Circulation of marriage goods

expressed in the form of a right to steal. The very peculiarity of the behaviour makes it difficult to believe that the privilege of the uterine nephew is purely and simply aimed at re-establishing the principle of reciprocity between the exchange partners, as one might at first think. However, this thesis with respect to the Dan is supported by Marie.[2] Among the Dan, as among the Tetela, 'the transfer of bride-wealth never ends'. The son-in-law is the 'debtor without redress' of his parents-in-law and of the elder brothers of his wife; on the other hand, the 'nephew has the right to take all that he wants from his uncle'. He can also have sexual relations with the wives of his uncle without the latter being able to complain (among the Tetela, he can only joke with the uncle's wife, but he will be able to inherit her on the uncle's death). Marie comes to the same conclusion that I formulated in 1958 when I drew attention to the asymmetry of the avuncular relationship in such situations; everything happens, indeed, as if, being creditor of his uncle, the uterine nephew was also superior to him. 'The relationship of uncle to nephew is therefore marked by the rights and the lack of constraint that are unilaterally allowed to the nephew, while the uncle has only his duties.'[3] But, he continues, this relationship, symmetrical to that between son-in-law and parent-in-law, and in the opposite direction, 'would have for its *raison d'être* not only to prolong it, but also to counterbalance it; to re-establish between the two groups in the marital relationship an equilibrium temporarily weighted in favour of the wife-givers'.[4]

Let us note that this argument applies only to those societies that create the unending debt of the son-in-law *vis-à-vis* his affines and thereby compromise the reciprocity of exchanges between the two groups. One consequently expects to encounter the privilege of the uterine nephew only in societies similar to the Dan and the Tetela where the bride-wealth is in some sense exorbitant, the transfer of valuables ending only when the alliance is broken by death or divorce. But such is the case neither among the Tsonga, where the receiving group receives merely a single transfer, nor among the Dogon, where the marriage can in no way be classed in the category of marriage regulated by the transfer of bride-wealth. Let us consider, one by one, the marriage systems of these two societies.

Let us examine first the case of the Tsonga.

Junod described the formation of any marriage alliance among the Tsonga as a veritable confrontation. The *lobolo*, bride-wealth, is the object of long discussion between the senior kinsmen of the girl and those of the young man; the two sides are separated from one another: they communicate by spokesmen in the form of two emissaries, who are their respective representatives; the latter go together back and forth from one hut to another. The *lobolo* consists of a relatively important sum, since Junod's informant, to whom we owe this detailed description, shows us the groom's family several days later dispatching a herd of fifteen head of cattle towards the girl's home. The village of the future affines is taken by storm: 'some of the invaders, the young ones, going steadily forward, the others, the adults, hiding behind the oxen and pushing them in under a show of blows'.[5] When the excitement has calmed down, the girl's male kin come out to criticise the received cattle while the groom's kin on the other hand contrive to emphasise their beauty. The alliance forms slowly, with infinite precautions. One month later, the girl, surrounded by women of her family, will shyly initiate the move towards the groom's group at the time of the ceremony called 'the beer that washes the hoofs of the oxen'. The father will only let his daughter finally leave the day when the family of the son-in-law has transferred all the *lobolo*. But the two parties will continue to exchange insults.

In this confrontation, neither of the two groups asserts its superiority over the other. The ritual aggressiveness that they display seems to abate after the marriage, when even the son-in-law should observe great reserve *vis-à-vis* his father-in-law. In fact, the greatest respect is not given to the male affines, who here play no role as creditors, but to two women, the mother of the bride and the wife of her brother.[6] This last, the great *mukonwana*, is the key figure in the Tsonga marriage system.

It can be seen that *ego*'s great *mukonwana* (*3*) has been acquired by the brother-in-law (*1*) thanks to *ego*'s cattle, thanks to the *lobolo* that *ego* has transferred to him in order to marry his sister. All familiarity between *ego* and his great *mukonwana* is rigorously proscribed. Junod asked one day whether a man could marry the woman to whom he is linked by such a relationship and received as a reply: 'What are you thinking of? Marry his mother?'[7] In the eyes of his informant, he states, 'that would have been incest, just as if this man had had

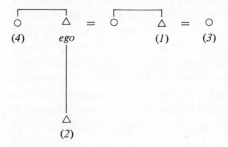

Fig. 3.2

115

sexual relations with his own mother'. In fact, as Lévi-Strauss has already observed in a brief discussion of some Tsonga data,[8] the great *mukonwana* and *ego*'s sister have been exchanged the one for the other: it is in giving his own sister (*4*) to another man that *ego* has been able to procure the cattle which have permitted him to marry the sister of *1*; he (the latter) for his part, has been able to marry thanks to this transaction. The sister and the great *mukonwana* find themselves therefore in positions of equivalence by reference to *ego* at the two ends of a link in the great marriage chain in which cattle circulate in the direction opposite to that of women. Whatever the reasons that the Tsonga identify the great *mukonwana* with a mother and not with a sister, the marriage with this forbidden woman would effectively signify the annulment of the exchange, that is to say incest.

Now, in violation of this great structural principle, which is the keystone of marriage exchanges in Tsonga society, *ego*'s son (*2*) comes to claim his uncle's wife, the great *mukonwana* of his father. He jokes freely with her, and, at the death of his uncle, will be able to claim her as wife. In order better to show the aggressive character of his claim, he does not hesitate to cast this joke in the direction of his uncle, who cannot protest: 'Please make haste and die that I may have your wife.'[9]

Nowhere better than here may the jocularly exorbitant aspect of the nephew's claim be seen. Let us consider the previous pattern from the point of view of the uterine nephew (*2*). The father (*ego*) has given cattle to *1* (maternal uncle of *2*) in order to obtain the mother of *2* in marriage. Cattle are passed from the lineage of *ego*, which is also the lineage of *2*, to the lineage of *1*. In exchange the lineage of *ego* has received a woman. In his turn, *1* has procured for himself a wife in another lineage. The right of inheritance held by the uterine nephew in the great *mukonwana* of his father introduces into this cycle of exchange a rupture, a true incestuous short-circuit, for, in the matrimonial dialectic, the wife of the maternal uncle is, truly this time, the equivalent of the mother; has she not been acquired with the wealth handed over on the occasion of the latter's marriage? Is it not precisely a reference to his mother that the Dan or Tetela uterine nephew makes so shamelessly to his maternal uncle when he demonstrates, with a suspect aggressiveness, his perpetual claim on the marriage goods and the wife of the uncle? Among the Tetela as among the Dan, the nephew invokes the fact that it is thanks to his mother that the maternal uncle has been able to obtain the wife that the nephew now covets for himself. Strange reasoning, in truth. Why does the Tetela uncle not retort: 'Your father and I, your lineage and mine, we are quits'? From all evidence the system countenances these petty violations of the law of exchange in the form of moderate pilfering of the marriage goods of the maternal uncle. Moderation is the very means to ensure that the system of marriage exchanges is not seriously weakened by the privilege of the uterine nephew: a Tetela adage advises one not to cut the rich manioc plant (the maternal uncle) at the root, but to let it regain vigour. As for

116

the Tsonga, they limit the damages by, as it were, sociologically sterilising the longing of the uterine nephew: when he inherits the widow of his uncle, he receives her usufruct, but the children to be born eventually of this union would escape from his lineage: they would belong to those who have paid the *lobolo*.[10]

A first conclusion: the privilege of the uterine nephew can by no means be seen as an expression of a delayed reciprocity but, on the contrary, as a derisory attempt at least partially to annul the exchange made in the preceding generation, taking back that which had been given. The aggressiveness that the nephew shows carries the mark of incest: it is, as it were, the replica, but in reverse, of the ritual tension found among the Tsonga between the two parties at the beginning of the marriage negotiations. In the first case, the feigned aggression marks the passage from a state of indifference or of potential hostility to the situation of alliance. In the second, the aggression is a sign of a regression, of the dissolution of the alliance into incest. Note the theoretical significance of this statement: the kinship systems that we are analysing from this particular point of view refuse secretly, as it were, truly and totally to transform the alliance with the maternal lineage into kinship; but neither do they intend to regard this tie as the continuation pure and simple of the alliance. And so the only solution is the partial dissolution both of the alliance and of kinship into incest.

It will be noted that all the patrilineal societies that have adopted this third solution, a somewhat comical one (that effectively invites trickery and obscene joking and at times gives rise to laughter), in order to regulate relations with the uterine kin, practise one or other complex form of the generalised exchange of women (usually by means of bride-wealth); they explicitly forbid (*de facto* and *de jure*) marriage with the cross cousin.

May I be permitted to recall that, from the perspective of Lévi-Strauss, 'elementary structures' are based on a primary marriage, which may be either preferential or prescriptive. 'Complex structures', on the other hand, decree only a system of prohibitions. In other words, they do not consist of positive rules, but only of negative rules. They replace with a statistical model of exchange a number of mechanical models that essentially characterise elementary structures. The interesting point is that complex structures permit secondary preferential marriages, always oblique, such as marriage with the wife of the maternal uncle. This observation is central to my thesis. It is a matter, historically and structurally, of a radical change. It is exactly as though the spectre of marriage with the daughter of the maternal uncle (that would transform the ambiguous relationship of the uncle and of the nephew into one of alliance, thus putting an end to its confused character) prowled around on the periphery of the Tsonga system. This shows itself among the Tsonga by a double displacement. Displacement, first, of the preferential marriage of the matrilateral cross cousin (which is prohibited) towards a distant classificatory cross cousin: 'to take a wife in the family where the father has found the mother', writes Junod, 'is recommended and approved of as long as she is not too near a relative'.[11] Secondly, transformation (in the structural sense) of the marriage with the matrilateral cousin into two preferential marriages which are oblique and complementary: the Tsonga permit not only marriage of the uterine nephew with the uncle's widow, but also marriage of a man with the daughter of his wife's brother (Fig. 3.3).[12]

It is clear that these two secondary unions conform equally to the matrilateral structural model: indeed the father (*1*) has a right to the matrilateral cross cousin of his son (prohibited to the latter) just as the son (*ego*) has a right to the great *mukonwana* of his father (rigorously proscribed). In both cases, the lineage of the father and of the son maintains a claim on the lineage of the brother-in-law—maternal uncle (*2*). However, these two oblique marriages are not symmetrical and reverse replicas of one another. In demanding the daughter of his wife's brother, *ego*'s father renews an alliance; in claiming with virulence the widow of his maternal uncle, whom he pretends to wish dead, *ego* destroys this same alliance by a regression to incest.

The prohibition of the matrilateral cross cousin and the employment of a substitute solution are the most noteworthy facts in our problem. It is more and more clear that those kinship systems in which the aggressive privilege of the uterine nephew is found occur at the point where the elementary structures (which call for one or the other form of marriage with the cross cousin) hinge with the complex structures which do not permit this primary union. Certainly preferential marriage still exists, but in an oblique and secondary form; it can therefore no longer play the same structural role as the marriages between cross cousins: in fact, logically, the marriage of the uterine nephew with the widow of his maternal uncle implies a preceding union. The 'preceding' marriage follows only negative rules: it complies with the prohibition of incest. It therefore rests firmly on the complex forms of generalised exchange. We will not be able, unfortunately, to examine here a last very significant characteristic of the Tsonga system that it shares with the Dan but not with the Tetela system: it uses a terminology of the Omaha type and by this states most clearly the strategic position that it occupies at the boundary of complex structures.

Junod has already noted that those southern African societies that practise

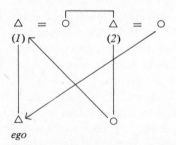

ego

Fig. 3.3   Oblique preferential unions among the Tsonga

marriage with the matrilateral cross cousin do not tolerate in any way the privilege of the uterine nephew.[13] The avuncular relationship there is entirely different from that of the Tsonga. The contrast is striking among the Lovedu: between the uncle (future father-in-law) and the nephew (future son-in-law), relations are harmonious and warm, lacking in aggression from either side.[14] Between the lineage that receives and the lineage that gives wives, there is no bargaining, even though the latter is bound to transfer, as among the Tsonga, cattle in virtue of *lobolo*. The accent is put on cooperation, the balance of the exchange. Certainly there exists some ritualised tension, but, most significantly, it does not oppose a demanding nephew to a tolerant or resigned uncle, but rather the cross cousins, the future brothers-in-law; as soon as the marriage negotiations begin, these joking relations, which allow for plenty of aggression, cease and are transformed into strict avoidance. One could not illustrate better how ritual tension expresses symbolically a claim for a wife. Our conclusion is reinforced by this: the aggressive claim of the nephew is only another indication of the closing of an elementary structure, that which establishes the marriage with the matrilateral cross cousin.

II

Let us examine now the privilege of the uterine nephew in the Dogon marriage system. The Dogon marriage could with difficulty be defined as bride-wealth marriage. The various gifts that the in-laws receive do not in any way constitute a bride 'price': their symbolic value is striking. The eight hundred cowries that constitute the fourth gift can on the whole buy only the indigo cloth that the girl will wear on her wedding day. We find ourselves therefore confronted by a new situation with respect to the previously examined cases, where the circulation of the marriage goods guarantees the proper functioning of the marriage exchange. At first sight, Dogon marriage seems regulated by preferential marriage with the matrilateral cross cousin.[15] But from recent information we have learned that paradoxically this marriage has hardly ever taken place, due, it is said, to too much sacredness; in fact, such a union would be indissoluble.[16] Like Dan, Tetela or Tsonga marriage, Dogon marriage in fact puts into operation a complex form of generalised exchange.

There is an extraordinary paradox in the mythical thought and social practice of the Dogon. They say explicitly that marriage with the matrilateral cross cousin is truly the perfect substitute for the ideal marriage, that is to say, for marriage with the twin sister. Now a careful analysis of Dogon genealogy, which I cannot develop here, would show that this ideal marriage, one that remains theoretically preferential, is no more stated in myth than it occurs in reality: a very small number of ancestors, and only in the fourth generation, are reputed actually to have married the daughter of their maternal uncle.[17] On the other hand, this genealogy develops a veritable theory of kinship that is at the same time both structural and evolutionist: it indicates how Dogon society would have passed from restricted exchange (expressed in the exchange of sisters) to the complex form of generalised exchange actually practised. The missing stage, at least in a systematic form, is, as I have just said, this particular form of elementary structure, which implies marriage with the matrilateral cross cousin.

Now, this paradox is cleared up if one accepts the unexpected (and even, I confess, a little preposterous) idea that this form, which is merely foreshadowed in the myth or found there only in a sketchy state, is expressed symbolically in the actual social system by the uterine nephew's claim for a wife. In order to develop this aspect of the problem, essential for a general theory of kinship, I will rely on the article that Griaule himself, in 1954, devoted to the uterine nephew in the Sudan. Griaule showed there that like Renard, the pale fox, the great fomenter of original trickery, all men claim the wife of the maternal uncle in an obscene way in order, in fact, to obtain his daughter. The aggressive behaviour of the nephew would of course cease if the marriage with the matrilateral cross cousin occurred. But we have seen that Dogon are paradoxically repelled by this solution. Why? To my knowledge, this has never been clearly explained. I think, however, that I can interpret the Dogon ideology in the following manner: the search for the matrilateral cross cousin as substitute for the twin sister means for all men, as much as for Renard, the pale fox, the return to the placental tissue from which he was prematurely torn at the beginning of the world, that is to say the return to the mother. This incestuous object being irremediably beyond possibility, the nephew finds a substitute for the mother in the person of the wife of the maternal uncle. In the last analysis, it is claiming the mother that obstructs the ideal marriage with the daughter of the uncle, which would be the only means of putting an end to this tension and agitation. The sole alternative, midway between the forbidden mother and the cross cousin, towards which the system is drawn, would be the oblique marriage with the wife of the maternal uncle, which is actually approved by the Tsonga. But in the eyes of the Dogon, who merely joke with her in an obscene manner, it is there only a matter of a derisory substitute. In formulating in this fashion the problem of the avuncular relationship, the Dogon show themselves extraordinarily conscious of the necessity of a decisive structural choice: either the harmonious round of permanent alliances with the same partners, thanks to marriage with the matrilateral cross cousin, that is to say an elementary structure of kinship where *a* gives *b* his sisters and receives his spouses from *c*; or else a complex structure, open to a multitude of combinations. The oblique preferential union, bitter substitute for the cross cousin, that such a system tolerates, is sometimes felt more or less sharply as a concession to the destructive urge of incest.

One finds among the Dan and the Tetela a formulation similar to that of the Dogon, but here in sociological rather than mythical terms. Nevertheless, here the first alternative (either the daughter of the uncle or his wife) is no longer permitted, but only the second. The Dogon admit, at least in theory, the possi-

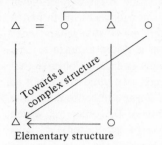

Elementary structure

Fig. 3.4

bility of marriage with the matrilateral cross cousin; this is certainly why, of course, they forbid marriage with the mother, with whom one can only joke. This ambiguous option indicates that the Dogon system oscillates around the critical threshold which separates elementary structures from complex structures. This is why the attitude of the Dogon nephew may be interpreted as derisory clowning, according to Adler and Cartry's reading of the myth. From a general point of view, the ritual thefts and cathartic jokes which he performs in the home of his maternal uncle are, as it were, the price paid for the passage from an elementary structure to a complex structure, that is to say for the abandonment, *de facto* if not *de jure*, of the matrimonial claim that every man has on his uncle when custom prescribes that he marry the uncle's daughter.

This statement does not necessarily mean that in a more or less recent period the Dogon have renounced the principle of matrilateral marriage. I assert only that, at the critical point where it now stands, the Dogon system is as if haunted by nostalgia for a marriage model that it proposes while at the same time makes impossible. I made the same observation about the Tsonga, among whom the encouragement to marry into the lineage where the father has already taken a wife (on condition that the relationship is not too close) may be regarded as a displacement of the matrilateral marriage (forbidden in pure form). It is no less true that a historical interpretation of these phenomena is tempting. Indeed, it is more likely that an elementary system develops into a complex system than the contrary. In any case, it would not be necessary to interpret the privileges of the uterine nephew as survival of the matrilateral marriage, but rather as transformation.

From the perspective that we adopt here, one may say that, being unable to obtain the status of son-in-law from his uncle, the uterine nephew symbolically short-circuits the system by claiming his mother, the key figure of the exchange made in the preceding generation, without idea of repetition or of return.

The reference to the former generation, in order to take part in the marriage affairs of this one, is one of the most significant attitudes of the uterine nephew in all the societies that we have considered. It is noteworthy that this confusion

121

of successive generations is only possible in the descent line of the mother, never in that of the father. The Tsonga refuse to transfer the widows of the father to his children, for these widows would risk having 'children of two generations'; on the other hand, a man can inherit the widow of a maternal uncle or of a maternal or paternal grandfather.[18] For their part, Adler and Cartry observe that among the Dogon, 'the category of time brings into play two opposed models of genealogical filiation: the one ... which is found in linear and continuous time (paternal line = regular succession of the generations), the other ... which assumes a dislocated time (maternal line: confusion of generations)'.[19] This opposition is vividly expressed in the sociological schema of the Tsonga by the adoption of an Omaha system of kin terms, which is characterised, as we know, by the adoption of a unique term to refer to the members of the same sex of the lineage of the maternal uncle, starting either from him or from the maternal grandfather. It is, in such a system, as if at each marriage alliance, time became fixed precisely in order to avoid it being repeated. This phenomenon is a sign of the passage from an elementary structure of kinship to a complex structure. The very movement that transforms the matrilateral cross cousin from the preferential spouse into forbidden 'mother' favours the useless and incestuous claim of the uterine nephew who tries hopelessly to regain symbolically his true mother in order to annul an exchange which, in the final reckoning, is apparently accepted as a kind of trick on the new generation; unable to find a spouse at hand, this generation turns towards the previous one in a sort of attack whose conclusion consists in confusing the matrimonial schema of the father and of the maternal uncle.

This attitude is often highly ritualised. It is evident among the Dogon where the impatience of the nephew exercises a cathartic influence in the home of the uncle.[20] Among the Tsonga, the nephew is the sacrificer *par excellence* for his maternal uncle in mourning rites. But, conversely, the uncle intervenes in favour of his nephew in private offerings to the ancestors.[21] It is significant that these religious duties are explicitly associated in Tsonga thought with the interdiction against preferential marriage. An informant explained to Junod: 'We have the special charge of sacrificing for our *batukulu* (uterine nephews); our sons also are priests to them, and can officiate in our place, even should they be younger than our *batukulu*. This is the reason why we do not marry them. We are their elders (*bakulu*).'[22] But it is perfectly evident that religious ideology cannot account for a marriage structure. Moreover, I would be tempted to reverse the explanation proposed by the Tsonga: should this not rather be that because the uterine nephew can never be a son-in-law (nor becoming in this situation a true kinsman) a ritual relationship rises in the ill-defined space that at the same time unites and separates him from the maternal uncle? In any case, the religious services that the nephew has the right to expect from the uncle add to the rights that the nephew exercises with a calculated lack of constraint in his uncle's home.[23]

122

Postscript: the Omaha system

Following the appearance in *Man* (1974, 9, 4) of the study above, R.H. Barnes criticised my presentation of the Omaha system.[24] I have taken account of one of his remarks in this new edition of my work. There remains a fundamental disagreement between us, but there is also a misunderstanding. Referring to the Gilyak, the Purum and the Kedang, whose systems are based on elementary structures, Barnes writes: 'if we take as crucial the fact that MB and MBS and other members of the line are called by the same term, then we must conclude that it provides no evidence of structural change of any kind ... If societies with elementary structures already make lineal equations in the mother's line, how can this feature be taken to indicate transition to a complex system?'

My own view is that the expression 'lineal equation' does not convey the distinctive character of the Omaha systems. If the terminology indicates the impossibility of repeating alliance with the mother's lineage, it does so by assimilating to mothers, who are prohibited, the daughter of the maternal uncle, the daughter of his son and all other women who are classificatory sisters of these two. It is clearly impossible to speak of the diversities of terminology of the Omaha type without referring to the matrimonial rules. Françoise Héritier laid strong emphasis on these in her remarkable study of the Samo of Upper Volta. She did not hesitate to describe their 'system of kinship and alliance' as 'Omaha'.[25] For three generations the Samo identify a maternal uncle and his male descendants, while the sisters of these men are identified as 'mothers'. The system is a highly refined one on the question of matrimonial prohibitions. Not only is each male *ego* forbidden to take a wife from the lineages of his four grandparents, but furthermore he is forbidden to marry 'into the lineages (Alter, Alter M, Alter FM, Alter MM) of his previous wives'.[26] In other words, each marriage creates a new network of prohibitions. And there are others besides, which we shall not consider here. Françoise Héritier demonstrates brilliantly that this superabundance of negative rules paradoxically allows 'the functioning of a system which aims to combine the classic Omaha prohibitions and village endogamy'.[27] To verify her thesis she had to run her genealogical findings through a computer. This exemplary method revolutionises the approach to the Omaha systems while most strikingly demonstrating that they constitute an autonomous structure of exchange. In view of this it is difficult to follow Needham when he declares peremptorily that 'no systematic comprehension is thereby provided, nor does the assignment to the Omaha type offer any clue to the analysis of the society which employs the terminology'.[28] The terminology certainly does not refer to a 'fictitious class'. Once again, the error arises from not seeing terminology and matrimonial rules as part of a single whole.

Françoise Héritier, in contrast, is concerned to 'understand and demonstrate by what mechanism a small community can be constituted in almost total matrimonial isolation, given the abundance of matrimonial prohibitions'.[29] Obviously, an enquiry of such precision has not been undertaken among the Tsonga or in other societies that, in whole or in part, present Omaha characteristics. The field of negative rules by which these systems appear, as a first approximation, to be defined varies from one region to another as do the terminological nuances. The Lega of Zaïre place the mother's brother in the same category as the uncles of the father, of the mother and of the four grandparents; they forbid marriage with their respective descendants.[30] On the other hand, the Tsonga appear to have developed only a rudimentary outline of the Omaha system, restricting their prohibitions to the lineage of the maternal grandfather. The Omaha themselves are less concerned than the Samo to multiply the prohibitions, since they, like the Tsonga, allow a secondary marriage with the daughter of the wife's brother, that is to say a renewal of the first alliance, but only for the men who actually contracted that alliance.[31] Radcliffe-Brown points out that in some systems this right extends to the wife's sisters (in the case of the Tsonga, for example) and even to the sisters of the wife's father.[32] So the Omaha system does not invariably forbid the multiplication of alliances with the lineage that is the giver of women.

The closing off of a number of networks of alliance is thus a common characteristic, but it is effected with varying degrees of rigour. For this reason it is impossible to apply a rigid universal definition to all Omaha systems. It is, however, possible to see that, as Lévi-Strauss noticed, they all obey certain fundamental structural principles. He provides what is perhaps the minimal definition of the Omaha system when he writes that such a system 'operates to change affines into kin' whereas general exchange effected by marriage with the daughter of the maternal uncle 'operates to change kin into affines'.[33] This formulation, which is perfectly valid for the Tsonga, was the basis for the remarks in my study above.

But Françoise Héritier's analysis raises new problems. In Samo society, the Omaha system clearly takes an infinitely more complex form. It is applied in large villages which are anxious to preserve their matrimonial unity. The villages regroup a large number of autonomous lineages into quarters. Gomboro, with 3,000 inhabitants, has about fifty of these.[34] Dalo has six for its 370 inhabitants, but this is a small village and 'traces of former habitation indicate that its past was more opulent'.[35] Given that endogamy within the village communities is respected in 75 per cent of primary marriages, the breaking up of lineages seems to be 'a necessary condition for the realisation of endogamy, in view of the prohibitive rules of alliance'.[36] The conclusion that Françoise Héritier's investigations bring out is that the Samo finally make marriage between distant relatives obligatory within a closed matrimonial system which would thus covertly be related to elementary structures. The end result of the superabundance of prohibitions is in effect to restrict choice to such an extent that the negative character of the system is in practice the equivalent of strict positive prescriptions.

The debt of the maternal uncle

The question posed is whether this is always the case. It will be possible to answer it only when other analyses of comparable depth and quality have been undertaken. But it is already possible to form a fairly precise idea of Tsonga society. Here the Omaha system appears only in an embryonic form, still to some extent constrained by matrilateral marriage. This is precisely the reason why I have proposed to interpret it as a state of transition from elementary to complex structures of kinship. Furthermore, the nature of the village here is quite different. The inhabitants are dispersed in small units that for the most part comprise one extended patrilineal family that is perforce exogamous. It is composed of 'the headman and the old people who have fallen to his charge, his wives, his younger brothers and their wives, his married sons, his unmarried sons and daughters'.[37] Thus dispersed, the exogamous lineage segments have little genealogical depth. In groups in the north, marriage is allowed between 'third cousins' and it may even be authorised between second cousins, provided the ritual for 'killing the family tie' is performed.[38] Although, on the maternal side, one does not marry one's *batukulu* (that is to say the members of the maternal uncle's group who are collectively assimilated to 'grandfathers'), nevertheless an alliance may take place with a more distant female relative. One informant declared: 'Where father has married I may also go to find my wife.'[39] The Tsonga feel repulsion at the idea of 'confounding and intermingling *bushaka* and *bukonwana*, relationship by blood and by marriage'. Nevertheless, the northern groups do not consider this with so much repulsion; according to one of their sayings, '*bukonwana* revives *bushaka* when *bushaka* has become weaker in the course of generations'.[40] There could be no clearer way of saying that, after a few generations, marriages are once again authorised between close relatives both on the paternal and on the maternal side. Moreover, there is nothing to suggest that prohibitions of the Omaha type affect the lineages of either the paternal or the maternal grandmothers. This strengthens the hypothesis that the Omaha system exists only in an embryonic form among the Tsonga.

Marriage among the Tsonga is controlled not so much by a restrictive body of negative rules, as it is among the Samo, but rather by *lobolo*; matrimonial exchanges are strongly marked by the transfer of wealth. It is from this point of view that Lévi-Strauss describes it: '*Lobolo* is nothing more than an indirect and developed form of marriage by exchange.'[41] This 'development' has seemed to me all the more remarkable in view of the fact that, within the same cultural zone, the Lovedu associate together the transfer of cattle and a strict respect for marriage with the matrilateral cross cousin. Lovedu marriage and Tsonga marriage share a number of common features which makes it possible to situate them within one field of transformations. In both cases a secondary marriage with the daughter of the wife's brother is allowed. I have elsewhere commented upon the strategic position of this oblique marriage among the Bantu of the south-east, in reply to criticisms addressed to me by Alfred Adler.[42] I will limit myself here to recalling to mind a few important facts. This secondary marriage with the daughter of the wife's brother is structurally compatible with the preferential marriage with the daughter of the maternal uncle, as Lévi-Strauss has already noted in connection with the Miwok.[43] But, as I have pointed out, the situation is threatened by potential conflict, since the father and the son theoretically both have a right over the same woman, who is for the one the daughter of his wife's brother and for the other the matrilateral cross cousin. If oblique marriage became the dominant form in an asymmetric system, the system would be threatened with a transformation. In such an event there could be only one outcome: the matrimonial right of the son would have to be deflected towards a classificatory female cousin. Now, this is exactly the solution adopted by the Tsonga. There is, naturally, nothing to prove that the Tsonga system is truly a historical transformation of the asymmetrical Lovedu system. However, one cannot exclude the possibility that an internal contradiction (the rivalry between father and son, who are both potential husbands of the same preferential wife) might be resolved by converting an elementary structure into a complex one which presents certain characteristics of the Omaha system. From this transformational point of view, the father's claim over the daughter of his brother's wife, who is forbidden to his son, leaves the latter with one other oblique solution: his maternal uncle's widow. The system, as such, in fact, authorises this new possibility. The fact remains, nevertheless, that such a solution is accompanied by a strange tension, a display of aggression towards the uncle, as if the nephew felt deprived. This is what gives us reason to believe that, in this particular form, the avuncular relationship bears the stamp of a critical state.

Radcliffe-Brown had already, many years ago, seen perfectly clearly that Omaha systems often, for their part, tolerate secondary unions with the daughter of the wife's brother, whereas they forbid marriage with the daughter of the maternal uncle.[44] He also noticed that some Omaha systems also allowed marriage with the maternal uncle's widow, but he rightly pointed out that this custom was far more widespread than the framework of the Omaha systems.[45] He did not venture a general explanation, although he could have based it upon a further, more meticulous investigation of the avuncular relationship that he described, among these very Tsonga, as early as 1924 in his famous essay 'The mother's brother in South Africa'.[46]

4

Structure and history: views on the Kachin

Some societies have the particular privilege of being the object of passionate controversy in the small world of anthropologists. One such society is that of the Kachin of Burma. The Highlands of Burma have become the focus of a major theoretical debate, the place where history appears to lay a trap for structuralism. Nobody would deny Edmund Leach the credit for having, in his remarkable book on the Kachin, dispelled a certain functionalist intellectual torpor. Nevertheless, the polemic he has provoked seems to me somewhat ambiguous. What exactly is the historical dynamic that makes the Kachin oscillate between two different types of political organisation, the one aristocratic, the other strictly egalitarian? Must one be content with saying that the empirical reality of archaic societies defies structural analysis because it fluctuates? If the 'model' is no more than a fantastic hypothesis on the part of the anthropologist, why do the politics of the Kachin display 'two quite contradictory ideal modes of life'?[1] Where are the roots of these fluctuating ideals? Could it be that this fluctuation represents the very essence of social life?

Let us briefly summarise the basic facts. In the egalitarian type of organisation called *gumlao*, local segments of patrilinear lineages of the same status contract alliances on a circular basis in accordance with the pattern of generalised exchange described by Lévi-Strauss. There is no sign of any dominant group, no tribute is due to the village chief – not, at least, so long as the system does not evolve in the direction of the *gumsa* type of organisation, which is the antithesis of this strictly egalitarian order. Historical instability comes into play between these two polar types. The ideal towards which the *gumsa* communities appear to lean is the social-class system characteristic of the neighbouring Shan societies whose official religion is Buddhism. Some *gumsa* communities *'under the influence of favourable economic circumstances* [my italics] tend more and more towards the Shan model ... other *gumsa* communities shift in the opposite direction and become *gumlao'*.[2] The *gumsa* system is presented as 'a kind of compromise';[3] but in an article written in 1951, Leach appeared to consider the *gumsa* model to be more important than the other two. He even went so far as

127

to declare — in contradiction to the essential thesis developed in his 1954 book — that this aristocratic model is stable.[4]

I shall be attempting to show that the dynamic of Kachin history can be more accurately interpreted as a shift away from a *gumlao* basic structure founded upon egalitarianism in matrimonial exchange and in the groups involved, towards a different type of society which, by introducing the principle of inequality into both matrimonial exchange and the organisation of lineages, attempts, in vain, to become like a class society, to wit that of the Shan. Why? And how? These are the questions that, following the information provided by Leach himself, I shall be attempting to answer.

Although he consistently stresses the economic factors affecting this structural flexibility, Leach does not follow the problem right through. He is even tempted by a psychological explanation: 'a conscious or unconscious wish to gain power is a very general motive in human affairs'.[5] Leach also appears to link the structural instability of the Kachin communities with an ill-defined cultural tendency which, he suggests, inclines them sometimes to imitate and sometimes to oppose themselves to their Burmese and Shan neighbours in the valleys who practise a developed agriculture (wet rice cultivation) whereas they themselves live on the high plateaux (in a state of relative poverty) off the resources derived from farming patches of burnt-over land.[6] In fact, the considerable theoretical problem posed by Kachin ethnography is none other than that of the emergence of social classes in an archaic economy, whatever the pressures exerted by the cultural model presented by their neighbours. The instability of the *gumsa* system lies, as we shall see, precisely in the refusal to make any radical alteration in a social structure based on the exchange of women and matrimonial goods and in its inability truly to transform itself into an irreversible class system. The aristocratic Shan model, towards which Kachin society of the *gumsa* type desperately strives without ever attaining it (constantly slipping back into a *gumlao* system), is astonishingly stable. The Shan culture is 'an indigenous growth resulting from the economic interaction of small-scale military colonies with an indigenous hill population over a long period'.[7] This highly diversified society presents an authentic stratification of classes in a different league from the hierarchy of status of the Kachin lineages, characteristic of the *gumsa* communities. Leach illustrates the economic situation of the latter with the example of Hpalang. The rich men own a few head of buffalo and zebu or several fields for wet rice cultivation in the valley. However, the standard of life of the 'rich' differs little from that of the 'poor'. Very little money circulates in the market of Lweje, where most transactions are carried out by bartering. So it is the system of land tenure that merits particular attention in Kachin society as a whole. In general, the land available on the high plateaux of the Kachin suffices, although farming on burnt patches of land does not give a high yield. Rights over the land belong to the local segments of the patrilinear lineages and are inalienable unless all the members of the lineage emigrate to the political domain of another chief.[8]

Land which is temporarily lying fallow is not abandoned. Meanwhile, the interplay of matrimonial alliances allows for the creation of a remarkable situation: many men are in fact dependent on others for the land. This relationship is expressed by hypogamy. In the last analysis, as we shall see, the status of lineages is defined by land-ownership.

What we need to discover is why the local segments of lineages which are strictly equal in the *gumlao* system relate to three different status in the 'aristocratic' *gumsa* system. They are arranged in a hierarchy of three 'classes' which correspond to an economico-political order that stamps the mark of historical contingency upon a structure of generalised exchange. But such an interpretation is alien to Leach's thought, in which the argument is, on the contrary, directed towards challenging the structural theory of kinship. In 1951 Leach thought that the analysis of kinship, considered independently from its economico-political aspects, was no more than a hollow dream, the product of a particular kind of formalist mind. I have already had occasion to counter this damaging interpretation of *The Elementary Structures of Kinship*. But let us follow Leach in his search for 'the structural implications' of marriage with the matrilateral female cross cousin among the Kachin.

Leach confirms the existence of the preferential marriage with a matrilateral (and generally classificatory) cross cousin both in the egalitarian *gumlao* system and in the aristocratic *gumsa* one.[9] But in the second case, the group relations between lineages which are givers of women (*mayu*) and those which are receivers (*dama*) have a political significance that they lack in the first. This is a crucial point. Whereas in the *gumlao* matrimonial system lineages of the same rank are linked through a generalised exchange between a limited number of partners (for example, A is a giver of women for B, which is a giver of women for C, which is a giver of women for A), in the *gumsa* system the *mayu* lineages tend to be superior to the *dama* ones. So if this idea became general, exchange could no longer be of the same circular type, for it is clear that if $A > B$ and $B > C$, C cannot be superior to A. In other words, C is unable to provide wives for A because it is lower in rank. But in practice true hypogamous marriage is a rare phenomenon among the Kachin. In *gumsa* communities, where there is theoretically a hierarchy of lineages, women either marry within their 'class' or into a 'lower class', never a higher. This hierarchy, without which there would be no hypogamy, is simply the product of an economico-political process which we shall have to work out.

Leach, for his part, appears – strangely – to believe that the domination of the superior lineages explains marriage with the female matrilateral cross cousin as such, among the Kachin, despite the fact that one also finds it practised between lineages of the same rank within the *gumsa* system and in an altogether general fashion within the egalitarian *gumlao* system. He writes: 'Matrilateral cross cousin marriage is thus a correlate of a system of patrilineal lineages rigged into a class hierarchy.'[10] But he immediately betrays his embarrassment: 'It does not necessarily follow that bride-givers (*mayu*) should rank higher than bride-receivers (*dama*); but it does follow that if class difference is expressed by marriage, then *mayu* and *dama* must be exclusive and one of the two must rank above the other.'

My own feeling is, on the contrary, that the explanation should be reversed. What we should do is start from the structural level common to the *gumlao* and *gumsa* systems and account for their different political aspects, expressed in particular by the presence or absence of hypogamy, by carefully analysing the land-tenure system and the circulation of matrimonial goods. To give Leach his due, I should point out that such a reinterpretation would be impossible had he not provided us with information of such high quality.

How is the social stratification of lineages organised in the *gumsa* system?[11] Each independent political domain (*mung*) 'belongs' to an overlord whose lineage is linked to others of the same rank through marriage with a matrilateral cross cousin. Within the domain, the village chiefs and their respective lineages constitute the second 'class'. They conclude egalitarian matrimonial alliances between themselves, of the same type as those of the lords, the domain chiefs; but they also receive a number of brides from the latter. Through these hypogamous marriages the village chiefs and their paternal kin thus become the *dama* of the lords, who are their *mayu*. Finally, the lineages of the commoners make up a third 'class'. These intermarry among themselves in accordance with the system of generalised exchange, in the same way as the other two classes, or else they receive brides from the lineage of the village chief whose *dama* they thus become. At one time the domain and village chiefs used to possess a large number of slaves.[12] No doubt this class of slaves considerably reinforced the economic position of the aristocrats, but it does not explain the social hierarchy of the whole body of free men linked together by hypogamous marriages. Hierarchy and hypogamy are the two indissociable aspects of this system of domination, which is, essentially, the statistical result of historical contingencies. They become established in a stable fashion within the structure of the generalised exchange of women, thanks to the successful or unsuccessful manipulation of prestige goods, which also serve as matrimonial goods. Let me develop this thesis.

The political domination of the overlords and village chiefs is not primarily expressed by land appropriation on their part, for all the villagers freely enjoy the fruits of their own labour. The land 'belongs' to the lineage which was the first to clear the virgin jungle.[13] True, the overlord has the right to claim a foot from each animal, whether wild or domesticated, slaughtered in his domain and also to use the labour of his subjects on certain occasions. In many cases he even has the right to demand one or two baskets of paddy from each domestic group every year. But this is not the essential point. And besides, this privilege disappears at the level of the village chiefs, who grant the use of the land for no visible return. Nevertheless, one cannot thereupon conclude, as Leach does, that there is no direct correlation between the stratification of the 'classes' and economic status.[14] In many passages of his book Leach quite rightly indicates the subtle economic mechanism which underlies the hierarchy of lineages. It is fully detectable at the level of the circulation of matrimonial goods, which I would go so far as to describe as bearing the stamp of potlatch.

Despite the apparent rigidity of the *gumsa* system, an aristocrat retains his rank only so long as he is in a position to maintain it, by meeting his obligations, his debts (*hka*). The scale of reparations for damages always varies in proportion to the rank of the debtor.[15] The full sum of legal compensation among aristocrats is fixed at a much higher rate than among commoners. Furthermore, 'the possessor of wealth objects gains *merit and prestige* mainly through the publicity he achieves in getting rid of them'.[16]

Cattle represent the essential item of prestige wealth, in particular the buffalo: 'it is the ownership of buffalo rather than any other single factor which is the mark of a rich man'.[17] The sum of the bride-wealth, like that of other ritual or legal prestations, is always expressed in terms of a number of head of buffalo. Other domestic animals (zebus, pigs, chickens) have no ritual value. Ritual wealth objects (*hpaga*) include, as well as the buffalo, various manufactured objects (gongs, swords, lances, pots, clothing, blankets etc.) the value of which in no way corresponds to their market value: for instance, the fact that a gong is rusty in no way affects its value in these circuits of exchange. Finally, other wealth objects which were also obtainable on the commercial market used to be included in the *hpaga* category: slaves, opium and ingots of gold and silver.

Nevertheless, it is clear that the determining factor for the Kachin is not the market economy but rather the use for matrimonial purposes of the whole category of wealth objects defined as *hpaga*, whatever their origin. It should be noted that the bride-wealth, which is expressed in terms of buffalo, must also, in the case of the well born, include a substantial list of manufactured objects that fall into the *hpaga* category. The great matrimonial game rests upon a complex strategy. The equality of the partners in the marriage alliance is defined by their capacity to give — and hence also to demand — matrimonial wealth of equivalent value. At the level of the overlord lineages the rate fixed for matrimonial wealth is extraordinarily high. The partner who is not in a position to meet this demand is not disqualified on that account but is seen as a handicapped player. He (and his descendants too) is threatened with a certain inferiority if the 'big' players, who hold all the economic trump-cards, present him with a bride at a cut price. Such a player finds himself as it were between two stools. The bride-wealth imposed on the son-in-law is, in such circumstances, fixed at a lower rate than would have been required from any other marriage partner of the same rank, but still higher than the going rate for the 'class' of the bride-seeker. For the latter can continue to enter into the marriage game with lineages of the same status, in the lower circuit, where the marriage stakes are not so high.

This strategy is implemented in the following ways.[18] The bride-wealth demanded from the husband is always higher between equals than it is on the occasion of a hypogamous marriage, in which the woman marries a man of lower status. It is the status of the bride-seeker — which means, in the last analysis, the amount of matrimonial wealth objects at the disposal of his local lineage — that governs the sum of the prestations. For example, in order to obtain the daughter of a lord in marriage, a suitor who is a member of a lordly lineage must have at his disposal more prestige wealth objects than a suitor who is a member of an aristocratic lineage. On the other hand, the aristocrat will have to give more to obtain this same bride than he would if he was content to marry at his own level, taking as his bride the daughter of a village chief. What, in economic terms, is the significance of this curious compromise?

For the bride-giver (of superior rank) hypogamous marriage in one sense means a loss, since he would have received more from a son-in-law of the same rank. It will be noted, however, that, as in poker, an element of bluff enters in demanding the highest price. Leach points out that in practice, in the ostentatious marriages of the highest 'class', the total value of the bride-wealth is, at any rate nominally, sometimes fixed at an exorbitant, purely fantastical figure.[19] From another point of view, all hypogamous marriages involve a considerable drain on the prestige wealth objects at the disposal of the lineages of lower rank who among themselves treat at lower marriage rates. So, as Leach observed, hypogamous marriages in practice deflect the wealth of the lower classes towards the upper classes.[20] What we still need to understand is why the former, who could quite well content themselves with egalitarian, endogamous marriages, agree to play the role of dupes in this game given that, to all intents and purposes, among the Kachin hypogamy favours the concentration of prestige wealth objects in the hands of the lineages that are of higher rank and in particular the overlords. I should point out that this 'class' strategy is played out only in the context of matrimonial wealth. It does not appear to affect the social relations of production. Every man, as a member of a local lineage segment, has the right to make free use of the land. However, this statement is contradicted by the principle according to which right of access to the land is in the last analysis held by the lord and chiefs of the village. What is the socio-economic reality that underlies this legal contradiction?

A village normally comprises a number of different patrilineages; one of these, however, is the 'owner'. At the entrance to the village a permanent altar is consecrated to the earth spirit.[21] The area available for cultivation, which the village chief calls 'our land', is generally ten to twenty times larger than the land actually used.[22] Each family independently cultivates its own parcel of land in the cleared area.[23] In the *gumsa* system a village cluster constitutes a *mare*. 'One of these villages is nearly always considered senior to the others. The principal lineage of this senior village can be said to "own" (*madu ai*) all of the territory (the sky and earth (*lamu ga*)) of the village cluster.'[24] Because its chief (*duwa*) has the right to levy the tribute of meat mentioned earlier, he is called 'thigh-eating chief'.[25] The political area placed under the control of such a chief is called *mung*, whatever its size, but the title of domain chief, *mung duwa*, is reserved for the paramount chief of a large area.[26] As opposed to this, an egalitarian *gumlao* society is composed of a group of independent villages; all the lineages involved enjoy the same rank; they owe no tribute to the village chief and they have equal rights to the land.[27]

To understand the coexistence within the same space of two social systems with such radically opposed philosophies of power, we must follow Leach into the historical domain. We shall see that any loss (or diminishing) of the available matrimonial wealth threatens to entail grave consequences so far as land tenure is concerned. Through the concrete situations that he describes, it is easy to perceive how it is that possession of prestige wealth objects affects land-ownership. A number of historical possibilities come to mind. Normally marriage is patri-local; the wife joins her husband in the local segment of his patrilinear lineage which owns cultivable land. But it sometimes happens that a man finds himself in conflict with the members of his lineage and, since he does not have at his disposal sufficient marriage wealth, he is obliged, in order to marry, to install himself with his father-in-law, placing himself at his service, in return for a reduction in the bride-wealth. Leach explains that the descendants of this émigré who has 'lost face' in his lineage of origin find themselves to some extent in a state of land-tenure dependency in respect of the lineage into which they have been received. They are permanently united with this lineage through a matri-monial relationship which also appears to be a relationship of subordination. In effect, the new segment of the patrilinear lineage descended from this matrilocal marriage will receive brides — as *dama* — from the lineage which has received them and which finds itself in the superior position of *mayu*, a perpetual giver of brides. The inferiority of the *dama* lineage 'rests on dual ground, firstly that the *mayu* "were there first" and therefore have a superior title to the land and, secondly, that the founder of the *dama* lineage by adopting matrilocal residence admitted his inferior status'.[28] But the sons of lords also enter into this interplay of accepted inequality. They often move away from the heir to the political domain — who is here the younger son — and settle in the domain of some other lord, at the cost of a similar loss in status, *mutatis mutandis*, to that suffered by commoners who marry matrilocally. In this case the emigration is prompted by the rivalry felt by brothers who have to choose between two modalities of sub-ordination open to them, either to a younger brother or to a father-in-law. The new aristocratic lineage which thus comes into being with an ancestor of lordly origins founds a new village and is united with the lordly lineage that receives it by a permanent matrimonial relationship in which the former, with the status of *dama*, is the dependant of the latter.[29]

This seems to explain how, historically, it is that the hypogamous relation-ship, whose economic significance Leach explained clearly in his article of 1951, recurs. When two lineages are united by a hierarchical *mayu*–*dama* relationship, the question of dependence is always expressed in terms of land tenure. At the higher level, when a lord's son settles on the land of his father-in-law, he becomes the latter's follower and client: 'If the *mayu—dama* relationship thus initiated continues for several generations with orthodox patrilocal residence, the ultimate position will be that the descendants of the father-in-law and the descendants of the son-in-law will be living side by side in the same community in landlord—tenant relationship. This probably is the most usual history of present-day Kachin villages.'[30] Generally speaking, 'it is fair to say that where the "tenants" or followers of a village headman or domain chief are not regarded as clan brothers of the "landlord", they are in the status of "son-in-law" (*dama*) to the "landlord" '.[31]

All that now remains for us to do is to discover the link between land tenure and matrimonial potlatch. Might hypogamy not be considered as an overvaluation of women, who are given at the same time as land is, with a view to maintaining the land-tenure privileges of the prior occupants? Leach hints at such an interpretation — although does not develop it — when he notes that payment of matrimonial wealth can be considered as a 'rent paid to the senior landlord by the tenant'.[32] On this basis, then, I shall attempt to reduce the *gumsa* political system to its economic factors, at the same time maintaining that the Kachin economic strategy would be incapable of setting up any social form at all without reference to a generalised exchange based initially upon marriage with the matrilateral female cross cousin. Thus, from the point of view of the structural articulation, it is, as Lévi-Strauss saw, ultimately kinship that constitutes the foundation of the system.

But let us proceed in an orderly fashion. The first analysis that needs to be made is an economic one. We have just seen that possession of land (at the level of the domain or of the village) and possession of prestige wealth objects are the major historical trump-cards in the great matrimonial game governed by marriage with a matrilateral female cross cousin.[33] The possession of land allows the lordly lineage to raise the stakes in matrimonial wealth objects to the disadvantage of the lineages of village chiefs, which, in their turn, benefit from a situation of land-tenure monopoly in relation to the emigrant commoner lineages. These historical positions of privilege are in essence expressed by an indirect land rent, received at the level of the matrimonial circuit. The highest local lineage — which enjoys a right to land tenure — is both a giver of land and a giver of women. Paradoxically, it uses matrimonial alliance, which is invariably strictly egalitarian between partners of the same rank (sharers of the same good fortune), to impose a matrimonial surplus value upon the *dama*, receiving lineage linked to it by land-tenure dependence. Let me explain this more clearly. The superior lineage (represented by its chief, either a lord or a village chief) appears in the role of a giver of women engaged in an act of self-interested generosity. He presents the emigrant, who is at a disadvantage (whatever his initial status), with a bride at a cut price and thereby engineers for himself an advantageous situation for the future. This initial favour will be paid for by the descendants of the emigrant to the extent that, in order to maintain the matrimonial alliance initiated by their ancestor, they will have to provide matrimonial wealth at higher rates than those demanded in egalitarian marriages between lineages of the same status. What we find here is, to some extent, the equivalent of a profit category within the matrimonial structure. The matrimonial rate imposed upon the *dama* lineage seems a kind of paradox: the ancestor, who was the beneficiary of a reduced marriage price, is in the long run alienated to the extent that his sons and grandsons will have to marry matrilateral cross cousins — from the superior *mayu* lineage — at a relatively high price, although they might have married, at a lower price, into a lineage of the same rank. Thus the hierarchy introduced into the *mayu–dama* matrimonial system is nothing other than an exploitation of the generalised exchange of women. In view of this, it would be interesting to know what statistical proportion of marriages takes place 'within the circuit' — between lineages of equal rank — and what proportion are hypogamous, imposed by land-tenure dependence. In this way it would be possible to assess the matrimonial surplus value of the aristocratic and of the lordly lineages in each *gumsa* community. These figures would make it possible to form an objective view of the evolution of an egalitarian *gumlao* community — in which, theoretically, alienation from land tenure does not exist — towards the *gumsa* type of society in which the aristocratic phenomenon is simply an expression of potlatch and matrimonial surplus value. Unfortunately, Leach does not provide us with this quantitative information. However, he does provide an extremely careful analysis of the *mayu–dama* system in the Hpalang community.

This concrete example shows clearly that the rigid schema of the three 'classes' connected by hypogamous marriages, as described in the 1951 article, needs some modification. The Hpalang community is an unstable *gumsa* society which, in Leach's own judgement, was in the process of evolving towards the egalitarian *gumlao* type of society.[34] These preliminary remarks will perhaps help us to understand better why 'some affinal links are associated with land tenure while others are not'.[35] The general ideology, according to which within a single community the *dama* are the vassals of the *mayu* despite the fact that in most cases there is 'no significant difference in the rank status' between them,[36] must then be recognised for what it is: an ideology that expresses the political function, real or latent, of matrimonial relations. It must be remembered that the theoretical article of 1951 clearly indicated that marriages within the circuit took place within each social 'class' in accordance with the egalitarian formula characteristic of the *gumlao* system, in which hypogamy is unknown. Hypogamy, that is to say the subordination of receivers of women to givers of women, only works effectively between 'classes', not within them, even when all *mayu* are considered superior to their *dama*. As we have seen, hypogamy is usually the result of matrilocal marriage, which implies subordination, in terms of land tenure, of the son-in-law to his father-in-law. Leach returns to this fundamental idea in his description of the Hpalang community: 'The basis of the *dama* inferiority seems to lie in the fact that where *mayu* and *dama* are members of one territorial unit the *dama* must, by implication, have broken the normal rule of patrilocal residence.'[37]

The Laga lineage, which gave its name to the village described by Leach, is allied to several *dama* and to several *mayu* lineages in a complex network that extends beyond the limits of the village and even of the political domain. The village was in fact founded by the Laga, who were accompanied by the Mahkaw, who were their *dama*. They were later joined by the Kareng, who were *dama* to the Mahkaw and who also became the *dama* of the Laga. The Jauji, clan brothers of the Mahkaw, soon settled in the village and became the *dama* of the Kareng etc. In this way a chain of hierarchical matrimonial alliances makes its appearance within a single local community: the Jauji are the *dama* of the Kareng, who are the *dama* of the Mahkaw, who are the *dama* of the Laga. However, this continuous chain of subordination is more theoretical than real.[38] It would in effect multiply the social status indefinitely and would at the same time fragment land-tenure rights. It evidently cannot be said that in the village of Laga the Jauji are the land clients of the Kareng, who are the land clients of the Mahkaw etc. Nevertheless, it is clear that the lineage of the village chief must maintain itself at the summit of this relative local hierarchy. The Laga – the dominant lineage and the true owner of the land – do in fact have *mayu* in other villages. However, although it is an unusual case, a family belonging to one of these *mayu* lineages (Hpukawn) lives among the Laga. But although its presence is embarrassing it does not affect the status of the chief.[39]

As we have seen, in migrations the *dama* follow their *mayu*. Although they helped to found a new village with the Laga, the Mahkaw continue to be their subordinates with *dama* rank. The Kareng lineage, the next to arrive, confirms its political subordination to the chiefly lineage by becoming its *dama* also, although it is already *dama* to the Mahkaw. The same goes for the Pasi lineage, which is *dama* both to the Kareng and to the Laga. One can summarise the picture provided by Leach as a whole by saying that the chiefly Laga lineage is united for reasons of land tenure with four of the six lineages which make up the village and that these relationships of relative privilege are the mark of political subordination. However, the same cannot be said of the other matrimonial relations that these same subordinate lineages may have amongst themselves. To arrive at a definitive demonstration it would obviously be necessary to compare the respective rates in matrimonial wealth imposed in each of the two alternatives (real or fictional hypogamy). However that may be, Leach does provide us with a most illuminating example of the difference between these two practices in connection with another village. When the Hpauyu settled at Hpalang they became the dependants (in terms of land) of the Maran. 'Later they became *mayu* to Sumnut and *dama* to Laga, but these later marriages did not involve any change of residence and the Hpauyu were not politically subordinate to Laga or superior to Sumnut.'[40] So it is clear that true hypogamy is a phenomenon limited by a certain number of concrete conditions.

However, Leach introduces a further suggestion which upsets the general argument that we have developed on the basis of his own premisses. Leach thinks that the political subordination of the *dama* to the *mayu* is eventually weakened when marriages take place in the orthodox manner, that is to say patrilocally, and with the bride-wealth paid in full.[41] We must examine this sibylline declaration with care. It appears to contradict the earlier thesis according to which the surplus value levied on certain occasions by the *mayu* is an indirect land rent, that is to say the mark of political dependence. Does Leach's suggestion imply that the high bride-wealth paid by the descendants of the immigrant who has married matrilocally at a reduced price effectively diminishes the initial dependence in which he found himself after he had 'lost face' in his own lineage? The converse extreme case of the immigrant who is totally without resources and for whom the only remaining possibility is voluntarily to become a slave would support this interpretation. He then becomes the *ngwam mayam* of an aristocrat who provides him with the matrimonial wealth necessary for his marriage in exchange for a permanent right to the labour of the slave and of his children. The master furthermore claims a share of the produce from his livestock and of the goods he receives when his daughters marry.[42] It will be noted here that voluntary slavery is simply the extreme form of the economico-political dependence in which the immigrant places himself when he receives a bride at a reduced price from the lineage which is the master of the land: 'The bride's people (*mayu ni*) then agree to a reduced bride-price in return for an agreed number of years' personal service from the bridegroom.'[43] A hint of slavishness weighs then on unorthodox marriages: one can thus better understand that the integral payment of bride-wealth eventually weakens political subordination.

But one must place oneself in the perspective of a potlatch. Does not Leach inform us that every family chief concerns himself with raising the rank of his lineage, by organising, for example, a 'wealth party' (*sut manau*) or, even more frequently, by arranging an advantageous marriage for one of his sons?[44] The case of the Hpalang community is particularly interesting. Two lineages, the Lahpai and the Maran, were quarrelling over the seignorial title of *mung duwa*. Of the nine village chiefs only four had the right to claim for themselves an aristocratic title. The chief of the village Sumnut was an ambitious adventurer.[45] By means of the competition that opposed the Lahpai and the Maran, he claimed to be the 'spokesman' (*bawmung*) for the whole community. The Sumnut had become the *dama* of the Maran. But the Sumnut ended up by quarrelling with them, claiming that the latter did not have the right to give their women to other lineages without their agreement. According to the Sumnut, the Maran had refused, in an insulting way, the bride-wealth that they proposed to them.[46]

This is a remarkable story. One sees in it a lineage of inferior standing deploying exceptional strategy: it deliberately multiplies the hypogamous marriages with the seignorial lineage while at the same time trying to monopolise them in order to heighten its own prestige. In a note published in *Man*, Leach clarifies this point: 'the game of hypogamous marriage is played with a view to raising the status (not class) of a man and his immediate descendants *vis-à-vis* other persons of the same class'.[47] He adds that the Kachin 'do not admit that a lineage can ever move into a higher class'.

It is more particularly the aristocrats, and not the commoners, who feel obliged to spend lavishly. They bring into play important bride-wealth in order to maintain their rank, to avoid falling from their status, indeed even in order to establish themselves one day as autonomous landlords, as we shall see further on. 'It is only persons of high status, such as the sons of chiefs and the sons of lineage heads, who need to conform strictly to the *mayu–dama* rules,' writes Leach.[48]

On the other hand, many of the Kachin live with a woman and have marital relations with her without being legally married to her. They may legitimise one or other of the children born from this union by paying a price (*numrai hka*) which does not create a *mayu–dama* link between the lineages concerned.[49]

So it seems that the commoners are reluctant to become involved in the great matrimonial game which enables the aristocrats to compete in gestures involving prestige wealth objects in order to establish their rights over the land. It is as if, when situations involving privilege such as these arise, the aristocratic lineages impose a number of hypogamous alliances on the commoner lineages, which try to avoid the obligation. Leach writes that the *mayu–dama* relation 'was [judged to be] adequately preserved so long as, in each generation, there was at least one marriage which conformed to the formal rule'.[50] This profoundly alters the very meaning of generalised exchange. If our interpretation is correct, the infrequent hypogamy of the commoners is, paradoxically, a statutory obligation. It implies an overvaluation of the brides given. Established on the basis of privileged economico-political positions, it favours their continuing existence, since matrimonial wealth objects circulate primarily upwards in the social scale, passing from the inferior *dama* to the superior *mayu*.

The economic power of those who find themselves, for the time being, to have the upper hand in this very chancy game is reinforced by the extra benefits that they can derive from various sources of legal compensation. As we have seen, these vary according to the rank of the injured party. The situation may be a threatening one for an aristocrat who is in debt to a creditor of equal status. The most enterprising debtors have, paradoxically, no hesitation in paying 'as much as they can afford rather than as little as they can haggle for'.[51] If the debtor is a commoner, the aristocratic creditor is still in a winning position, for the compensation demanded will be extremely heavy: 'the penalty for offences against persons of high rank is more expensive in terms of *hpaga* than for similar offences against persons of low rank'.[52] In this way a legal surplus value is added to the matrimonial surplus value. In such a situation the effects of the initial overvaluation of wives are multiplied.

Structure and fission

The structural order must be apprehended at two levels, that of alliance on the one hand and that of descent on the other. Marriage with a female cross cousin produces a generalised exchange of women within the egalitarian *gumlao* system which we are bound to take as our logical point of departure, since the *gumsa* system uses the same matrimonial model, investing it with a spirit of potlatch directed towards political ends, although it is never successful in producing a class society of the Shan type. Within the *gumlao* system, where marriage takes place in a circuit between non-hierarchical lineages, the way that matrimonial wealth is manipulated has no repercussions on the society as a whole. It is interesting to observe that, in a system such as this, both matrimonial wealth and legal compensation (*hka* debts) are kept at a relatively low level.[53] Eventually one begins to suspect that it is the overall volume of matrimonial goods available that dictates the choice of the one or the other society. However, the *gumsa* system also implies a *structural* decision that is different from that adopted by the *gumlao* system, to wit the statutory superiority of one of the brothers.

In a society of the *gumsa* type there is a hierarchy in relationships of kinship as there is in those of marriage alliance, whereas both types of relationship are egalitarian in a society of the *gumlao* type.[54] In his 1951 article, Leach allowed this structural order of consanguinity to emerge quite clearly. In the *gumsa* view, the aristocratic lineages (of the village chiefs) are called 'lineages of the older brother' by reason of a diachronic law governing lineage fission that expresses the 'class' hierarchy in the structural terms of kinship: 'When a lineage has acquired a "depth" of four or five generations it tends to split, but of the two residual lineages only one retains the class status of the parent lineage; the other tends to "go downhill" (*gumyu yu ai*). In theory the senior lineage is always the youngest-son line — i.e. the youngest son of the youngest son etc. — hence lineages which have split away from chiefly lineages and thereby resumed a subordinate status are eldest-son lineages, i.e. aristocrats. Similarly, the lineages which split away from aristocratic lineages tend to "go downhill" and become commoner lineages.'[55]

So there exists a structural hierarchy of lineages distinct from the economico-political dependence that operates in a *dama—mayu* marriage alliance. In 1951, Leach even appeared to consider the former hierarchy more important than the latter, for he thought that marriage with the matrilateral female cross cousin maintains these inequalities of status by defining 'feudal' relationships between lords, village chiefs and commoners. In reality it is a matter of two distinct but complementary structural orders, the one governing descent and the other marriage alliance, in an economy dominated by competition between different groups for land (through the intermediary of wives) and for wealth objects. This structural order of descent and consanguinity is conceived as such by the Kachin themselves since 'in Kachin theory the status of a lineage is defined absolutely by genealogy so that a lineage can only lose status and never gain it'.[56] We have seen how and why it is that the great matrimonial game and the manipulation of wealth objects confer considerable flexibility upon this rigid ideology.

However, Leach seems in his book to take up a somewhat different position from that assumed in his 1951 article, where the structuring role of the principle of ultimogeniture was clearly asserted. Adopting the point of view of Frazer, who discussed the problems in *Folklore in the Old Testament*, Leach proposes a strictly economic explanation.[57] Both assume that giving precedent to the youngest son is the social result of a rudimentary agriculture that implies constant migrations. In the particular case of the Kachin, Leach points out that in the *gumsa* system the eldest brother is, ideally, the warrior who departs in search of a new domain with followers and kin who belong to his lineage, while the youngest son remains at home in his father's house where he assumes responsibility for the altar of his ancestors. However, Leach admits that the rule of succession devolving on the youngest son was far from being 'sacrosanct'. Influential chiefs whose dominant position in practice is at odds with their legal status find themselves faced with an alternative: either to manipulate the genealogy or to deny the very principle of the sacredness (*tsam*) of the youngest son. In fact this observation itself shows clearly that the rule of ultimogeniture is structural in kind and cannot be reduced to an economic explanation. The converse, rather, is true: the elder brother may reverse the rule or ride roughshod over it. The fact that a society may choose to transmit power to the younger rather than to the elder son is in no way determined by the economic regime.

Of course one wonders how this hierarchical system of lineages, founded on the principle of ultimogeniture, can come into being in a *gumlao* system which does not recognise any opposition between the younger and elder brother in just the same way as it rejects the relative hierarchy of *mayu* and *dama* in the circuit of matrimonial exchange. The two phenomena are concomitant and call for a general interpretation. The *gumsa* society is clearly totally opposed to the *gumlao* as an inegalitarian system to egalitarian. The latter refuses to tolerate the emergence of a dominant lineage, and, for it, the function of headman 'is not, strictly, hereditary'.[58]

It is quite possible for a hierarchical order to occur in a lineage system without its affecting the relative autonomy of the segments involved, as I have indicated in connection with an African society, the Tetela of the Kasai, where the elder segments are, in theory, superior to the younger (see p. 7). But among the Kachin, the existence of a hierarchy of lineages is indissolubly linked with the emergence of a sovereign power situated at the very heart of the society, whereas, among the Tetela, the most senior lineage is simply juxtaposed alongside the others without its chief (the eldest son of the eldest branch) being able to claim any matrimonial surplus value or any levy on foodstuffs or labour. Ultimogeniture erupts into the egalitarian fabric of the Kachin lineages as an integral part of the hierarchical system that can be detected in the matrimonial exchanges: the lineage hierarchy is an indispensable complement to the inequality of matrimonial status. The lineage system must necessarily produce inequality in its structure in order that acquired privileged situations can reproduce themselves in the matrimonial sequence. The rarity of prestige goods calls for the introduction of a hierarchical order within the lineage structure. Here I am merely translating Leach's idea: 'Since the commoners greatly outnumber the aristocrats and the aristocrats greatly outnumber the chiefs there is necessarily procedure whereby the upper classes shed their surplus into the class below.'[59] This procedure is but an affirmation of the youngest son's privilege in the transmission of inheritance. The process of lineage fission among aristocrats is therefore conceived as 'going downhill'. The possibility nevertheless remains for the elder brothers to 'climb uphill' again, since the sovereignty around which the society henceforth revolves is not a sacred royal power. It is always legitimate for a Kachin elder brother to buy from his youngest brother the ritual powers connected with lordship[60] and thus to become an 'eater of thighs' with full rights (that is to say, the one who levies tribute on slaughtered animals).

In this way lineage fissions have the effect of proliferating autonomous chiefdoms of varying importance. A hereditary aristocracy is created on this lineage basis. It becomes subdivided into a hierarchy of two categories based upon the genealogical position, that is to say upon an arbitrary structural order that is not reducible to the economic order: the chiefly lineage, which is always the issue of the younger son, is *du baw amyu*,[61] and the segments that are the issue of the elder sons are *ma gam amyu*; they are 'sufficiently close to those of the chiefs for their members to be able to claim that they are descended from chiefs and to feel that their descendants might one day become chiefs again'.[62] Of course they will not be able to realise this hope (relating to their genealogical, structural position) unless they can maintain their rank in the manipulation of rare wealth objects. It should be remembered, in this respect, that the total volume of prestige wealth objects cannot increase indefinitely without issue towards the outside world, and meanwhile those with pretensions to aristocratic rank continue to multiply.

If this is indeed the way that relations between the hierarchy of lineages interact with the circulation of matrimonial wealth, it becomes easier to understand how it is that Kachin terminology is content to oppose two non-servile 'classes' when it is a matter of establishing the formal rules relating to the payment of *hpaga* (prestige wealth objects): commoners (*darat*) on the one hand and chiefs (*du*) on the other.[63] There always remains the possibility of distorting the structural hierarchical order by deliberately putting about a genealogical lie. To do such a violence — one which can be absorbed by any political system

141

– is, after all, not very revolutionary so far as the structural order, which is not thereby changed, is concerned.

Hierarchy, hypogamy and class societies

Finally, following Leach, we must examine the structural reasons that prevent an aristocratic society of the *gumsa* type from truly changing into a class society of the Shan type even though the latter is a cultural model in the eyes of the Kachin chiefs. Here, all we need do is simply reproduce Leach's excellent argument. The social hierarchy of the Shan kingdoms comprises the nobles (kin of the sacred sovereign), the peasants and a lower class which includes a series of professions regarded as inferior according to the Buddhist code: fishermen, butchers, sellers of alcohol, pig-farmers etc. The local community, the endogamous village, is the basis for social life. Neither marriage nor lineage allegiance plays the same role as among the Kachin. The main reason why the Kachin chiefs have always failed to convert their principalities into kingdoms of the Shan type is that the very principles of matrimonial alliance in the two societies are contradictory. The Shan kings consolidate their political power by making matrimonial alliances that are in opposition to the hypogamous structure of the Kachin; they receive many brides of inferior status as tribute.[64] Leach interprets this intake of women as a form of land rent incompatible with that which the Kachin lords levy by, in contrast, giving their daughters to aristocrats in order to provide a basis for their economico-political domination. By conforming with the hypergamous and polygamous matrimonial model of the Shan kings, the Kachin chief 'offends against the principles of *mayu–dama* reciprocity'[65] and encourages the development of revolutionary tendencies which threaten to sweep the aristocratic *gumsa* system towards the *gumlao* system. So one may well wonder what new economic factors introduce a movement in the direction of the Shan model of a class society. Leach believes that trading in iron probably made it possible for a number of Kachin chiefs to become feudal satellites to the Shan princes, whom they then attempted to imitate. Elsewhere, following a study of the ecological distribution of the *gumlao* and *gumsa* systems, he notes that the latter tends to become general in areas where the archaic mountain farmers depend for their subsistence upon the more developed agriculture practised by the Shan in the valleys. In this zone B, either the Shan chiefs are the overlords or the Kachin or vice versa.[66] Finally, analysing the economic transformations that underlie the transition from the *gumsa* system to the Shan system in the strict sense, Leach points out that the only way for the Kachin lord to free himself from the permanent bonds of matrimonial alliance imposed by the *mayu–dama* relationship (in other words, to pass from hypogamy to hypergamy) is to rely on the support of his slaves in order to strengthen his privileged economic position.[67]

Passing beyond Leach's conclusions, one could say that slavery marks the partial intrusion of a system of authentic social classes into an archaic structure of exchange. Slavery may contribute to the disruption of the political order, but this is exceptional. The majority of slaves were voluntary, their status resembling that of poor sons-in-law. Slavery is not the dominant mode of production among the Kachin. The social system is ordered more directly by the marriage arrangements and the manipulation of prestige objects of value.

In such a context, land and cattle give a man power over others, but their accumulation has no economic significance. The supreme prestige of the chief is linked with an ostentatious squandering of his wealth. The lord – and he alone – as frequently as possible organises great ritual sacrifices enjoyed by the entire community so that 'the ultimate consumers of the goods are the original producers, namely the commoners who attend the feast'.[68] One can understand why this ritual privilege is a monopoly of the sovereign.[69]

In all Kachin communities, the lineage chiefs offer sacrifices to the spirits of the earth and to certain minor celestial divinities; only the landlord has the right to slay cattle in honour of Madaï, the principal spirit of the sky. This bestower of wealth and prosperity is considered to be a relative by marriage of his farthest-removed ancestor. The right to sacrifice to Madaï appears, then, as the logical development, on the religious level, of the transformation of the *gumlao* system in the *gumsa* system: it constitutes merely an amplified lineage ritual. The ritual position of the landlord does not bear in any way the mark of this symbolic rupture by which I have previously defined sacred kingship (see p. 22).

The entire system is self-limiting. Its development, even its continued existence are undermined by the very political religious order that the chiefdom sets up. The chief, who is a giver of women and the beneficiary of matrimonial surplus values, finds himself obliged, in order to maintain the advantages he has acquired, to make a permanent display of ostentation and regularly to sacrifice a proportion of his cattle. The agricultural tribute that accumulates in his barns is not directly convertible into rare wealth objects. Ambitious 'eaters of thighs' are forced to seek some other outlet if they wish to extend their domination. Leach makes this quite clear. The neighbouring Shan model – that of fully developed kingship – implies for the Kachin the reduction of 'his subordinate tenants from the status of son-in-law (*dama*) to that of serf or bond-slave (*mayam*)'.[70] Leach suggests that such an attempt could only result in a *gumlao* revolt, unless the Kachin chief is himself a feudal vassal to a Shan sovereign. At all events, the demands made indeed seem finally to be the cause of the system collapsing: 'The mythological justification of *gumlao* revolt concerns rebellion against chiefs who "rated as commoners even their own relatives who had not the right to collect dues, and insisted on the payment of dues, labour and otherwise, from these relatives as from other commoners".'[71] The *gumsa* system collapses because it can only reinforce its power by denaturalising kinship, having already distorted the network of matrimonial exchanges. It would be destroyed from above if a younger brother opposed the segmentation of the chiefdom by force, forbidding his elder brothers to set themselves up as his peers and refusing to allow them access to ritual power. The involution of the *gumsa* system is governed by these political limitations. When the pressure becomes too great, the interplay that the system sets up starts again from scratch: all 'debts' (*hpa*), all matrimonial over-bidding are annulled. It is significant that a *gumlao* community fixes the levels of matrimonial wealth as low as possible.

There is, however, one other solution which makes it possible to break this circle. But it implies external economic relations. By offering their military protection to the cultivators of the irrigated rice fields in the valleys in exchange for tributes of rice, equivalent to 'thighs', and by levying a tribute on Chinese caravans, certain Kachin chiefs acquired 'real economic strength' and became veritable autocrats.[72] There is a striking contrast between this extreme situation and the picture Leach paints of a small *gumsa* community comprising 130 domestic units engaged in the process of reconverting to the *gumlao* system, to wit Hpalang.

Thus the aristocratic *gumsa* system continues in most cases to be founded on archaic forms of production and exchange, whereas a true class system necessarily forces the mode of domestic production and the structures of kinship into a new stage of development. Despite its flexibility, Kachin society ultimately demonstrates an inability to escape from the structural model of generalised exchange, whatever the transformations hypogamy imposes upon it. You could say that social change comes full circle. Besides, it should be remembered that the productive forces remain unchanged in the *gumlao* and *gumsa* systems, and that the social relations of production, which are dominated by the question of land tenure, undergo only insignificant transformations from one type of system to the other. These transformations are essentially contingent; they are the expression of the economic play tolerated, up to a certain point, by the kinship and marriage structure. Slavery, which is a move towards a regime of authentic social classes, is not an integral part of the Kachin social system, since it was abolished, with very little adverse effect to the communities of the *gumsa* type, by the British administration.

The Kachin and the 'Asiatic mode of production'

Since this essay first appeared in French, in a somewhat different version, Jonathan Friedman,[73] taking his inspiration from the theses proposed by Godelier, has put forward a strictly Marxist analysis of Kachin society, in a paper which has considerable theoretical ambitions. My own point of view was that of a structuralist alert to the possibilities indicated by Marx. It seemed to me impossible, in any event, to submit the evolution of traditional Kachin society to the rigid rules of historical materialism. Friedman's analysis will enable me to make this point more precisely.

Friedman admits, as I did, that the egalitarian *gumlao* system is the 'structural origin point'.[74] He makes a clear distinction between the 'household', the smaller unit of cooperation and consumption, and the local lineage segment, 'the main unit of appropriation and exchange'.[75] He appears to rally to the structuralist thesis when he admits that marriage is 'the dominant politico-economic relation'.[76] He also recognises that 'the motive of the rise and fall of the brideprice can only be found outside the sphere of circulation'.[77]

According to Friedman, it is by defining this area external to marriage that one might have some chance of discovering the moving cause behind the historical dynamism that interests him. But, far from finding it within the political dependence occasioned by the question of land tenure, as I suggested, following Leach's information, Friedman tries to find a "last resort" explanation in line with the theory of historical materialism. He believes he has discovered this in the production of an agricultural surplus on the part of the lineages.

He draws his inspiration from the model provided by the big-men societies of Melanesia. It is well known that these heroes of archaic production capitalise on their prestige through prodigality, increasing their own production and that of their closer relatives. Friedman introduces a mediatory factor, namely religion. This recognition of the fact that belief in ancestor-worship is an integral part of the social reality will be hailed as a stroke of audacity in the evolution of Marxist thought.[78] Friedman starts by examining how the ancestors of a 'strong' lineage might become the gods of a larger political community, to the greater advantage of those who mastermind such a coup. In a *gumlao* society, the production surplus would be drained off by the ancestors in the course of communal sacrifices. Starting with an organisation of this type, how is it possible to end up with the *gumsa* system, in which the house of the chief is known as the 'paddy store'?[79] By a route that Friedman considers entirely natural. He believes that the great religious festivals (*manau*) organised by the chief of a large political domain are simply the final result of a continuous process: at the starting point we find a candidate for the role of big-man, displaying exceptional generosity in the course of festivities given in honour of his ancestors. The *manau* 'links production directly to social differentiation'. How? The answer is simple, although the Kachin have not mentioned it: 'The capacity to produce a surplus demonstrates the importance and influence of lineage ancestors with the higher spirits who appear as the source of all prosperity and wealth. Prestige so attained is converted into relative rank in the matrimonial circuit.'[80] And that is how men allow themselves to be fooled by religion, until such time as the wisdom of Marxism enlightens them.

But sketching out a theoretical schema is not enough. We must examine the literature relating to the Kachin to find arguments capable of supporting such a thesis. It is true that Leach states that a commoner who desires to raise the prestige of his lineage in a constituted *gumsa* society can always give feasts and display a prodigal hospitality, but he takes good care not to suggest that this factor lies at the very basis of the formation of *gumsa* society or, above all, that the credit for holding these festivities goes to the host's ancestors. Leach only implies that lavishness in itself does not necessarily imply aristocracy but that 'when it comes to social climbing the cunning ones are at an advantage', class hierarchy not being rigid.[81] Friedman carelessly extrapolates from this observation as if the whole *gumsa* society springs necessarily from this strategy. Now the Kachin historical data hardly allow us to believe this. One never sees, within *gumlao* society, a cunning big-man 'convert' his alimentary prodigality into land rights. On the other hand, one finds those lineages that have acquired prestige by their prodigality manipulating the constituted *gumsa* genealogies by claiming a higher status. But this process of readjusting the previous aristocratic order apparently does not proceed via the affirmation that the ancestors of the prodigal man favoured his production. This kind of politico-religious mystification in any case does not work in Melanesian big-men societies. Marshall Sahlins showed perfectly that the display of generosity by ambitious men, who endeavour to overproduce, does not place anyone in a state of dependency. The big-men fail to establish any domination or capture any surplus.[82] In such circumstances, recourse to the mystical power of the ancestors, such as Friedman alleges, is purely hypothetical, the product of historical guesswork. It is perfectly true that a transformation in the religious system can be noted in the transition from a *gumlao* to a *gumsa* system: we find a claim being made that the chief's ancestor is related to the greatest spirit of the sky, Madaï (see p. 143). An increase in spiritual power accompanies political sovereignty, that is to say the theoretical seizure of the land, but there is nothing to indicate that among the Kachin it is the instrument whereby this is accomplished. All Leach's indications point in the same direction, suggesting that the distortion of the original egalitarianism is connected with the question of land tenure and takes place on earth, not in heaven. On this point Marx will bear me out against Friedman. Besides, the religious rites carried out on the one hand by the *gumsa* lord and on the other by the commoner lineage chiefs in the *gumlao* system are very similar. They differ only by slight nuances within the same symbolical space. The *gumsa* lord makes sacrifices to Madaï and to Shadip, the earth spirit, while the commoner lineage chiefs make sacrifices to certain sky spirits (but never Madaï) and to a particular earth spirit who is held to be distinct from Shadip.[83] For that matter, the Kachin lordly system has, as I have already stressed, never experienced the veritable break in the symbolical order that is introduced by sacred kingship. I should point out that the prestige and wealth of the aristocrats does not, *ipso facto*, confer upon them the right to organise the supreme ritual in honour of Madaï. So how could the hierarchy of status be derived from the automatic high valuation set upon ancestors of clever big-men contriving to spend a surplus the better to ensnare others?

One could just as easily reverse Friedman's theory and hold that the (altogether relative) development of agricultural production is the consequence, not the cause, of the *gumsa* system considered as a new political order. Anyway, the alleged development may equally well never take place: the Kachin lord is defined, first and foremost, as an 'eater of thighs', and the levy that he operates on the economic circuit consists essentially in prestige wealth objects. If there must indeed be a 'last resort (*dernière instance*) analysis' why neglect dependencies resulting from land tenure? Why forget that the Kachin lord can only remain at the summit of the prestige hierarchy by displaying an ostentation and generosity that precisely define the limits of his economic power?

The undeniable originality of Friedman's thesis lies in his appeal to the ancestors, attributing to them functions that are 'critical for social reproduction'.[84] But can he convince the Kachin that a lineage only needs to show an increased productivity (expressed in celebratory feasting) for the other lineages automatically to bow down before it, believing this wealth to be the 'work of the gods' of the most generous group?[85] Do the Kachin really think that this beneficent spiritual influence can only be 'the result of a closer genealogical relationship' with the distant ancestor of the favoured group, who thus becomes the 'territorial deity'?[86] Hypotheses are piled one upon another in order to explain what is supposed to be a 'perfectly natural' process.[87]

The purpose of this ingenious theoretical construction is to show that 'the internal logic of the fetichised presentation of the work process determines the form taken by political development'.[88] In this schema, primary importance is attached to the establishment of hierarchical relationships between different segments of a lineage, in accordance with the formula of the younger being superior to the elder. As a result, matrimonial alliance is supposed to follow the same path by virtue of the fact that 'the *mayu—dama* relation is re-presented simultaneously as an elder/younger relation between lineage ancestors'.[89] This theory has the merit of referring back to a Kachin model developed by Leach in his 1951 article: by 'going downhill' the elder lineages become possible partners in hypogamous marriages. However, the model is entirely theoretical. There is nothing to guarantee that it has the slightest historical value. Its function is quite other: to produce a visible harmony between the hierarchical orders of descent and of alliance. Leach later makes the point that it is not possible to be precise about the levels of lineage segmentation associated with exogamy.[90]

Next, Friedman introduces a number of equally unverifiable demographic and ecological factors to account for the involution of the *gumsa* system. He thinks he has shown 'how the economy is based on an increasing or even accelerating demand for surplus'.[91] He boldly concludes that this demand necessitates a territorial expansion entailing demographic growth; this in its turn provokes an ecological decline, while the increasing demand for a surplus leads 'to an inflation of all prestige goods (*hpaga*) and all prestations including bride-price and indemnity payments, which in turn threaten every level of the social structure with increasing indebtedness'.[92] It is this critical situation that, in his view, provokes the break with the *gumsa* system. The *gumlao* system that then takes its place makes a regeneration of techno-ecological conditions possible. With this ecologico-Marxist argument, based upon a total dearth of precise evidence, Friedman thus re-establishes the doctrinaire schema according to which a 'contradiction between forces and relations of production is manifested at the level of the social relations'.[93]

Is not the ecosystem, magic panacea as it is, the new 'last resort', making it possible for contemporary anthropological thought to get rid of a number of embarrassing problems? They are embarrassing because, at first sight, they do not appear to fit with the materialistic interpretation. Harris uses the ecological argument to account for the warfare and violence among the Yanomani, Godelier for the amazing equilibrium that prevails among the Pygmies and Friedman for the failure of the *gumsa* system among the Kachin. I myself, from having several times visited the Rwanda am — alas — all too familiar with the ravages caused by soil erosion in the highlands of central Africa. But it is precisely in this milieu, particularly unfavourable to agricultural development, that a political system particularly oppressive to the peasants has been developed — a veritable system of social classes, without, however, the slightest degree of technological change. On the contrary, the traditional herding which the Tutsi aristocracy has systematically intensified and which is economically unproductive has been a major contributory factor to the impoverishment of the mountain soil; but through the instrument of domination that cattle represented, the Tutsi were successful in dominating the peasant masses over five hundred years from three points of view, social, economic and political; and this they did despite overpopulation and despite appalling famine.

For Friedman's theory to conform with Marxist orthodoxy all that remains to be done is to explain how the *gumsa* system, despite its internal contradictions, heralds the 'Asiatic mode of production' of the neighbouring states. Naturally, a factor here has to be the increase in productivity which makes for vertical and hierarchical relations. One question is not considered: whether, on the contrary, we are not faced here with the phenomenon of a political break, with an overthrowing of the order of lineages, that has the power to found a new type of society: a class society, precisely. However, Friedman, who is certainly very little concerned with the analyses of Leach, decides that the transition from Kachin hypogamy to hypergamy (as practised by the Shan) is, all in all, 'only a change in dominance'.[94]

I find it extremely difficult to subscribe to the reassuring evolutionism of Friedman, who concludes that 'the Asiatic state evolves directly out of tribal structures in the process of verticalisation of the relations of production'.[95] I have already expressed my opinion concerning this mysterious Asiatic State that is so ubiquitous yet nowhere exists.

I have the greatest respect for Marx, the anthropologist of nineteenth-century capitalist society, and for his provocative ideas on class societies. But the attempt to apply historical materialism universally seems to me decidedly a failure. Reading Friedman reinforces this conviction.

148

PART II

Religion

5

Possession and shamanism[1]

In every religion dialogue with the gods calls for specific physical techniques. Catholic prayer insists upon humility and self-collection, the body in a state of silence. On the spiritual level as on the physical it is a preparation for death, the gateway to salvation. The body's activity is suspended, turned down low, and this is in keeping with a dualist metaphysics which has always been current despite theology's persistent attempts to diminish the dizzy distance that separates the soul from the body. In Christian prayer the body is condemned to self-effacement; it crouches down, the face is buried in the hands: man prostrates himself. Laughter is banished, silence reigns in the sanctuary, the faithful speak softly in whispers. They take no part in the sacrifice; each is merely a spectator. There is only one actor: the priest, with the support of the organ and the choir. The joy aroused in the congregation by the sacred music has no physical manifestation: it is purely internal. At a very early date the beginnings of drama were banned from the church. Seen from this point of view, any derangement of the senses in communication with the sacred is essentially diabolical. Nevertheless, mystics venture, not without incurring the distrust of the clergy, to communicate directly with God using unorthodox means and dispensing with the priest. In doing so, they enter the zone of shamanism and possession which is also the province of the diabolical. They strive to become satiated with God, anticipating the condition of Paradise. Like the one possessed by Satan, the Christian mystic is a figure considered foreign to the Christian system. His behaviour has much in common with ecstatic religions, the typology of which I shall attempt to describe briefly.

Each of the physical techniques of the Christian religion that I have mentioned is opposed, in every respect, to the African and Afro-American techniques characteristic of many cults of possession. Religion here is danced theatre, a dramatic explosion, Dionysiac exuberance, physical joy. The human body is the vehicle used by the sacred, the gods appear on earth, become incarnate, 'ride' the faithful one, forcing him to start and leap and lending him their voice. The devotee's own personality is effaced; it offers no resistance to the irruption of the god's personality. The priest is no more than the organiser of a ritual spec-

151

tacle in which it is impossible for the actors to evade their vocation: they are the elect, the chosen.

But authentic possession, as most typically exemplified in the Haitian cult of voodoo or its Dahomian equivalent, is part of a complex body of religious phenomena which has not yet been the subject of a systematic study. The expression 'ecstatic religions' could serve to cover them all regardless of the particular cultural features of the societies in which they appear. This expression would include two opposed religious structures which observers sometimes confuse, shamanism on the one hand and possession on the other. Let us, at this point, limit ourselves to a few general remarks.

Both shamanism and possession are ways of approaching the gods by means of physical techniques of greater or lesser violence which sometimes lead to trance. These techniques exploit a curious disposition of the human mind and body, considered in our own culture to be abnormal or neurotic, namely personality change. It is brought about in the course of a nervous crisis of varying intensity which is not unlike hysterical 'disturbances' as defined, somewhat confusedly, by western psychiatry. The peculiar feature, which has not failed to attract the attention of ethnographers, is that this nervous crisis can, in a social context, sometimes affect a considerable number of men and women, as in the case of Haitian voodoo. In view of this, the ethnographers (Métraux, Bastide, Herskovits, Verger and many others) have dissociated themselves from the interpretations of the psychiatrists, emphasising the sociological characteristics of the phenomenon: the trance seizure is never anarchical; it is regulated, like a role in the theatre, and integrated into an organised cult with its own priests and pantheon and its own strict rules. The recognition of these facts, which stand in marked contrast to hysteria pure and simple, has been salutary. But although these distinctions have been clearly recognised, this does not of itself solve the recalcitrant problem of the strange coincidences that subsist between the behaviour of hysterical subjects in the West and that of the African in a state of possession or the Siberian shaman. The time has come to seek out common ground for a discussion among ethnography, the history of religions and psychiatry, and to suggest a perspective in which all 'hysteria-like' manifestations could be accommodated within a coherent psycho-sociological structure.

I shall confine myself here to suggesting the desirability of such a collaboration, which would no doubt result in a simultaneous revision of both psychiatry's definition of hysteria and ethnography's definition of the trance seizure.[2]

Shamanism and possession appear as a pair joined together head to tail, in symmetrical and inverted positions. In their purest forms shamanistic cults seem to be peculiar to Mongolian and Amerindian peoples, while authentic cults of possession are mostly typical of the black world in both Africa and America. These two poles provide a structure for a huge network of physical techniques that are similar or comparable despite the evident differences in their cultural contexts.

Shamanism develops entirely within the domain of magic. The shaman enters into competition with the gods, sometimes fights them, cheats them, and ascends towards them in a movement of pride which sets him up as their equal or rival. Shamanism is an ascension and is usually founded on a tiered cosmology. The existence of an axis for the world makes possible the mystic voyage, the dizzy journey of the shaman's soul through space, the ascent to Heaven and the descent to the Underworld. The shaman leaves his body behind; his soul escapes, leaving the 'yourte' where the drummers are gathered together with the rest of the congregation beset with its troubles and prisoner of its evils. The shaman is above all a healer, a magician. The quest for the stolen soul is a constant shaman-istic theme among the peoples of Siberia. The sick man has been 'dispossessed' of his soul and the shaman sets out to win it back in mythical space. He flies through the air, crosses abysses and descends to the Underworld. He owes these extraordinary magical powers to the benevolent spirits which protect him and with whom he enters into dialogue. In this way the shaman retains his psychic personality intact but at the same time its powers are increased tenfold. He is a seer, a hero. In some cases, it is true, the protector spirit which selects the future shaman reveals itself to him during a fit of frenzy which could be confused with a seizure of possession. But, in fact, it seems that the spirit reveals itself simply by appearing, not by taking possession of the body of the one elect. This revelation is a violent meeting, not the substitution of one soul for another. Furthermore, in the course of the shamanistic cure, the shaman invokes the pro-tector spirits. Sometimes he summons them imperiously. Sometimes the spirit appears to make, at most, a partial use of the shaman's body: for instance, it sometimes happens that the protector spirit speaks through the mouth of the shaman—medium who is interrogating him. Mircea Eliade[3] and Marcelle Bouteiller[4] have made an excellent collection of all these features.

The ecstatic technique of the shaman is necessary as a counter to the patient's dispossession. The patient is diminished, dispossessed of his soul. The shaman sets out to regain it. The reintegration of the soul is often symbolised by the patient's eating some substance: thus the pueblo healer puts a grain of maize, the symbol of the refound soul, into a drink which the patient has to take.[5] How-ever, the shamanistic societies of Asia and America also profess a second theory of sickness which is the symmetrical converse of the first, namely that the sick-ness is provoked by the untimely absorption by the patient of some foreign body. In this case, which we shall call shamanism B, the evil is an addition, not a subtraction. In the earlier case (shamanism A), the cure consisted in an adorcism, whereas in shamanism B it consists in an exorcism. The second theory seems more common among Amerindians. Lévi-Strauss has brilliantly demonstrated that shamanistic adorcism is an inverted psychoanalysis: 'Actually, the shamanistic cure seems to be the exact counterpart of the psychoanalysis cure, but with an inversion of all the elements. Both cures aim at inducing an experience and both succeed by recreating a myth which the patient has to live or relive. But in the one case, the patient constructs an individual myth with elements drawn from his own past; in the other case, the patient receives from the outside a social myth which does not correspond to a former personal state. To prepare for the abreaction, which then becomes an "adreaction", the psychoanalyst listens, whereas the shaman speaks.'[6] This pertinent observation prompts another that is complementary: if adorcism (the return of the soul) in shamanism A is indeed a perfect inversion of psychoanalytical techniques, the exorcism practised in shamanism B is more like psychoanalysis pure and simple; the ill (or the complex) is torn out. In the case of shamanism B the exorcist—shaman delves into the patient's body, which is weighed down and troubled by an alien presence. On completion of this internal exploration, which is symmetrical to the voyage into mythical space that characterises the search for the soul in shamanism A, the exorcist—shaman eradicates the cause of the ill. He sucks it out, tears the pathogenic element from the patient's body. But Lévi-Strauss draws our attention to another important observation which bridges the gap between the two therapeutic procedures associated with shamanism. He shows that among the Cuna Indians the mythical world which the shaman fights in the course of a long and difficult confinement is located both within and without, inside the woman's uterus as well as outside in mythical space in the strict sense of the term.[7] Here, then, the cure appears as a dialectical synthesis of adorcism and exorcism. To Lévi-Strauss's suggestion one might add that, conversely, in ascensional shamanism pure and simple (type A), it is the body of the shaman himself, not that of the patient, which merges with mythical space. Indeed, among the Yakut, the struggle against evil spirits is a protracted anguish for the shaman, who is obliged to take the spirits into his own body. He suffers more than the actual patient; he becomes the image of, and assumes, the sickness himself.[8] So sometimes it is the body of the sick man, sometimes that of the doctor into which the projection takes place.

Shamanistic exorcism and adorcism alike can be paralleled in the mythical structures peculiar to the African cults of possession. These, however, are characterised by a different point of view. Possession is opposed as a whole to shamanism in the following respect: we have seen shamanism to be an ascent of man towards the gods. Possession, on the other hand, is a descent on the part of the gods and an incarnation.

A first type of possession must structurally be coupled with the shamanistic view of sickness as the adjunct of some pathogenic element, that is with shamanism B. In both cases a presence alien to the patient must be eradicated by exorcism. But in the case of possession the patient is not just any kind of patient. He is clearly understood to be mentally sick. The 'possessed' person is totally overwhelmed (not partially, as in shamanism B) by an extraordinary, harmful, abnormal presence. What was, in shamanistic thought, a general theory of disease becomes in this case — in particular in certain Bantu regions of Africa — a limited psychiatric theory applicable to a restricted number of cases. It is clear that here we pass from the domain of psychosomatic medicine practised by the doctor—madman (shamanism) to a mental medicine intended for the use of the patient—madman (possession). In this instance it is the patient who suffers from the nervous agitation, not the doctor; the patient falls into a trance because he is ill.

H.-A. Junod has given us an excellent and full description of this first type of possession among the Tsonga of Mozambique.[9] The Tsonga live in terror of finding their bodies invaded by the ancestral spirits of neighbouring peoples, the Vandau or the Zulu. This particular sickness is called 'the madness of the gods'. The sick man suddenly passes into a state of unconsciousness, behaving in an eccentric manner; these first symptoms foreshadow a sudden state of aggression accompanied by a fit of trembling. When consulted, the diviner indicates a healer who specialises in this type of complaint, an exorcist who has more in common with a psychiatrist pure and simple than with a shaman. This doctor acts collectedly, with both feet on the ground. Following a precise ritual procedure, he tries to provoke a decisive crisis in his patient. He proceeds by assaulting the patient's nervous state, manipulating it as if using electric shock treatment. The vehicle for the exorcism is a violent Dionysiacal sacrifice. During his possession, which is provoked by chanting directed by the healer, the patient falls on the wound of the sacrificed animal and greedily sucks its blood. The blood is not intended to be swallowed but is a vehicle for the evil spirit. It is spat out so that the spirit is expelled. The specialised healer is a kind of cut-down shaman. He retains one of the shaman's fundamental characteristics: he is the master of evil spirits. But he controls them calmly, like a psychiatrist who is also an authentic psychoanalyst, questioning the possessed patient and eliciting the name of the evil spirit that is the source of his psychic disturbance. This attenuated shamanism has lost its ecstatic character, which passes altogether into the sickness of the patient. At this critical point in our structural analysis we can clearly perceive the way in which shamanism and possession are linked 'head-to-tail'. The passage from the one to the other is effected through a radical semantic alteration of the trance itself. The Tsonga trance is both an epiphany and a sickness, a sickness but at the same time a therapy. Thanks to the doctor, the nervous attack is given a cultural form; he integrates it into a religious sacrifice and, by exorcising it, provokes a permanent release for the patient, thereby curing him. Once he is healed, the patient undergoes a religious initiation. Now that he is definitively calmed he becomes a seer, a magician. He will be possessed and tormented no more.

This first type of possession (B) may be described as an evil possession, undesirable, inauthentic. Inverted, a number of its characteristics put one in mind of shamanism B, which also resorts to exorcism. The sickness and the trance, which are carefully dissociated in shamanism, are closely fused in this evil possession, where the trance is both the sign of the sickness and the means of curing it. This type of shamanism and this type of possession culminate in the same way, with exorcism.

In contrast, the other type of shamanism, the type that employs adorcism (shamanism A), has a structural converse in a second type of possession which I will refer to as authentic possession (A). Here the alien presence is no longer considered to be a pathological state but rather a pure epiphany. Far from being rejected as an evil (as in possession B), the spirit is accepted as a blessing. This is desirable possession, authentically religious and wholly accepted through initiation, which is, in effect, adorcism. Under the guidance of a priest, the devotee selected by the god learns how to be periodically inhabited by him. Sometimes a permanent bond is created during the initiation between a particular god and the devotee whose soul is placed for safety on the altar (as in Haitian voodoo). I trust that I am not here distorting the thought of the many ethnographers who have devoted penetrating studies to these phenomena, in particular Michel Leiris, Pierre Verger and William Bascom. This authentic possession is to be found among the Songhay of the Niger, the Ethiopians of the Gondar region, in Dahomey, among the Yoruba of Nigeria, in Haitian voodoo and among the blacks of Brazil. It represents an inversion of all the values and symbols of shamanism A, the type which is consistently based upon the ascent of the shaman, the conquest of the stolen soul and the magical and heroic character of intervention by the human being. In authentic possession (A), the African devotee does not ascend towards the gods as the Siberian shaman does; instead, the gods descend to him and — in the strongest sense of the term — take possession of his body, completely taking the place of his normal personality. Far from restoring the equilibrium of the original personality, as is the case in shamanistic therapeutic practice, this adorcism introduces a new personality, thereby creating a beneficial social situation by establishing a direct communication between men and gods. Furthermore, the patient undergoes the trance passively, religiously. He does not seek it deliberately, by magical means, as does the shaman. This time the transition from magic to religion is very clear. The priest appears at the devotee's side, supervising the manifestations of the trance. He initiates the elect and teaches them how to play their dramatic role correctly. Michel Leiris has given an excellent account of this particular aspect.[10] Whereas the shaman is a solitary actor, the devotees who are possessed form cult groups which bring the gods on stage. Periodically, they offer them the vehicle of their own bodies, which become 'mounts' for the gods. It is easy to see the links formed, by the inversion of elements, between these two ideologies of adorcism: shamanism A and authentic possession. In the course of his search for the stolen soul, the shaman deliberately seeks to reconstitute the original, deformed personality of the patient who begs for his help. The subject authentically possessed submits to the presence within him of a new divine personality, passively, for the sake of others and the good of the whole community (in order that the gods may communicate with men).

Jean Rouch has described this desirable type of possession among the Songhay of the Niger as a kind of sacred drama expressed in dance, a Dionysiacal epiphany. The fits of possession take place in public, in front of the house of the priest of the cult, the *zima*. The dancers are seated opposite the musicians and surrounded by the spectators. Preparations are made amid a general mood of good humour. The band starts to play and for a long time, indefatigably, it continues to play tunes for all the spirits (*holey*) without any of the dancers becoming possessed. The *zima* encourages the band and rouses the apathy of any dancers who become exhausted. 'In general, however, after an hour or two (sometimes less when the *zima* is particularly skilled), a dancer shows the first signs of possession: he ceases to dance and begins, imperceptibly, to tremble. Calm women cluster round, ready to help him. The *zima* priests . . . now intervene more actively than before. They come up to the dancer and recite the sayings of the spirit manifesting itself, whom they have identified from certain details in the behaviour of his mount. The band now plays the tunes of this spirit only, while the other dancers continue to dance. Soon the selected dancer shivers violently, groans softly and weeps. The priests are all solicitude towards him. This is the *tunandi*, the "raising", whose purpose is to "raise" the spirit on to his "mount". The fit becomes increasingly acute, the tears and groans become sobs with a characteristic low pitch (a kind of "wawawawa" . . .). Then, all of a sudden, the dancer falls to the ground, staggers to his feet again, opens his eyes brimming with tears and breathes with difficulty, moaning continuously. The dancer is no longer master of his panting body; it is now the spirit who inhabits him and makes him move, groaning in this way, and who in a moment will speak.'[11] The god greets the priests and all those present. The calm women who attempt to quieten him with gentle words clothe the spirit in his ritual costume and prepare a seat for him. The spirit speaks with the priest in a 'muffled and trembling' voice. He supplies the information requested of him. In short, the devotees who are possessed play the role of medium. From time to time their words are interrupted by a violent fit. When the priests have finished, the spectators put questions to the god or offer him presents. The atmosphere is nothing like that of a Christian service. Instead of taking place in the solemn contemplation and gravity that western minds associate with religious devotion, 'these ceremonies, which were already taking a jostling form, become a veritable "carnival", noisy, dusty and violent, during which the most intimate confidences are shouted aloud by the spirits'.[12]

Possession hardly ever lasts longer than a quarter of an hour. The spirit leaves the subject's body in the course of another fit, less violent than the first, after which the 'mount' is left immobile, panting, like a corpse. Soon he comes to his senses, removes his divine ornaments with the assistance of the calm women and then staggers away from the dance and, without the slightest recollection of all that has happened, simply goes home. 'Even if he has eaten burning coals or burnt himself on a torch or fallen repeatedly on his head, neither his body nor his mind will bear the slightest trace of it.'

Thus we can see that shamanism and possession, the two structural poles for ecstatic techniques, operate within an overall system of representation comprising four types which, since one pair corresponds to the other, can be reduced to two fundamental procedures. This 'geometry of the soul' could be synthesised in the following diagram, which manifests a double inverse symmetry both horizontal and vertical:

Adorcism	*Exorcism*
Shamanism A	Shamanism B
(return of the soul)	(extraction of a presence that is alien to the subject)
Possession A	Possession B
(injection of a new soul)	(extraction of a soul that is alien to the subject)

The god—man relationship is inverted when one passes from shamanism to possession. Furthermore, the structures peculiar to the two types (A and B) correspond to each other, head to tail. Both shamanism A and possession A (Songhay) are modalities of adorcism, while shamanism B and possession B (Tsonga) are modalities of exorcism. Shamanism evolves essentially on the level of magic; possession is a religious or magico-religious system necessitating collective rituals and a more respectful attitude to the sacred than shamanism. Through their primary or secondary therapeutic aspects shamanistic techniques are related to psychoanalysis; authentic possession should rather be compared with electric shock treatment. The latter suggestion was proposed by Pierre Mabille in an important posthumous and as yet unpublished study on voodoo.[13] For these reasons these physical techniques deserve to be considered the most important contribution that the archaic world has made to psychiatry. It is perhaps interesting to note in this respect that (according to Jean Rouch) among the Songhay those subject to fits of possession make up less than 6 per cent of the population, although the entire population takes part in the cult in the capacity of spectators. But authentic cults of possession go far beyond any psychosomatic therapy. The trances are usually experienced one after another, presenting a spectacle that has something of the *commedia dell'arte* about it. Each person who is possessed is familiar with the general pattern of his divine role.

Among the Songhay of the Niger, as in Haiti, the initial violent, anarchical fit of possession is not a sickness but the sign of having been chosen. The god does not seek to torment but to communicate through the intermediary of a human body. So the purpose of the initiation is not to expel the god, to exorcise him as in inauthentic, undesirable possession (Tsonga), but instead to accept him, to accommodate oneself to him, to deliver oneself up, body and soul, to him after learning how to do so.

Nevertheless, the starting point is the same whether for authentic or for inauthentic possession. It is only the outcome and the meaning that society gives to these manifestations that differ. Among the Songhay, for instance, the possessed subject who has not been initiated indeed looks, during his first fit, as if he is mentally sick. He is prostrated, does not speak and is every so often shaken by terrible attacks. But unlike the Tsonga, who, presented with such a case, attempt to bring the patient back to normal life, thereby adopting a typically western procedure, the Songhay try to imprint a religious character upon disorder. They set out to create order from psychic chaos, to transform the mental sickness which is disorder, confusion and silence (the patient no longer speaks) into language. The master of speech here, the theatrical director for the gods, is a priest, the *zima*. The new language and role that he teaches the sick man are beneficial both for the whole group (who thus communicate with the gods) and for the patient himself. The psychiatric efficacy of this technique (which is a radical inversion of the fundamental concepts of psychoanalysis, since it accepts the evil, channelling it towards new ends) cannot be doubted: the initially continuous fits now occur at intervals. The spirit now only possesses his 'mount' during the ceremonies, at the sound of the specific drumbeat associated with this particular spirit. Thus, in this religious system too, the *zima* imposes his magic will upon the gods; or at least he manoeuvres the gods, not seeking to negate their action but simply to force them to submit to the human order. Far from taking the form of an exorcism, as do psychoanalysis and the technique adopted in the cases of inauthentic possession, here the cure lies in adapting to the disorder itself and in changing the sickness (which is defined as a lack of communication) into a structure of communication. Authentic possession is the language of the gods. The Tsonga who, like western psychiatry, have opted for exorcism say on the contrary that possession is the madness of the gods.

The Songhay possessed are taken into the charge of the *zima*, who initiates them into this language and teaches them to play — or, more precisely, to dance — the role of the gods. They let themselves go during public ceremonies in accordance with certain rules and under the supervision of 'calm women'. These, from a psychiatric point of view, act as nurses; from a theatrical one, as costume-makers and dressers; and, finally, from a religious one, as the servants of the gods, helping them to blow their noses, wiping away the foam at their lips and the sweat from their bodies and at the same time seeing that seemliness is respected.

I should point out that an unexpected nervous fit is not always the initial reason why a man or a woman joins a corybantic association. The ritualised dance of possession appears in many cases prompted by troubles which have nothing to do with mental sickness. It is as if the field of application of an extraordinarily effective cure for mental sickness had been extended to include neigh-bouring domains all of which have one common characteristic, namely that the evil which must be got rid of or, rather, controlled is seen as a kind of spell, that is to say an attack from the outside world which painfully changes the psychic personality.

Among the Ethiopians of the Gondar region described by Michel Leiris we find at the outset a man or a woman disturbed by a sickness or distressed by a misfortune which he or she believes is caused by the action of some spirit or *zar*. So the presence alien to the subject, which is the cause of the action taken, can equally well be a malevolent presence around him. Leiris writes: 'In most cases, far from being the sign of the original trouble which needs to be cured, fits of possession only appear after the intervention of the healer. In order to parley with the supposed persecutor, so as to reach an agreement, the healer has caused the latter to take possession of the patient in a manifest manner or, to be more precise, has accustomed the patient to show in his behaviour (usually during assemblies of the devotees) the signs recognised to be those of possession.'[14] The healer—priest who intervenes by interviewing the spirit certainly acts like a psychoanalyst during the first stage of the investigation. However, it must be repeated that his therapy differs considerably from Freudian techniques. In the case of the Ethiopians it is a matter of — literally — incorporating the 'evil' in the psychic personality of the client. In this connection Leiris goes on to note that the one possessed will be 'mounted' during subsequent ceremonies by a spirit — or several of them — these being the ones that declared themselves during the initiatory therapy. They have been attached to the one possessed, through sacrifice.

In the initiatory ritual of Haitian voodoo it is also a personal link between the god and his 'mount' that is established, although subsequently the devotee may from time to time be possessed by other gods too.[15] Not only does initiation ensure the protection of a particular spirit (*loa*), but it also confers the extra strength needed to withstand the violent manner in which the spirit gains entry during the trance. There are various motives which may prompt a devotee to offer his body as a 'mount' to the god: initiation often appears as the decisive remedy for a sickness or as the complement to some medical treatment. The *loa* himself manifests his desire to be embodied in the devotee. He may express himself through the mouth of one possessed during his fit or he may appear in a dream to the devotee in question. But most neophytes have already been spon-taneously possessed before their initiation; they dedicate themselves to the *loa* who was the first to descend upon them or to the one who has manifested him-self the most frequently.

The significance of voodoo initiation goes far beyond a therapeutic treatment. One priestess of the cult has declared that the ceremony 'brings luck'.[16] It con-fers new vigour upon both body and mind. It is a shock therapy and/or a personality transformation. It follows the true pattern of authentic initiation: retreat, purification, a symbolical killing and resurrection.

The Dahomey initiation into the *vodun* cult (which is known to be the historical model for voodoo) takes us even further away from therapeutic preoccupations. I shall be basing my remarks on this subject upon the work of Pierre Verger, Geoffrey Parrinder and Melville Herskovits.[17] What strikes one immediately is the extremely long duration of the initiatory retreat in Dahomey. This takes place in religious institutions that have been termed 'convents'. In the old days it would last for as long as anything between a few months to three or eight years. Nowadays it is usually much shorter. It is characterised by an initial short period of between seven and sixteen days which is followed by the public 'resurrection' of the neophyte. It would seem that this preliminary phase alone was repeated in Haitian voodoo. Clearly a society condemned to slavery could simply not afford to copy the institution of convents.

Among the Fon of Dahomey, even more than in Haiti, the therapeutic aspect of the fit of possession becomes secondary. In many cases it even ceases to appear as a desirable by-product of hysteriform modes of expression. For instance, Herskovits describes the initiation of a child who had been promised to the gods by his mother even before his birth, following a vow made after his mother had been sterile for a long time. Consecration to a particular deity may also be inherited: the heir to the deceased devotee is chosen by the family. Tradition has it, moreover, that each god (*vodun*) used to be the particular property of one family group. While in both these cases the motivation seems purely religious, in the third it is indirectly based on therapeutic aims: faced with a mysterious sickness, the diviner who is consulted diagnoses an epiphany. The god desires that one member of the family should be initiated.[18] It is remarkable that, in this last case, the therapeutic connection between sickness and possession is made through an intermediary; it is not necessarily the sick person himself who undergoes the religious 'treatment'. Here again it is the family that chooses the future initiate. It has been noticed that there are more women than men in the initiatory convents. Unfortunately, Herskovits does not provide any information on the factors determining this choice. It is disturbing to note, in this respect, that a child of five or six, when led by its mother before the altar of the gods to fulfil the vow she made when she was sterile, falls into a trance at the mere sound of the drum.[19] Although he does not indicate the personal reasons for their recruitment, Parrinder tells us that the candidates are assembled at the beginning of the rainy season during the procession in which the gods are exhibited.[20] The postulant is possessed in the course of a dance and eventually falls suddenly to the ground 'as if prey to an epileptic fit'. This is the first phase of initiation, symbolic death; the 'corpse', wrapped in a shroud, is carried to the convent. Only the pressure exerted by the group can explain how it is that candidates chosen for such diverse and arbitrary reasons suddenly acquire the faculty for depersonalisation required in authentic possession. We should also note an observation made by Herskovits: this sudden 'death' is brought about by the god who 'kills the wife' (the candidate, regardless of sex, is assimilated to a bride for the god) following a period of secret instruction which lasts for forty-one days.[21] In Haiti, as in Dahomey, a large number of initiates are taking up a family religious heritage, but initiation is also open to anyone who seeks it for personal reasons — as a therapy or protection or a means of improving their social status. In such cases the candidate has often directly experienced being chosen by the gods in the course of 'savage' possessions, even before submitting himself to the initiatory discipline. Possession of the voodoo type appears at least in part to be a response to a personal need or desire as it also does among the Songhay of the Niger or the Ethiopians of Gondar. The situation is different in Dahomey, where social pressures affect not only the dramatic presentation — the form taken by the fit — but even the choice of the initiates. It may even happen that a man decides to consecrate one of his children to a *vodun* in order to gain protection against the risks of war or some other dangerous enterprise. But Herskovits himself notes that this 'regimentation' of religious life weakens the intensity of the trance as compared with the more spontaneous fits of possession that may be observed elsewhere in Africa. In Dahomey, 'even when the frenzy is unleashed it seems that the dancer is seldom, if ever, completely in a state of trance'.[22] The realities of the situation in Dahomey push the boundaries the Africans themselves usually set up between the psychic and the sociological much further back. At the beginning of this rapid investigation we came across the theory that possession is a sickness, a spell, an irruption within oneself of a malevolent, alien personality (Tsonga). Next we found a mixed concept where possession was regarded by the possessed themselves as an uneasiness cured by being transformed into sacred drama (Songhay, the Gondar Ethiopians). Finally, with voodoo, we found theatricality extending beyond the medical treatment to which it was often complementary: voodoo possession is deliberately sought after for its beneficial, comforting effects. Initiation becomes a means of medical, psychical, even metaphysical salvation. Finally, right at the historical sources of voodoo, we are confronted with pure theatricality, which is not to suggest that the Dahomians are frauds. All acting falls halfway between possession and simulation and is connected with the general phenomenology of possession.

We must not lose sight of the fact that, in Dahomey, the fit which starts the initiation is described as being particularly violent and similar to epilepsy. The 'corpse' remains in the convent for seven days before its 'resurrection' (according to Parrinder;[23] seven, nine, thirteen or sixteen days according to Herskovits[24]). At the end of this initial retreat, which is all that Haitian voodoo requires, the candidate reappears. He is publicly resuscitated in front of the temple when the priest or *voduno* repeatedly pronounces his new name, that of the god who inhabits him.[25] At the seventh call the 'corpse' gives a grunt and comes to life.

Still staggering, he moves seven times around the drums. But he is still a long way from being an initiate, a *vodunsi*, and is taken back to the convent for a long period of secret apprenticeship.[26] Parrinder believes that its most important phases can be reconstructed. During the first phase of initiation the candidate's head has been shaved. The initiator—priest keeps the hair in a secret place. The body of the neophyte is regularly anointed with palm oil in order, it is said, that the god may take pleasure in contemplating his 'wife'. The importance of the priest's activity in remodelling the personality is profound. It is a lengthy task. The initiate learns to speak a new language, to chant the canticles of the god and to dance his steps. It should be emphasised that each temple devotes itself exclusively to the cult of deities of a single type grouped into a homogeneous pantheon and served by specialised clergy. In this respect too, the religious system of the Fon of Dahomey is noticeably different from that of Haitian voodoo, where all the gods are honoured in the *houmfo*. The neophyte appears as a passive, feminine object in the hands of the skilful engineers of his or her psychological conditioning. As I mentioned earlier, there are noticeably more women than men in the initiatory convents. Men and women are kept separate from each other, and, for the duration of this period of almost monklike seclusion, sexual relations are strictly forbidden. The neophytes are obliged to undergo special exercises about which we know nothing but whose purpose is to bring about possession under the control of the priest. We do, however, find in the Dahomey ritual the central rite of adorcism practised in voodoo initiation: after an initial period of instruction the candidates wear on their heads or on the nape of their necks the sacred 'parcels' of the gods. As in Haiti, these sacraments are truly the seats of the gods. Pierre Verger particularly stresses the importance of the part played by herbs in establishing the close mystical link between the initiate and the deity to whom he is consecrated. During the period between his resurrection and the giving of his new name 'he is plunged into a state of numbness and mental apathy; he has forgotten everything, can no longer speak, and can only express himself through inarticulate sounds'.[27] In voodoo, the constitution of the new personality seems a very slap-dash job if we compare it with the painstaking efforts and unremitting discipline of the priests of Dahomey. Their extraordinary and amazingly effective labour used in the old days to last for years, sometimes as many as eight. These periods are shorter nowadays but still incomparably longer than the single week of retreat imposed upon the future *hounsi* in Haiti. This seclusion, during which vigorous young people undergo an enforced chastity and allow themselves, whatever their sex, to be 'made effeminate' as they achieve increasingly close contact with a god whose substance gradually absorbs them, is interrupted only by a few ceremonial occasions outside the convent. By the time they eventually leave the convent they have altogether lost their original personality; they have become 'other' and no longer understand the language of their country. They are symbolically offered for sale as slaves, and their family 'buys them back' from the priests. They remain strictly dependent upon the priests who have transformed them, and from time to time they work for them. They dance and enter into a trance only at the bidding of the priest, on the occasion of festivals held in honour of the god to whom they are consecrated and subjected just as a bride is to her husband.[28]

Perhaps it would not be irrelevant to return to our starting point to situate a number of marginal Christian procedures in this structuralist perspective. At the two poles of the orthodox system, at the bottom and at the top, the person possessed by Satan and the mystic both come close to the sacred (whether diabolical or divine) by paths similar to those we have just described. I would suggest that satanic possession, the reality of which the Church has never ceased to maintain, should be compared to the forms of undesirable possession that call for the intervention of a specialised exorcist. In Tsonga thought, as in the Catholic system, the one possessed finds himself in the power of an evil spirit which the priest attempts to expel. At the other end of the scale, the Christian mystic effects a curious synthesis between shamanism and possession. If I may, for the time being, neglect some of the nuances, I would suggest that the initial procedure of the mystic, on the threshold of ecstasy, takes the form of a shamanistic ascent. The Church is, in fact, suspicious of this first movement and condemns the pride which threatens to engulf anyone venturing in this direction. But following this ascent the mystic feels himself invaded, possessed by the presence of the divine. The vocabulary used by mystics to describe this state of beatitude which follows trials of a shamanistic type is potentially misleading. The fact is that this is an ambiguous state of possession. The intrusion of God into the human personality is not exactly an incarnation: such an idea would be considered sacrilegious in the Christian system. The mystics prefer to declare that in the intermediary sphere which they suppose themselves to have reached, they are absorbed into God. Midway between Heaven and earth, they thus achieve the state of depersonalisation that is characteristic of authentic possession, which differs from it only by being earthly, immediate, intimate, joyful and collective. One can hardly expect African Christianity quite simply to absorb the theatrical, Dionysiacal techniques of the traditional cults of possession. The joy of the Christian mystic is something purely internal, static, corpselike. Haitian voodoo has produced a syncretism between the African gods and the Catholic saints. However, this assimilation is quite superficial; it does not affect the strong personalities of the African gods nor in any way modify the meaning or significance of the ritual fits of possession. Although they belong to the same structural level, there is an opposition between the solitary, painful path of the Christian mystic and the sacred drama of the African possessed whom the missionaries have always ascribed to Satan.

6

The madness of the gods and the reason of men

Sickness, misfortune and religion

The debate on the psychological or sociological nature of religion to which Evans-Pritchard has, with some eclectic and disenchanted scepticism, referred[1] is a sterile one to the extent that this apparent contradiction masks one of man's fundamental experiences, that of misfortune and the finite. The functionalists do justice to only one part of reality when, forgetting to treat religious utopia as such and without adducing any evidence to support their view, they describe it simply as an instrument of social control. Now, religion concerns sometimes the individual, sometimes society as a whole. Whether individual or collective, rituals can be defined as an autonomous category of spoken and enacted language. They introduce a plan for order to protect or reinstate the degraded, to increase their vital potential or, conversely, to destroy others. These various modalities, which can be applied equally well to individual and to collective ritual, take place within time. Within that context there would appear to be only three possibilities for the performance of rituals.

1. They may be cyclical and as such are, *par excellence*, structurally ordered. The plan for order in this case becomes a plan for eternity: the rituals create the very structure of time, at the price of negating history.[2] They counter the historical flux, since they are concerned to maintain production and reproduction at the same level. It goes without saying that this kind of periodicity, which provides a framework for time and also for its negation, concerns the community as a whole, for, by reason of the simple fact of the renewal of the generations, only a community can be thought to provide a spectacle of cyclical permanence.

2. However, the group as well as the individual is subject to the bitter experience of events that are unpredictable and shocking. Rites connected with particular events, of irregular periodicity, are sporadically fitted into the framework of time. They provide an adequate response to the historical disturbances that beset the collective, cyclical order. War and famine offer the most immediate examples of this second aspect of the theory of ritual, which cannot be reduced altogether to a metaphysical dive into the ultimate and primordial

165

reality, *in illo tempore* as is suggested by the phenomenology of Mircea Eliade. (The very meaning of individual ritual activity is profoundly distorted by this philosophically tendentious hypothesis.) The universal religious practice of so-called archaic societies shows clearly enough that at the individual level ritual is very often a response to misfortune and lack of success. And the most painful personal experience of misfortune has probably always been sickness. Theories of disease and religion are always closely welded together in prescientific societies; and it has not been possible to dissociate these two domains altogether even in Christianity.

3. Time punctuated by events and cyclical time are not the only temporal modalities in which ritual can develop. Once the dangerous event has been warded off, the structure of time as defined by cyclical rites is no longer threatened. But many religious actions establish time that is irreversible, sometimes for the group but more generally for the individual. Here we must of course refer to at least a part of the immense domain which Van Gennep takes the credit for first exploring under his somewhat ambiguous heading 'rites of passage'. One may wonder whether the formal position adopted by Van Gennep was not too general in that he paid insufficient attention to differentiations on the axis of temporality. Agricultural and seasonal rites (which are cyclical) were thus put on practically the same footing as the rites of birth, puberty and death that he particularly had in mind.

To refer to those magico-religious actions — usually individual but occasionally collective — that are linked with an irreversible time, it would, to avoid confusion, perhaps be helpful to substitute for the expression 'rites of passage' the one 'rites of transition'. Neither cyclical rites nor those linked with particular events take place within irreversible time in this way. Even though the Tsonga healing ritual may manifest the three phases described by Van Gennep (separation, marginal activity, reintegration), being clearly directed towards effecting the passing of a victim from the status of a sick man to that of a healthy one, the operation does not have the same significance as the initiation of young people. A sick man can always fall sick again, whereas a circumcised man, introduced into the society of adults, will never repossess his foreskin; he cannot go backwards in socio-biological time. Similarly, as Marcel Griaule used to point out, the deceased relinquishes his function as a living man to acquire a definitive and different status within the community of the generations.

However, the problem becomes more complicated when one reflects that a number of the therapeutic rituals appear to be irreversible initiations into the cult of a pathogenic spirit. Such is the case, in particular, of an impressive number of cults of possession in Bantu Africa. So we must introduce a new distinction. The fact is that there are two types of irreversibility, one socio-biological, the other spiritual, and the two correspond to two different meanings of the term 'initiation'. The first is necessary and general; the second, contingent and relatively unusual. All children grow to be men but only a very few of them accede, for different reasons, to communication with the spirits. The initiation of the priest, magician or sovereign and that of young people do not belong to the same type of irreversibility. The opposition is nevertheless not as clear-cut as appears at first sight, for the initiation governed by socio-biological necessity and the irrevocable acquisition of a new spiritual status may go hand in hand, as is clearly shown by the *kimpasi* ritual undergone by the young people of the Kongo.[3]

From the point of view of groups devoted above all to cyclical time, the idea of initiation to a new irreversible status is difficult to understand unless as the point of departure for a new cycle. This is no doubt the significance of the village foundation rites connected with changes of site among the Bantu, or of the enthronement of kings among the Rwanda, which involves taking cyclical possession of both time and space.

These preliminary remarks do not aim to exhaust the complex problems posed by the theory of ritual in general. Their sole purpose is to situate in their correct place — one that is more important than is generally admitted — the occasional rituals that are triggered by the unpredictable irruption of misfortune and sickness. There can be no doubt that one of the three sources of religion lies in this ill-starred field, while the second springs more spectacularly from the idea of eternity, easier to assert at a collective level than at an individual one, where man is confronted with his own transience and death. (Christianity would recognise the second source only.)

Because of the scope and universality of the disasters it causes, sickness, whether organic or mental, lies at the heart of the magico-religious preoccupations of archaic religions. The medical dimension of a large number of religious facts opens up a fertile and so far little-explored path of enquiry for structural analysis, as also do the connected representations of body and spirit (framework for intellectual operations with a therapeutic purpose). In the United States, ethnoscience has begun to explore medical taxonomies, taking good care, however, not to infringe cultural frontiers between different languages. What I should like to do is make a modest contribution to the anthropology of religions in general by attempting to show that such an infringement is exactly what is called for.

Not long ago, psychoanalysis was inviting us to explain away the obsessiveness and apparent absurdity of magico-religious rituals as neurotic behaviour. Now we are beginning to suspect that, on the contrary, many aspects of archaic magico-religious systems may be seen as an answer to disorders of both the mind and the body. It has, perhaps, not been sufficiently recognised that both types of disorder belong to the same semantic field. We must, in a manner of speaking, turn the Freudian interpretation upside down. If anxiety lies at the base of religious illusion, it does not allow it free rein but rather sets up, in opposition to it, a rational if utopian system of interpretation and defence. Religion is not so much an illusion as a rational utopia.

The principles of therapeutic ritual remain remarkably constant across the many kinds of views of disease in archaic societies. Sickness results either from the intrusion of pathogenic objects or spirits into the patient's body, or from his soul being captured.[4] These two kinds of explanation are universally countered by two therapies, the one the reverse of the other. In the first case medicine employs techniques of extraction and exorcism; in the second it sets out to recapture the lost soul. This simple structure is based on two poles; on the one hand, intrusion or 'possession' (a presence within one that is alien to oneself) and, on the other, dispossesion of oneself. We can therefore see just how equivocal the expression 'possession' is, as used in French or English ethnographical literature. In its widest ideological sense the term conveys the fact that the body of the patient is weighed down, weakened or changed by a spiritual being and/or a dangerous material object of supernatural origin. The passage from organic sickness, physical languor or suffering to a disorder of the mind is simply a question of degree and intensity, usually expressed in African languages by the declaration that the pathogenic spirit has lodged in the patient's head, forcing him to change his personality. At this point the spirit of the patient is affected, either totally or partially. Thus, seen from the archaic point of view, mental sickness is simply the strongest expression of the general idea of sickness, which is conceived as the intrusion of a pathogenic agent. One could even say that mental sickness is sickness *par excellence*, for in it the 'supernatural' quality common to all sickness is most strikingly manifested. It is here, in mental sickness, that the link between sickness and religion is seen at its clearest, when a spiritual being momentarily, periodically or definitively takes over the being of a man in the most upsetting of epiphanies.

Sickness, the experience of partial or total alienation, the opening towards death, is the constant threat to any human order. To respond to it effectively and to transform his despair into hope, man's only means are pharmacopoeia and the language of ritual. Thus appears a first relationship between science and religion, which had seemed set for a definitive divorce. There seem to be no archaic societies in which certain morbid states at least are not invested with a magico-religious significance, whereas the memory or fear of the dead who invade men's dreams is far from being the universal basis for an ancestor cult. On this point it is worth bearing in mind the pertinent remarks of Meyer Fortes, which have definitively undermined Spencer's speculations.[5] On the other hand, the fear of sickness and man's magico-religious response to it are not unconnected with the prohibition of murder which Georges Bataille[6] has suggested to be the basis for all moral and religious order. Is not sickness, in the archaic universe, a mystical attempt at murder, a shocking, intolerable violence done to man? It always implies a pair: an aggressor, whether a spirit or a sorcerer, and a victim.

From a magico-religious point of view, the physical experience of pain is continuous with the moral experience of evil and misfortune. Evil, misfortune and sickness are manifestations of the same disorder, of the same negation of being. Any magico-religious system could be considered to be a dialectical whole based on a denial of history: it can only ensure the continuity of being by repeatedly denying its inevitable destruction.

There is a painful contradiction between the relative permanence of a society and the irremediable fragility of the individual, with the latter desperately striving to resemble the former. Hence the widespread idea of the reintegration of one part of the personality into the eternal clan either here, in the Underworld or in the beyond.

The horror of sickness is perhaps comparable with the horror of incest. Sickness, the threat of death, of corruption, is in the final analysis, like incest, a return to nature. It is not surprising that one of the principal agents responsible for sickness and death is the sorcerer, whose initiation is marked by incest and murder. Let us hazard the idea that any archaic medico-religious system is founded upon a prohibition of sickness, an ill-starred prohibition that can never be fulfilled and from which stems a set of variable rules, some positive, others negative, with which sometimes men and sometimes the gods play tricks. A fair illustration of this ambiguity is the Dahomian figure of Legba, the trickster god, whose clay figurine is destroyed in anger when he, the god who presides over divination, without speaking allows the death of a man he is supposed to protect.[7] Right to the end, even to the point of absurdity, religion refuses corruption, defilement, death. Natural violence done to man is considered supernatural only on account of man's inability to admit that nature works inexorably towards his destruction. So-called higher religions were, in their turn, also to struggle to deny the scandal of the interruption or degradation of human life, by indicating the routes by which the individual might attain salvation. Archaic societies, on the other hand, are preoccupied essentially with the salvation of the group. However, in response to the anxiety of the individual, they also introduce the language of magico-religious medicine, through which men can exercise a measure of control over the violence of the gods. The capricious nature of this violence presents a problem of a psychoanalytical order the difficult investigation of which has been initiated in the fine book produced by the Ortigueses in 1966.[8]

Following Collomb and Zwingelstein,[9] the authors note that depression 'is probably the most characteristic feature of African psychiatry'. They then point out that, within the limits of their Senegalese experience (Lebu and Serere), traditional doctors could choose between 'three interpretative models arranged in ascending order': the first is the action of soul-eating sorcerers; the second, a spell cast through a magic technique (*'maraboutage'*); the third, 'possession' by ancestral spirits.[10] These three types of diagnosis are used to define the origin of organic diseases as well as that of diseases which, in a western view, fall into the domain of psychiatry. It is as if the traditional magico-religious representations were at the service of a veritable generalised mental — that is psycho-

169

somatic — healing. Thus possession by *rab*, an ancestral spirit, can manifest itself equally well either through particular mental disorders ('running off into the bush, undressing, having visions or hallucinations, being agitated or violent') or through gastro-intestinal infections, through sterility or through miscarriages.[11] It is suggested that these three Senegalese diagnoses can be translated into psychoanalytical terms. The Ortigueses write as follows: 'To put it very schematically, to claim to be attacked by a sorcerer is the equivalent of feeling threatened by death and exclusion; to claim to be affected by *maraboutage* is the equivalent of expressing a castration complex; to claim to be tormented by the *rab* spirits is the equivalent of feeling urged to form closer links with one's ancestors' (which is a type of Oedipus complex).[12] It is as if the Lebu and the Serere of healthy mind had based their medico-religious ideology on clinical models of anxiety. Naturally this hypothesis would need to be widely verified in other societies. If it was confirmed, the thesis of Kardiner and Linton would suffer a startling reversal. Far from being a 'projection' of affective conflicts peculiar to one particular type of personality formed in every case by a similar upbringing, the magico-religious system would be seen as a way of countering men's anxieties, first by identifying their nature and origin and then by dispelling them. Within a restricted field, I shall attempt to show that the cults of possession on the one hand and the various aspects of shamanism on the other precisely correspond to the overall structuring of the experience of mental sickness which is sometimes transformed and sometimes eliminated but invariably seen as an epiphany.

These remarks would run the risk of being purely speculative were it not for the fact that at least one African society, the Tetela of the Kasai, of which I have first-hand knowledge, provides a measure of evidence to support them. Their entire religion is based on a fear of spirits and sorcerers. There is very little speculation about the supernatural world, what there is being contradictory and reticent. The sacred manifests itself in and through sickness, failure and death. It is as if any dialogue with the sacred (such as prayers, sacrifices or offerings) is impossible. Religion, thus stunted and as it were reduced to its lowest common denominator, resolutely turns its back on the language of positive ritual and becomes nothing more than a procedure for escape, for which the justification is a terror of any contact between men and spirits. In these circumstances the action of the diviner—healers has virtually no effect except upon evil spells cast by men. Magic takes the form of a vast anti-sorcery system. There is a striking absence of cyclical rites. Although the Tetela society is segmentary, there is no sign of ancestor worship at all. The only way of making contact with the sacred is by being possessed by the *Odyenge* spirit. No one can become a diviner—healer unless he has undergone this dangerous experience, which is characterised by mental disorder, either genuine or simulated. Among the Tetela religion is a positive experience of mental health for some, and a negative experience of sickness and misfortune for everybody. To put it more precisely, it is the relationship established between these two experiences.

This relationship illustrates the need to construct a general model of disease which is able both to overcome the opposition between mental and organic sickness and to make some contribution to the study of grand ideological schemata, conceived as transformational systems.

From sickness to epiphany

Sickness is a sign. It refers one to a visible signifier (the symptoms), which may be somewhat variable (the taxonomies of disease are often vague), and to what is signified, which is invisible and supernatural. The function of divination is generally to reveal the latter. The science of divination fills in the gap, the linguistic gulf between the imprecision of the signifier and the specific character of what is signified. Divination is as much a precursor of medical science as is 'folk' or popular pharmacopoeia, the only difference being that medical science presents a detailed inventory of signifiers connected with relatively well-defined diseases. In the widest sense of the term divination appears to be a science of intermediary signs. Among the Lebu of Senegal, for whom 'sickness is not a clinical entity',[13] the place and time at which the onset of the disturbance occurred make it possible to establish the correct diagnosis. Among the Tetela of the Kasai the intermediary signs are placed in the diviner's calabash and submitted to a 'chance draw' not unlike our own types of lottery.

Sickness, the sign of untimely action on the part of the gods or of sorcerers, calls for a medico-religious reaction. Its purpose may be limited to restoring the afflicted being purely and simply to his state of wholeness. But it may also reinforce his vital potential. In this case the sickness, which started off as a way to death, a death-plan plotted by the gods, paradoxically acquires a positive dimension. The Lunda of central Africa believe that all sicknesses are epiphanies. Every sickness, everything that goes wrong contains the obscure promise of a better life; sickness is simply a demand that the links between men and the spirits should be tightened, or it can even be a sign of election opening up the path to a career as a healer or diviner. This extreme case shows that misfortune is the necessary and sufficient condition for the development of communication with the sacred. Turner, a meticulous observer of the Lunda, describes this aggression which is at once good and evil in terms which call to mind the wider meaning of spirit 'possession'.[14] Organic sickness, mental disorders or lack of success in hunting all constitute different ways — of varying intensity — in which the sacred breaks out through excessive closeness in the medico-religious domain. Each different affliction, whether physical or moral, calls for the performance of the appropriate ritual by a medico-religious group made up of all those who have previously benefited from the same therapy. The therapy

establishes precious links with the pathogenic spirit while at the same time eliminating the evil or dispelling the misfortune.

At this first level, then, 'possession' is a general explanation for sickness and
misfortune, an alternative to the explanation of 'dispossession' or loss of the
soul. Among the Luvale an etiological distinction is made between organic sickness and mental disorders: for them psychic disorders originate outside the
group.[15] They are provoked by pathogenic spirits which belong to a foreign
tribe, whereas organic sickness and lack of success are attributed to ancestors.
Here, the 'possessed' victim singles himself out by his behaviour: he falls into a
trance, speaks the language of the spirit in question and imitates the customs of
the group to which the spirit belongs. Alienation in this case takes the form of
an imaginary and spontaneous incorporation into another culture. Some of these
psycho-sociological disorders are clearly connected with the colonial situation.
The *sitima* (train) affliction causes the victim to play at trains. He is the victim
of a spirit of mechanised civilisation and imitates the noise of a steam engine,
dragging his feet along two rods suggesting rails, and pulling baskets (imaginary
carriages) behind him.[16] Whatever the impact of colonialism on these manifestations of possession may be, the opposition the Luvale establish between
endogenic family spirits and allogenic spirits foreign to the kinship system
certainly corresponds to a structural division in the world of sickness. Whether
physical or psychic, the disorder establishes communication with the world of
spirits through various pathological forms of contact. The patient himself is,
par excellence, the place into which the sacred is projected, the place where the
enigmatical manifestations of the sacred appear as the basic pattern of possession.

This epiphany is first and foremost an act of aggression on the part of the
supernatural world. Thus the first — and strictly therapeutic — step taken consists of an exorcism. The Lunda, like the Luvale who belong to the same linguistic and cultural world, expel the pathogenic spirit, taking all the necessary
reverential precautions. The excessive and harmful contact by which the sickness
is defined is to be transformed into a social relationship: the cure is also an
initiation and creates a lasting link between the pathogenic spirit and the cured
patient, who has now acceded to the status of a devotee or even a magician. In
Africa, the transformation of psychic disorders into events of religious value is of
the first importance in their treatment. In a very large number of cases it
accounts for the emergence of cults of possession, in the strict sense of the
expression. Anthropologists show a remarkable tendency to underestimate the
significance of the transformation of mental sickness into religion. They are
afraid of being crudely trapped into positivism. Perhaps they, in their turn, are
often unconsciously possessed by the powerful ghost of the religion that they
themselves have abandoned — as if the death of God did not also imply the
death of the gods. It is a strange and surreptitious return from monotheism to
scientific polytheism. I should like, within this wider perspective of disease, to

develop and if possible refine the general model for ecstatic religions that I suggested in an earlier study.[17]

First we must note that possession in the strict sense of the word, whether undisciplined or controlled within the trance, often appears as a special case in the general ideology of sickness seen as supernatural aggression. We must first explore this field and define its boundaries and then, working gradually outward, examine how neighbouring areas relate to it and to each other. Meanwhile we naturally acknowledge that, however far-reaching it may be, this study can as a whole explore no more than a limited sector of the language of religion. I am in no way proposing a general anthropology of religion. Our most daring step will be an incursion into the domain of shamanism, which we shall make despite the caution which a specialist as wise as Eveline Lot-Falck has — no doubt advisedly — expressed, believing that the time has not yet come to reduce 'the operations of the human mind to equations'.[18] As a measure of prudence I shall limit myself to the reconsideration of the difficult problem of shamanism within the African context, beyond which my specialist training does not allow me to venture. My aim, however, will be to argue that where psychic disorder exists it is always understood in relation to religious ideas. Psychic disorder may be conceived of either as illness or as therapy across a continuous spectrum of different kinds of epiphanies.

Forms and transformations of possession

In a study written in 1962 I suggested grouping the various ideologies of the ecstatic trance within a structural whole defined by two sets of fundamental and interlocked oppositions, namely possession/shamanism on the one hand and exorcism/adorcism on the other. This was, however, only a provisional starting point. Now I should like to refine this hypothesis and resolve a number of equivocal points. There is no way of distinguishing *a priori* between one who is possessed (*stricto sensu*) and a shaman except in so far as society confers upon them different status. From a purely external point of view, both have the faculty of entering into a trance in conformity with a particular cultural model. One could say that they are, in a sense, the object or subject of a ritualised fit of depersonalisation. I certainly do not wish deviously to suggest the idea condemned by Michel Foucault, that religion is a response to 'the fantasising powers of neurosis'.[19] But at the same time I would radically dissociate myself from Foucault's rash declaration that 'the complex problem of possession stems directly from the history of religious ideas rather than from the history of madness'. Why should there be such an epistemological break in the realm of the imaginary? In medico-ethnographical experience there are, quite to the contrary, two extreme positions: the trance may appear as a cultural aspect of mental sickness, of the 'madness of the gods', as the Tsonga put it, or, on the contrary, as a result of a radical reversal on which the structural symbolic order is based, as a generalised instrument of therapeutic action. Thus at a first approximation it would seem that the reign of the mad patient (or at least of the patient afflicted by a number of mental disorders which turn out to be curable) is opposed by that of the mad doctor in this particular region of intercommunication between Heaven and earth defined by ecstatic religions. In general, ethnographic usage assigns the term 'possessed' to the mad patient and the term 'shaman' to the mad doctor. Two inverse and complementary ideologies characterise these extreme medical positions. For example, the Tsonga define possession-sickness as an invasion of spirits into the body of the victim, whereas the soul of the shaman leaves his own body to seek out the pathogenic powers and battles heroically within them in a mythical space that is now Heaven, now the Underworld and now the body of the patient himself.

I have been criticised for drawing too absolute a set of distinctions here. I accept the criticism without, however, abandoning my structuralist thesis. In particular it has been pointed out to me that among the Eskimo and the Tungus the ideology of possession coexists with that of shamanism. In a Tungus initiation, an old and experienced master calls upon the spirits one by one and sends these into the body of the shaman-candidate seated before him: 'At the moment when he is possessed by the spirits the candidate is questioned by the elders and must tell the whole story (the "biography") of the spirit in all its details, in particular who he was before, where he lived, what he did, which shaman he was with and when that shaman died . . . all this the candidate must tell in order to convince the spectators that he is truly inhabited by the spirit.'[20] This poses the whole complex problem of the shaman's auxiliary spirits. I shall come to this later, although without claiming to resolve it definitively. In every case, the shaman's relationship to these auxiliary spirits is different from his relationship to the evil spirits that he is called upon to fight. Thus even within the framework of the classic Tungus shamanism — at one level anyway — we can detect a particular form of possession, the type that I have ventured to call authentic and desirable, which in Africa in particular is the basis for the true cults of possession. In my earlier study I opposed the possession-sickness of the Tsonga, described as inauthentic and undesirable (type B) to the type of possession accepted as an epiphany by the Fon and the Songhay (type A). Type B is rejected or warded off; it calls for exorcism of the pathogenic spirit. Type A is sought after through the converse techniques of adorcism which establish a recurring magico-religious link between the possessed devotee and one or more spirits selected for the greater good of the community as a whole, thus making intimate and regular communication with the gods possible. This is the point at which, if we are to make further progress, we must ask ourselves whether there is any connection between the pathogenic spirits of the first type (B) and the gods of the second (A) or whether, on the contrary, they belong to two different, irreducible procedures.

At all events, the theory of disease and religious metaphysics appear to us from the outset as a closed system in which there is a correspondence between exorcism and adorcism. A choice must be made between the two in ideologies both of possession and of shamanism. In the case of possession, exorcism expels the undesirable presence of something that is both a sickness and a spirit, while, in contrast, adorcism creates a positive and highly valued link between the profane and the sacred (the latter frequently, although not necessarily, manifesting itself as a pathogenic spirit). In shamanism, which is committed above all to medical action, the shaman in some cases extracts the pathogenic spirit (or object) from the patient's body (exorcism), in others endeavours to bring about the return of the soul to the body so as to re-establish its lost wholeness (adorcism).

Shamanism and possession are thus played in the same key, with medicine providing the keynote, but they do not have the same score, at least never at the same time. To be sure, the performer may be now a shaman and now one possessed, but a careful distinction should nonetheless be made between the two roles, as I shall now show, using an African example. I shall attempt to establish that the amazing variety of African forms of possession truly constitutes a field of transformations that can help us to understand how it comes about that shamanism may, albeit exceptionally, be the end result of a pattern of behaviour that forms a single, continuous whole even though based upon greater or lesser differential variations.

From possession-sickness to the trance: the Tsonga and the Kongo

As we have seen, the literature of African ethnography uses the term 'possession' in a most ambiguous way, a faithful reflection, in this respect, of the Africans' own ambiguity. In its widest sense it refers to a generalised theory of disease and is some kind of expression of an aggression on the part of the spirit world, manifesting itself in a sickness, no distinction being made between organic and mental disturbances. Even so, the Lunda—Luvale do make an etiological distinction between the two. Among the Tsonga the distinction is more radical: for them, possession in the widest sense (*lihamba* among the Lunda) and mental disorder (possession in the strict sense) no longer belong to the same category. H.-A. Junod specifically limits the term 'possession' to the psychopathological phenomena that the Tsonga themselves describe as a mental 'sickness', 'the madness of the gods'.[21] The pathogenic spirits responsible for the disturbance belong to neighbouring tribes; they are not ancestors. The latter also attract the attention of their descendants through sickness — thereby inviting them to renew links that have weakened — but they can also appear directly in human shape in dreams or in immediately recognisable animal forms (as mantises or small, harmless, blue-green snakes). Although it is an epiphany, here ordinary sickness is not, as it is among the Lunda, a mark of being chosen but simply of being recalled to order.

In contrast, mental disorders provoked by foreign spirits are believed to result purely and simply from aggression.

Whether provoked by angered ancestors or by sorcerers, the sickness is 'dispersed' by means of an unvarying ritual procedure which culminates in the reintegration of the now cured patient into the community. The 'madness of the gods' is also treated with a ritual of expulsion, but the culmination of this is initiation into the cult of the initially pathogenic spirit with whom the patient had no positive links until the sickness. The treatment is, in the strongest sense of the word, an exorcism, the expulsion of a presence doubly alien to the self, lodged in the most inopportune manner at the very heart of the personality, which it totally disrupts. It should, however, be noted that this expulsion ritual is not purely and simply a rejection, negation or destruction.

In all cases the signifier, the sickness, refers to the signified, an epiphany that cannot be denied or reversed (the spirit) and that can only be understood when deciphered. The decipherment is always carried out by the diviner manipulating his collection of knuckle bones. But in the case of a sickness provoked by a foreign spirit this preliminary analytic phase is followed by a second – and much more important – linguistic operation, namely the interrogation of the spirit during a trance. The patient who is 'possessed', in the strict sense of the word, lives in chaos, deprived of any kind of language. He behaves in an eccentric manner, trembles, is subject to fits of aggression. A specialised doctor imposes upon this disordered agitation the cultural discipline of the trance, calling upon the spirit signified to appear openly, in public. When urged to speak through the mouth of the patient himself, the pathogenic spirit reveals its identity that it had hitherto been concealing. It is in and through the trance that the signifier, the 'mental sickness', refers clearly to the spirit signified, becoming for a brief moment indistinguishable from the latter. After this, the therapy consists in treating these two aspects of the sign in different ways so that the sign, as such, is destroyed. The Tsonga exorcism consists in bringing about the disintegration of the anomalous sign represented by the disorder of the mind: the signifier, that is the sickness, must be abolished, but the signified must be transferred to the altar, where it plays a role in a normal linguistic procedure, that of peaceful, comforting (and usually unproblematic) communication with the ancestors. But the altar in question is a marginal one, different from that erected in honour of the spirits of the dead around which all religious life gravitates.

This ritual tragedy or 'conflict with the forces of the invisible world', as Junod describes it, comprises two phases. At first possession is a personality disorder, an alienation of a human soul tormented by an evil spirit that is characterised by being alien in both senses. Once the patient is cured by exorcism, by means of the trance, he is – paradoxically – initiated into the cult of the pathogenic spirit, which thereupon loses its pathogenic quality. But the paradox is no more than apparent. It is resolved as soon as one considers the two sides to the sign of 'possession' among the Tsonga. Mental sickness is not, as such, considered to be sacred; it is no more than a temporary, discomforting and distressing signifier. The sacred, which falls on the side of the signified, can only be reached through therapy based entirely on exorcism. The state of possession is unacceptable in the eyes of the Tsonga precisely because it is both a mental sickness and an epiphany. The trance induced by the exorcism is still connected with both these categories, but it represents a decisive stage in the resolution of the contradiction. The trance unequivocally reveals the unity of the signifier and the signified while at the same time heralding their definitive dissociation. This is effected by means of a violent sacrifice. The one possessed, in a trance, falls upon the animal's wound and sucks greedily at the blood; then, immediately, he spits it out. The pathogenic spirit leaves the patient's body and is transferred to the altar. At this point its function is reversed: it confers powers of second sight upon the cured patient, now a devotee of a marginal cult. Once the sickness has been dispersed, all that remains is the epiphany of which it was a sign. Possession-sickness does not result in a veritable cult of possession. Even if, as usually happens, the patient suffers renewed fits 'particularly during the first weeks following the exorcism', he is now in a position to 'calm his gods'. The normal form taken by relations with the spirit is that of an offering and prayer before the altar. The mad gods have become reasonable, have come round to the reason of men.

The Tsonga trance is a dialectical stage in between disordered and confused possession and the sacrifice of exorcism. Possession is an anomaly, undesirable, rejected. It needs to be converted into another type of religious practice. The pure and simple confusion of man with spirit must be replaced by a separation that makes dialogue possible. In psychological terms one could say that the mental sickness is stabilised in a neurotic ritual prompted by the society itself. The Tsonga treatment for mental sicknesses is a psychoanalysis of expulsion aimed at forcibly eradicating a false identity (the patient's erroneous idea of himself). Basically it is a cure that involves the dispossession of the spirit and the repossession of the self. It is a very constrained psychoanalysis, subject to a ritual protocol.

Nevertheless, the Tsonga system presents structural analysis with one major difficulty which cannot be avoided. Junod's description suggests that some mental illnesses are connected neither with this treatment nor with this religious etiology. The type of delirium known as *mihambo*, another form of dementia called *rihuhe*, and epilepsy are all treated by magico-pharmaceutical methods aimed at killing the evil (in the first two cases) or chasing it into the bush (in the third case). It should be noted that the dementia known as *rihuhe* does not appear to be ascribed to the activities of sorcery or of angered ancestors. It is 'the sickness that comes from far away with the wind'.[22] There is reason to believe, despite the vagueness of the information, that the Tsonga are perfectly well aware of the essentially modern distinction to be made between neuroses that can be successfully treated by psychotherapeutic methods and psychoses which call for a different kind of medical treatment. Another Bantu society, the Luba of Shaba, seems equally aware of this distinction. They practise possession in its mediumistic form (see below), refusing to assimilate to this phenomenon incurable madness, which is the work of a wayward, irremediable spirit, Kibanda, who never responds to the diviner.[23] Similarly, Nadel noticed that the Nuba never consider epilepsy to be a sign of mediumistic possession.[24] On the other hand, six out of ten mediums whose biographies he studied numbered epileptics among the members of their families. He concluded that possession (which, in contrast to the Tsonga, among the Nuba appears in recurrent form) might constitute an institutional catharsis whose purpose was to stabilise 'hysteria' and associated psycho-neuroses.

I do not here intend to reopen a debate calling for a close collaboration between psychologists, psychiatrists and anthropologists; such a debate has been most auspiciously set on foot by a team of research workers in Senegal (Zempleni, Ortigues, Collomb and Martino). I shall simply point out that Africans themselves are often deeply conscious of the proximity of madness and religious possession. The boundary between the two is vague for the Zulu, who always hesitate before pronouncing a diagnosis. When a man begins to cry out and sing bizarre songs there is always an argument: some say that the patient is quite simply mad; others maintain, on the contrary, that an Itongo spirit inhabits him. The question can only be settled by a trial of clairvoyance.[25]

Bantu Africa offers other examples of possession-sicknesses that are cured or stabilised by a religious ritual with a therapeutic purpose. The case of the Kongo is all the more interesting in that this time the spirits that torment their selected victims (women more frequently than men) are endogenic (rather than allogenic as among the Tsonga). These are the spirits of nature (*nkita*); magicians extract them from the water and quite literally capture them in a fetish (*nkisi*) by applying the appropriate rituals, which vary according to the character of the spirit one is setting out to master. A number of *nkita* spirits, referred to by name, cause specific 'sicknesses' which all demand the same type of treatment. They have one distinctive characteristic in common: all are temporary mental derangements which take the cultural forms that are described by Van Wing as 'possession'.[26] I have noted only one significant difference from the case of the Tsonga: it is the absence of any separation between the signifier and the signified. Here there is no need to bring on a trance nor to question the spirit in order to discover its identity. It reveals itself immediately in the behaviour in which the possession expresses itself, due account being taken of the particular circumstances. If a woman runs to the river lightfooted as a partridge (or rolls on the ground, eating sand) it is plain for all to see that the Malari *nkita* has taken possession of her heart and given her the wings of a bird. If she is consumed with fever and suffering from convulsions, having gathered the red manioc from the river on market day, the immediate diagnosis is that Mvumbi-Masa is present.

The ritual to exorcise Mvumbi-Masa follows (despite the apparent differences) the same structural pattern as the expulsion of foreign spirits among the Tsonga. It is in both cases a matter of transferring the pathogenic spirit, who is greeted with all due reverence, to another place. Here normalised magico-religious relations can be established for the future between it and the patient, who is both cured of the morbid state of possession and at the same time initiated into a cult that in no way differs from the magic practices usual for the other *nkita*. The essential feature of these practices is the making of a *nkisi* fetish for the use of its owner. As among the Tsonga, the ritual healing of possession-sickness is a separation of the signifier and the signified. However, the operation of exorcism here is less easy to interpret than that of the Tsonga. Here it could even be thought to be the converse, namely adorcism. In the first phase of the operation the one possessed is in some measure consecrated to the Mvumbi-Masa spirit. But the ritual never fails to pass into a second phase. The first part of the ritual consists in an unequivocal declaration of the presence of a particular spirit within the body of the patient. What is signified is made visible, whereas in the Tsonga ritual the trance brought on by the doctor made it audible. The patient, who displays on her person the ritual colour of the *nkita* spirits, takes a potion containing the symbolic ingredients of Mvumbi-Masa, which have been extracted from the *nkisi* fetish owned by the magician-healer who is directing the ceremony. The patient is in this way 'incorporated into the *nkita*', in the words of the formula used by the Kongo to describe possession. It is a curious reversal of language, as if the patient was absorbed by the spirit (a formula reminiscent, *mutatis mutandis*, of that used, with poetic variants, by the Christian mystics when they attempt to convey their own dizzy experience that also bears the burning stamp of fusion).

However, the second part of the Kongo ritual radically transforms the initial situation. An analysis of the symbolism shows that now it is a matter of expelling the spirit and locating it in a new fetish which is made from the first and of which the patient is to become the master (*nganga nkisi*). It is apparent that, in this clearly magic context, the possessing spirit is, in the end, itself possessed. All the symbolism of this second phase indicates repulsion of the spirit. Whereas *nkita* spirits belong to the sphere of water and mythology indicates that they belong to the side of the raw, the non-cooked, the anti-fire,[27] the patient now undergoes a treatment characterised by fire and overeating. She is copiously fed and kept in seclusion in a hut where the fire is kept constantly burning. Two or three months later, a festival to mark her emergence is held 'around a blazing fire fuelled by three time nine faggots' in which all who take part eat and drink as much as they want. The patient lies down on the hot ashes of the fire while the participants dance round her. When the master of ceremonies bids her rise she begins to sing, begging the spirit *to be appeased*. The next day a celebration is held for the definitive return to the world of the living of this body now liberated (through the interplay of symbolic antagonisms) from the painful although highly prestigious presence of the *nkita* spirit. She now receives the appropriate *nkisi* fetish and henceforth controls it.[28]

The trance (which appears with the beating of drums, during the cure) does not recur any more than it does among the Tsonga. It is no more than the opportunity of making the spirit as manifest as possible before it is transferred to the *nkisi*; it is a temporary way of controlling, by rhythmical means, certain mental disorders that are regarded as sickness. For the Tsonga, as for the Kongo, the human body is not the normal dwelling place for the spirits. When a spirit establishes itself there, it must be dislodged and located on an altar. The new dependency that is then established is for the Tsonga a religious and for the Kongo a magic one. But in both cases possession, considered to be an anomaly, is eliminated from the magico-religious scene and integrated into another system by means of techniques of 'displacement', in the mystical and psychological sense of this term. The trance is not systematically sought after as the product of the epiphany of a possessing spirit. This latter alternative, which marks the point at which system B (Tsonga and Kongo) changes to system A (Fon and Yoruba), the structural transition from exorcism to adorcism, is exemplified in Africa in a second series of cases all of which can be said more or less to involve therapeutic possession.

Therapeutic possession: the Sukuma and the Lovedu

In the previous cases possession in the strict sense of the word was found to be the mental sickness which had to be cured by effecting a transfer of the spirit in question. Among the Sukuma it is, in contrast, considered a therapy. A number of organic disturbances that Tanner believes to be of hysterical origin, although they are ill defined (sterility is one of them), are treated by the intervention of a healer practising a veritable psychomatic medicine.[29] He provokes (or 'induces', to use Tanner's word) an ecstatic trance by ringing little bells close to the head of the patient, whom he interrogates in a loud and aggressive voice in order to obtain the name of the pathogenic spirit. The patient, who has apparently never suffered a fit of possession (in the Tsonga sense of the word) but who now finds himself in an indefinite state of 'possession' in its widest ideological sense, is projected into a trance whose purpose is strictly therapeutic. To appreciate the full significance of the difference, we must re-examine what the trance means from the two different points of view. Both for the Tsonga and for the Sukuma the trance is provoked by the intervention of the healer in an atmosphere of rhythmic excitement. It is the linguistic instrument of communication between the profane world and a pathogenic form of the sacred. From a medical point of view, however, its mediatory position between the sickness and the cure is significantly different. In the Tsonga ritual the trance prolongs the sickness – I have even suggested that it took the purest form of possession-sickness, in which the signifier and the signified are united. The action of the healer is limited to giving a cultural form to the already existing fit of possession, which is quite undisciplined and wild and which the Tsonga themselves see as a kind of dementia (the madness of the gods). Among the Sukuma there is no such preliminary signifier. The sickness is a totally indeterminate state, truly a floating signifier, to use the expression with which Lévi-Strauss describes the category of *mana*.[30] In the case of the Sukuma the spirit that is signified is concealed, hidden deep within the silent body. The trance, which is induced, appears as in the previous case to be the way to discover the meaning. But it is also and above all the occasion for the diagnosis which must precede medical treatment. Although it should not be confused with the cure itself (Tanner is quite categorical on this point), it is nevertheless true to say that it is a part of the therapy that it introduces, whereas the Tsonga trance follows and brings to a conclusion the manifestation of possession-sickness. The two positions in the ritual sequence are assuredly very close; the interval could be described as a semitone or even a musical comma. In both cases the trance can be described as an operation of naming, preliminary to the cure itself. A new threshold is crossed by the Lovedu of southern Africa, who, strangely enough, bring us back to a geographical and cultural region close to that of the Tsonga, from whom, nevertheless, they differ radically on a magico-religious level.

The Lovedu introduce an increasing element of differentiation within the semantic field we have been exploring.[31] A series of diseases intractable to all treatment but not necessarily mental are diagnosed by the Lovedu as being forms of 'possession' in the widest sense of the term: an ancestral spirit is lodged in the body of the victim, causing the disturbance from which he is suffering. To rid the patient of this intractable, anomalous complaint, a specialist doctor induces, through the excitement of dancing, a trance which in this case is clearly regarded as a cure, not just a method of diagnosis as in the case of the Sukuma. The trance has become the actual treatment. The doctor who is directing the therapy is himself a former subject of 'possession' who has personally undergone this magico-religious procedure. He begins to grunt and tremble in the presence of his client, whom he urges to dance to the point of exhaustion in order to force the spirit to manifest itself ('to come out', as the Kriges put it). To facilitate the epiphany, medicines are applied to the patient's body and he is urged to drink infusions. The first time the pathogenic spirit emerges it is painful for the patient. When he feels it coming on he falters; then his movements become increasingly frenetic; he drags his feet with difficulty and finally collapses in a state of trance. At this point he begins to sing the song for the arrival of the spirit, which is greeted by all those present. After this treatment the patient feels better. The spirit has not been expelled; on the contrary, it will return periodically to the body of the initiate but without doing him any harm. The cured patient — sometimes when oppressed with guilt for neglecting some prohibition — seeks the return of his ancestor deliberately: 'thus, very often, when a possessed person does not feel well he will ask for the drums, saying he must 'dance'. The dance is central to the cult, and it no longer has anything to do with exorcism. This modified, sedative, recurrent trance is the indisputable mark of the structural transition from the B type of possession to the A type, where it is the constant instrument for beneficial communication between men and the gods. The ancestors speak in the course of possession, sometimes in a foreign language.

This cult of possession remains a marginal one among the Lovedu. It affects only a limited number of individuals, not the whole society. The personality of the possessed is not altered in the course of the dance; only the initiation brings on the trance; as in all the preceding examples, the trance constitutes an exceptional, stunning revelation of the spirit which has taken possession. The only fundamental (but consistent) difference is that the ancestor is not definitively separated from the patient after initiation: on the contrary, here initiation counts on the power of adorcism. The spirit returns periodically, but calmly. At all events, the transition to the recurrent epiphany trance characteristic of authentic cults of possession is no more than a question of degree. The decisive step is taken in Gondar. The cult of the *zar*, brilliantly described by Michel Leiris, is constructed on the same premisses as the curative trance of possession of the Lovedu.[32] A number of diseases or misfortunes are attributed to the action of a *zar* genie. Leiris writes: 'In most cases, far from being the sign of the original trouble which needs to be cured, fits of possession only appear after the intervention of the healer. In order to parley with the supposed persecutor, so as to reach an agreement, the healer has caused the latter to take possession of the patient in a manifest manner or, to be more precise, has accustomed the patient to show in his behaviour (usually during assemblies of the devotees) the signs recognised to be those of possession.' In Gondar the resolution of the sickness truly introduces the spectacle of possession which is based on the abandonment (real or simulated) of the patient's personality and the incarnation of the gods who 'mount' their devotees during the ceremonies.

In authentic cults of possession where the trance, regarded as most prestigious, is recurrent and much sought after for its virtues as a means of communication, the link between sickness and ritual may be weakened or even disappear completely. This would appear to be the case in Dahomey or among the Yoruba of Nigeria. But here another question arises concerning the candidates for initiation — that is the future vehicles for the gods — who are always restricted in number even where the cult is central to the magico-religious scene. Where access to the cult is free, are they not, in some way, the victims of another kind of alienation? It is a question that has often been posed, in particular by Lewis, who has no hesitation in situating phenomena of possession within the field of psychosociological frustrations. He particularly emphasises how many women or other marginal groups are involved and how, in many cases, possession is the symbolical expression of their desire for compensation.[33] Drawing on their ethno-psychiatric experience of the Lebu of Senegal (where the cult of the *rab* is based on an alliance), Collomb and Martino emphasise – in more general psychological terms – that 'the need for possession (to be possessed) is connected with a fear of solitude or of loss of identity as well as with an illusion of or an attempt to bring about a fusion'.[34] Zempleni, for his part, underlines the 'therapeutic' element in the rituals of possession practised by the Lebu and the Wolof.[35] Thus it is quite possible for a mixture of positive and negative motivations to be at work within the structural field that I have attempted, albeit rapidly, to indicate. Complex historical problems are raised by the two poles (exorcism and adorcism) that define this field. It does not seem quite correct to suggest, as Collomb and Martino do, that 'African cultures which are community-focussed and prone to fusion within the community, prepare the way for and facilitate possession', since it is also a fact that a striking number of these cultures reject possession, either transforming it into another system (Tsonga and Kongo) or eliminating it entirely (although this is less common).

In view of the consensus of evidence that indicates that possession of type B (undesirable, inauthentic and rejected) appeared at a relatively recent date in a number of Bantu societies, I may suggest another hypothesis. The magico-religious system of the proto-Bantu is based on the permanent struggle between a beneficent agent, the magician, *-ngang*, and a harmful one, the sorcerer, *-dog*.[36] As we shall see, this fundamental opposition is rooted in the shaman ideology, with the evil sorcerer taking the role of a black shaman. In such a field, cults of possession in the strict sense of the expression are not considered desirable. And, in fact, in central and southern Africa (with the possible exception of the Cameible exception of the Camerouns) possession more often takes a mediumistic form which, as I shall try to show, exhibits a pre-shamanistic structure.

With an overall perspective such as this it is easier to understand that the new psycho-sociological disorders provoked by colonisation and intensive population migrations in central and southern Africa might, for many individuals, find expression in the loss of a sense of identity, attributed to spirits that are not a part of their traditional framework but either belong to neighbouring tribes or are connected with the European world (as happens with the Tsonga and the Lunda). This explains why these harmful powers must first be exorcised and then integrated into the traditional system. There is no evidence to suggest that possession-sickness is a regressive form of the cults of authentic possession which are found to be characteristic of a certain number of West African societies. It certainly seems likely that cults of possession within the historical Fon–Yoruba grouping are of considerable antiquity, and I, for my part, would not support the bold hypothesis put forward by Lombard, suggesting distant Mediterranean or Semitic origins.[37] A study in depth of the historical traditions of the Fon and the Yoruba might shed some light on the difficult problem of the formation of cults of possession in the Gulf of Guinea. Among the Fon, at any rate, this appears to have taken place along with the development of centralised power, and right from the start the cult appears to have had a syncretic form. In the

Songhay empire, well known to have played an important historical role in the Niger valley, the Sohantye magicians consider themselves the spiritual successors to their founder Sonni Ali (the king described as 'always the victor, never vanquished', who was overthrown by the Askiya dynasty). It is interesting to note straight away that these magicians still claim to go back to a tradition of magic quite foreign to the spirit and to the manifestations of the cult of possession (which is currently attracting a large number of followers).[38] The rituals of the Sohantye are clearly shamanistic in character; their function is to ward off the sorcerers who are eaters of souls. So it is not without interest to note that Songhay traditions claim an oriental origin for the cult of possession dedicated to the *holey* genies.[39] However that may be, and this time from a synchronic point of view, the Songhay magico-religious system demonstrates the coexistence, at separate levels, of the ideologies of both possession and shamanism. We still, however, need to enquire whether it is possible to give a structural definition of shamanism *vis-à-vis* the terms of possession and to do so preferably within the framework of the same historico-cultural area; for clearly a comparison between Siberian or Amerindian shamanism and the African cults of possession could, with some justification, be regarded as a somewhat sterile intellectual exercise. Now it so happens that Bantu Africa provides us with a positive answer to our question.

Towards shamanism

Mediumism: the Sukuma (once again), the Kuba, the Luba and the Nuba

The system of ideological transformations in the trance becomes more complex if we envisage the possible variations in the paired terms doctor—patient. The patient has so far always appeared as the passive subject of a trance controlled (or, more precisely, induced) by the spirit, with or without the mediation of the doctor. With the possible exception of the Lovedu, where the healer, equally, is in a state of possession (showing the patient the path he should follow), in every case the doctor treating the possession-complaint acts with cold self-control, without himself becoming agitated. One may well enquire whether any examples of the converse exist in Africa, in which the doctor — rather than the patient — assumes the state of trance, becoming in this way its active subject. This theoretical possibility does in fact find concrete form in the second kind of 'possession' to be found among the Sukuma. Here, the 'auto-induced' trance, to use Tanner's expression, coexists with the earlier type ('induced' or provoked by the doctor, in the body of the patient). This new use of the trance seems to be an attenuated or rudimentary form of shamanism within a society in which, what is more, the patient can also be induced in trance by the medicine-man.

An authentic shamanistic trance, in its Amerindian or Siberian forms, is entirely therapeutic in character: the doctor is the general healer who gains recognition as such during — and using — the trance. In this respect the Sukuma mad-doctor is only a cut-down shaman. He puts himself into a trance in order to get a clear view of the case, to make a diagnosis, not to effect a cure. The operation of second sight represented by the doctor's trance is quite distinct from the subsequent treatment, as indeed was the case in the other, 'possessive', form of trance (that undergone by the patient).

Despite this similarity, what we have here in fact is a spectacular reversal of possession within one and the same society. The Sukuma doctor in a trance is not, as Tanner implies, possessed. He is not submerged by the spirit. He retains his own strong individual personality when confronted with the ancestors whom he interrogates within himself, that is to say on a mythical level. Tanner himself writes: 'Suddenly he stops rattling and starts to pronounce as his diagnosis what he had been told by the ancestor spirit while he was in his trance.'

This seer, whose consciousness is extended rather than obliterated during the trance, nevertheless finds himself in an ambiguous position in relation to the spirits: although he has the power to induce a trance within himself, he does not have the power to arrest it. This decision depends entirely upon the spirit. This attenuated shamanism represents the field of medical mediumism in Africa. It appears in the Bantu world, in particular among the Kuba and the Luba. Vansina has no hesitation in describing as shamanistic the periodical ecstatic fits of Kuba priests 'possessed' by whichever of the spirits of nature they are specifically linked to.[40] Once again, the form this 'possession' takes needs to be described in detail. The medium puts himself into a trance in order to diagnose the origin of sicknesses; but this trance has no therapeutic value for the consultant. The medium is not a soul-doctor. The spirit simply reveals the remedies to him and imposes prohibitions. The mediumistic trance is not a dramatic unleashing of spiritual forces, a heroic duel within the body of the seer—doctor. This rudimentary specimen of shamanistic activity lacks the element of violent mythology that involves coming to grips with the enemy spirit in the course of the trance. The Kuba medium is simply in the presence of the protector spirit, who, for others, may also be an evil spirit. The spirit guides him in the best interests of the local community. For the medium is in the service of the group as well as of individuals: the spirit reveals to him the means of wiping out the calamities which befall both. From a religious point of view sickness and misfortune are treated alike: the medium is sometimes called the 'healer of God'. The spirit appears to the medium it has chosen in what amounts to a veritable annunciation: it teaches him the details of the cult and tells him how to make a fertility charm which will itself be the token proving he has been selected. The trance is not the only way in which the protector spirit may appear: the medium also enters into communication with it in dreams and in intense meditation practised close to a spring. Emphasis should be laid on the face-to-face nature of the communication between the medium and the protector spirit. In this respect mediumism points towards shamanism and moves out of the zone of possession in the strict sense of the word, in which the two partners involved are confused together in one mind. Vansina has recorded many accounts showing that the spirit speaks to the medium and gives him instructions.

Mediumism also lies at the heart of the religious preoccupations of the Luba of Shaba.[41] The great heroes of the past, the *vidye*, communicate with men through the intermediary of the medium, who may be either temporary or permanent. Temporary mediums make their prophecies at the spot where the spirit is living; those who are permanent are consulted by clients, they 'arouse' the spirits. This function of arousing indicates the active nature of the mediumistic trance and, from a structural point of view, sets it squarely within the zone of shamanism.

Like Vansina in the case of the Kuba, Nadel has no hesitation in classifying — rashly, but with some justification — the mediumistic 'possession' of the Nuba within this universal magico-religious category.[42] In effect, this pseudo-shamanism is simply a logical stage in the transformation of possession into shamanism. Under the influence of the trance the Nuba medium makes prophecies, relays the wishes of the spirits and discovers the causes of sicknesses. Nevertheless, no more than in the case of the Kuba is the trance identified with the treatment itself. It is simply the means of discovering the correct therapy. The ideology is still to some extent that of possession in the strict sense of the term, for the spirit 'mounts' the medium or 'enters his head'. Each spirit stamps its 'mount' with a particular pattern of behaviour. But in contrast to one possessed, who loses his own personality completely during collective ceremonies, the Nuba medium holds séances of consultation, privately, inside his hut. Furthermore, the cult appears to be predominantly male. All the spirits are male; if they should happen to possess women the situation is regarded as incongruous, as this possession distracts the women from their duties.

It is clear from these remarks that, both from a linguistic and an operational point of view, African mediumism lies on the borderline between shamanism and possession. In the latter the gods make their presence brutally felt, speaking unsolicited, at random, at times even at the cost of a man's sanity. It is easy to see how mediumistic speech differs from the babbling of the gods in authentic cults of possession that is spontaneous and often — to use Jean Rouch's expression — 'insipid', even if the profit individuals and the community as a whole derive in the end may be similar. The structural position of mediumism clearly makes it possible, theoretically, for it to evolve either in the direction of overt manifestations of possession or, on the contrary, to slip into authentic shamanism.

In the interlacustrine Bantu civilisation, whose collective cults of possession are the subject of one of my own analytical studies,[43] the former development seems to have been the case. Beattie's evidence concerning the Nyoro kingdom suggests that the sacred drama of the Kubandwa is a recent transformation: previously there was only one accredited medium to each lineage. This connection between mediums and family groups is attested in other places too, while there are other cases again (for example among the Kuba) where one possessed priest is attached to a particular territory. Among the Shona we find examples of both possibilities simultaneously: there are minor mediums in the service of single families and major ones in the service of the whole region or sub-region.[44]

We ought, rapidly, to consider the position of the complex phenomenon of prophets pure and simple on this scale ranging from possession to shamanism. We shall limit ourselves to the case of the Nuer, which has been well described by Evans-Pritchard.[45] The dialectical relationship between men in a state of trance and the spirit in question already suggested by mediumism is strikingly evident here. Although 'possessed' by a spirit of the air, the Nuer prophet at the same time 'possesses' the spirit. The Nuer make a distinction between the passive and the active aspects of this 'possession'. From time to time the prophet undergoes a nervous fit during which he makes no pronouncements: this is simply the sign of the exceptional powers conferred by the spirit upon its medium, who, for his part, always makes his prophecies in a state of cold self-control.

Now authentic shamanism precisely represents the difficult conjunction of these two states and the resolution of the antinomy between them. For a true shaman the state of trance is one in which he operates in the heat of inspiration, in a frenzy of hyperlucidity. There is one very rare Bantu example of the shaman-istic fit which will presently help us to understand this heroic tragedy which is intensely played out in Asia and America but on which the African societies have, in general, turned their backs.

The institution of Nuer prophets can to some extent be seen as one of the divergent paths leading from mediumism to shamanism. But perhaps this repre-sents, as it were, a royal road in the history of religions. It is significant that Moses received the tablets of the Law from God after an ascension which may, with justification, be interpreted as a proto-shamanistic journey.

An African case of authentic shamanism: the Vandau

A radical transformation of ideologies of possession into shamanistic ideology is exemplified in one African society at least: the Vandau of southern Africa.[46] The case is all the more remarkable given that the Vandau live among the Tsonga, among whom the theory of possession-sickness is maintained so strongly. Through a structuralist irony it fell to the son of H.A. Junod, the brilliant ethnologist of the Tsonga, to make a study of this extraordinary reversal of possession. An exaggerated filial respect prevented the younger Junod from see-ing that the trance of the Vandau exorcist magician is something quite other than a particular case of the kind of 'possession' his father described among the Tsonga.

187

The Vandau trance is not, as it is among the Tsonga, the ultimate expression of the mental sickness, that is to say the clear manifestation of an epiphany that heralds the patient's being freed from possession. Among the Vandau the trance is undergone for general therapeutic purposes by the doctor himself. Here, the mad-doctor is an authentic shaman. He is the 'clairvoyant', 'the one with the head' (a literal translation of the word *nyamusoro*), 'the one who has the extraordinary faculty of seeing the spirits, of finding them out, knowing their secrets; the one who, in a word, has the power to exorcise them'.

It will no doubt be remembered that the figure of the exorcist also exists among the Tsonga within the framework of possession-sickness. But the point is that their respective positions in the ordering of the ritual form a system of oppositions. In the case of the Vandau the exorcist appears to practise general medicine, regardless of which spirits are responsible for the sickness, which is defined, in the widest sense, as 'possession' (of the patient). Among the Tsonga the exorcist in question is very clearly a specialist in the treatment of mental sickness. The Tsonga magician who confronts the madness of the gods is neither mad nor agitated. He is not supposed to be, any more than the western psychiatrist is, although it is quite possible that either of these may be former patients, now cured, or seeking a cure via their professional specialisation (as is attested among the Tsonga, at least).

Be that as it may, the Tsonga psychiatrist operates with a cool head, if not coldly. He is not in a trance as is his Vandau colleague, who has the responsibility of curing all sicknesses at his own risk and peril. The Tsonga doctor transforms his patient's mental sickness into a trance; the Vandau doctor puts himself into this state. The Vandau ritual is worth analysing in detail. The exorcist doctor kneels before his patient, who lies motionless before him, and gradually puts himself into a trance. A crucial problem of interpretation arises here. The younger Junod believes that the doctor is 'possessed' by his protector spirit, *bzoka*. We have seen, in connection with mediumism, that such an opinion needs to be evaluated with great care. The description goes on to tell us that the magician (*nyamusoro*) 'feels the weight of his protector spirit on his shoulders'. This contact should be distinguished from the identification, pure and simple, that possession is supposed to precipitate between the possessing spirit and the man possessed, an identification that is linguistically expressed equally by metaphors of marriage or of horse-riding. In the peculiar state of protection in which he finds himself the *nyamusoro* waves the tail of a hyena or of an eland several times around the patient's body. Suddenly he stops trembling. Then, in the heat of an inspired condition, in a state of hyperlucidity, he practises exorcism by suction, using a typically shamanistic method: 'He abruptly raises his eland tail to his nostrils and breathes in, sniffing hard. He has seized hold of the possessing spirit.' There could be no clearer way of declaring that, protected by the spirit which inspires and guides him (in a relationship whose closeness cannot be confused with a state of possession in the strict sense), the Vandau shaman suppresses the state of possession (in the wider sense of the word) of his patient. The exorcist then leans over a sacred basket and sneezes violently. This procedure is repeated several times while the exorcist is all the time firmly grasped by the belt by his assistant. Eventually those present interrogate the pathogenic spirit, 'which replies through the mouth of the exorcist'. This paradox calls for a diachronic explanation. The exorcist has absorbed the pathogenic spirit of his patient and so finds himself in a state of possession in the strict sense of the term. Having been a shaman in the first stage of the ritual, the doctor himself suddenly, and dangerously, becomes 'possessed'; he changes roles but at the same time tries to overcome this contradiction: his sneezing is a prodigious effort at self-exorcism by which he attempts to free himself from the evil spirit that he has taken over. Suddenly, at the moment of possession, the medium of language is rediscovered. Through the mouth of the possessed exorcist the spirit reveals to those assembled how they can appease its wrath. This strange interrogation-possession of the shaman now carrying the pathogenic spirit of his client takes place during a break in his shamanistic labours: he stops trembling when he breathes in the pathogenic spirit and is not overtaken by frenzy again until the interrogation is over. After this intermediate episode — which underlines the difference between possession and shamanistic action, between passivity and activity — the medicine-man in a trance enters into dialogue with the spirit whose dwelling place he has reluctantly become. His body is the stage for a dialectical struggle between two personalities, his own and the spirit's. The shaman seeks to persuade the latter to enter into the object that his assistants now offer it, almost as if it were a trap. While in the grip of an authentic shamanistic fit he asks this spirit which is also within him (for his body has become a mythical space where the doubling of the personality is fully played out) where it wishes to be led (or led away to). When he has come back to his senses the shaman administers some medicine to his patient and deposits the offering in the desired place. This offering has finally, after a transfer, become the dwelling place for the pathogenic spirit, which is now kept well away from its victim.

A new problem arises from the fact that the Vandau declare the shaman to be in a state of total somnambulism throughout the ceremony. They claim that the attentive assistant to the unconscious exorcist plays the role of interpreter. When it is all over it is he who explains to his master what has happened. But neither this nor any other detail can justify calling the *nyamusoro*'s trance a 'possession'. It simply suggests that shamanistic power can be exercised in the same psychophysiological conditions as the state of possession, with which, as we have seen, it can coexist in different ideological contexts. The fact is that, for all that, these are two divergent if complementary attitudes. When the Vandau healer assumes his role as exorcist he is a shaman, the active subject of a therapeutic trance. When he takes over this same spirit into himself he temporarily becomes the passive subject of possession (and now needs to be supported by his assistant), even while he struggles against this alien presence, striving to expel it from his own body. During the third phase he once again takes over his full functions as a shaman and reassumes the initiative, interrogating the spirit so as to remove it definitively both from his patient and from his own body.

The irruption of the shamanistic procedure within the cultural zone of the Tsonga seems clearly the product of a desire to be different. Everything would suggest that it was the Tsonga who took the initiative in making this structural reversal from Vandau shamanism. The Tsonga despise the Vandau but live in terror of being 'possessed' (in the strict sense) by the ancestral spirits of the latter. For this reason certain Tsonga clans set about learning the propitiatory rituals of the Vandau exorcists. But, as the younger Junod points out: 'What for the Vandau represented a sacrifice aimed at winning the good favour of their ancestors became, for the Tsonga afflicted with "possession", the outlet for their complaint.' What he failed to see is that the basis for the reversal of Vandau shamanism is logical and structural.

Vandau	*Tsonga*
'Hot' exorcist, 'cold' patient	'Cold' exorcist, 'hot' patient
The exorcist breathes in, then spits out the pathogenic spirit	The patient sucks the blood of a sacrificed animal, then spits it out
The spirit is directed into some object which is deposited far away	The expelled spirit is fixed on the altar

African sorcery seen as hollow shamanism

What is still unexplained is why shamanism in its positive, curative, beneficent form remains the exception in Africa while possession is seen to flourish there in all its forms. A careful re-examination of the magico-religious evidence seen from a theoretical point of view might to some extent correct this initial impression. Thus, in western Africa, the great magic of the Songhay is, at least in part, connected with this ideology of shamanism (although the role of the trance here is a minor one) even within a culture where the centre of interest is an authentic cult of possession. There is a striking contrast between the religion of possession and the practices of 'a haughty elite whose unique speciality is their magic'.[47] The difference between the two 'paths' is defined by Jean Rouch in the same terms that Mauss and Hubert used to differentiate between the domains of religion and magic: the former is characterised as consisting of public ceremonies, the latter of solitary activity in the bush or in the privacy of the hut. But this criterion has never seemed a very decisive one to me.[48] What is more remarkable is the particular mode of action of the Sohantye magicians who are the spiritual heirs to the first sacred king. The interpretation of the term *sohantye*, given by a Songhay dignitary, refers directly to the gift of clairvoyance and the power that stems from it: 'the wise men of Songhay, those who know everything that happens'. This hereditary power takes on a key form that is typically shaman-istic: a close link is established between the Sohantye and vultures, which are the only birds capable of crossing the seven skies to reach God. The Sohantye communicate with the vultures in dreams. They are themselves capable of making a mystic journey in pursuit of sorcerers who are eaters of souls, the much-feared *tyarkaw*. What in effect we have here is the antagonistic pair magician–sorcerer, constructed upon the shamanistic model. The *tyarkaw* has the power of metamorphosis, can fly with wings of fire and ravish souls away. The struggle that the Sohantye takes up against the *tyarkaw* is similar to that between the white and the black shamans in the Siberian world. When all normal treatments have proved ineffective, the magician sets off in pursuit of the stolen soul. There is just one important element missing in this classic shamanistic picture: the trance, which is the sign of the magician's journey through space. The Songhay ideology of shamanism has lost the element of ecstatic drama. Not entirely, however, as this is still present in an attenuated form in the collective activity of the Sohantye, the *sohantye hori* or dance of the magicians: it takes place in especially serious circumstances, in particular for the purification of a village. Jean Rouch distinguishes precisely how this ritual ceremony differs structurally from dances of possession: 'True, it culminates in a sort of ecstasy but, far from being a transfer of the personality, the ecstasy instead reinforces it, giving the magician extraordinary powers of perception and action: for a few seconds he can see what is happening all round the village "more than two hundred kilometres away", he can detect evil and dangers and "lances" or deflects them. This sudden surge of power ... is emphasised by the music and dancing and manifests itself through two characteristic signs: the *gyigiri*, the trembling, a prolonged and violent kind of shudder, and the *sisiri*, the metal chain that the magician has in his stomach, which he "vomits up" and which floats for a few moments before his mouth. This chain is the sign of his power but also a weapon to be feared, and most dangerous when used.'[49]

This disturbing, 'uncertain struggle against the forces of evil' entered into by 'the magician, who may be secret and solitary or who, in this dance, becomes part of a community', also epitomises the ideology of the majority of Bantu magico-religious systems in central and southern Africa. However, the shaman-istic character of the opposition between the magician and the sorcerer (which I have studied elsewhere)[50] is much attenuated. To be more precise, it is wholly associated with the second, evil, pole in the relationship, so that Bantu sorcery seems to be a hollow shamanism: shamanism is driven altogether into the realm of the imaginary. Once it has ceased to be a spectacle it becomes, literally, a hollow dream. The powers attributed by the Songhay to the sorcerer who eats souls are widely attested in the Bantu world, the whole of which is dominated by a panic-stricken fear of sorcery. The Tsonga sorcerer (*noyi*) communicates with owls and will-o'-the-wisps; he possesses the (shamanistic) power of dividing into two at night: a part of his personality leaves his visible body and sets out on sinister mystical voyages.[51] The struggle against this abhorred and much-feared being is carried on principally by the *mungoma* magician (the root *-ngang*, which refers in most Bantu languages to this beneficent agent paired with the sorcerer, is restricted, among the Tsonga, to the specialist in pharmacopoeia, whose magic character is less pronounced). Of the procedures adopted by the *mungoma* to deflect the criminal sorcerer, whose action has previously been denounced by divination, only one really deserves to be considered shamanistic in that it implies a certain form of trance. It is put into operation in the capital when a chief has decided to round up all the sorcerers in the district in a wide dragnet. Surrounded by the crowd, the magician, holding in his hand an animal tail and a lance, dances tirelessly until he enters a state of nervous hyper-excitation. 'He brandishes his tail, dilates his nostrils, inhales the air on all sides, as if to smell the spot from whence the evil influence has emanated, then takes to his heels in a certain direction, the assembly still clapping their hands and singing. He approaches a hut, enters, and triumphantly plants his assagay in one corner.'[52] Evil spells are then discovered to be hidden there and are destroyed by burning.

The part played by the trance is clearly minimal in this ritual, the ideology of which is extremely rudimentary. All existing descriptions of Bantu magicians bear witness to the same poverty of imagination. We should, however, bear in mind that many of our sources of evidence have reached us in a fragmentary form — as if the description of magic did not demand at least as much care as that of the attributes of the Supreme Being of which, following Father Wilhelm Schmidt, the missionaries have provided full, self-indulgent and fastidious accounts.

Seen as a whole, this comparative picture, imperfect as it is, nevertheless suggests that the shamanistic counterattack of the Bantu magician is reduced to its simplest form. I have, quite by chance, been lucky enough to come across some information concerning a little-known tribe of Zaïre, the Mbala. It confirms what we have learnt from the younger Junod's original study of the Vandau, namely that we should not underestimate the shamanistic foundations of Bantu cultures despite the fact that they have, more or less recently, assumed forms of inauthentic religious possession. My Mbala informant tells me that a female shaman, the *nganga-ngombo*, moves from village to village, giving séances for the deflection of sorcerers (*ndoki*) in a state of trance while her soul voyages in the disquieting world of the stealers of souls. Among the Mbala a form of mediumism (also female) coexists with this authentic shamanism. The expression *nganga-ngombo*, in which we find the proto-Bantu root *-ngang* that designates a beneficent agent, refers, in the neighbouring Kongo ethnic group, to the diviner who indicates the origin of evils and sicknesses.[53] It will be noticed that in Bantu religions the function of diviner and that of magician are, for the most part, both distinct from each other and complementary. Thus, the Tsonga first consult the 'thrower of knuckle bones' (*mbula*) to establish a preliminary diagnosis and find out whether or not the sickness is caused by a sorcerer. Only then does the magician intervene to make a specific accusation, by name. The divinatory-magic system thus proceeds from the general to the particular. The Mbala shaman seems to combine these two successive functions in a single action of second-sight-and-pursuit analogous to that of the Sohantye magicians among the Songhay. But such a combination — characteristically shamanistic — is not common in Africa. From a linguistic point of view it seems that there used to be two distinct proto-Bantu terms to refer respectively to the diviner and to the magician, the beneficent agent devoted to counter-sorcery.[54] We may conclude that, in Bantu societies, there is relatively little chance of finding a fusion of divination and the ritual counteroffensive that is characteristic of shamanism in the sense of absolute 'clairvoyance' in the Vandau sense. This would account for the structural imbalance in the magic—sorcery system and also for the triumph of the latter over the former. The aggression that is typical of the shamanistic sorcerer is replaced by a much-weakened reaction spread over two successive phases: both positive interventions seem to relate to analysis rather than action. Accordingly, to resolve the situation, a number of Bantu societies secretly claim that the only effective magician is one who, having been initiated into the authentic shamanistic mysteries of sorcery, fulfils both functions according to the social, or the antisocial, demands of his clients. From this point of view it is perhaps easier to understand the strange confusion of values that obtains among the Bolia, where sorcery is the initiatory source of all magic activity.[55]

John of the Cross and the devil

The figures of the devil and the mystic, in Christianity, are in a dialectical relationship that is reminiscent of that which obtains in possession and shamanism.

Christian myths in effect bring together two concepts of sorcery which are assimilated at the heart of the theological theory of temptation. One is rooted in the ideology of inauthentic possession (type B), the other in that of shamanism. The church recognises the possibility of demoniacal possession, although the progress made by psychiatry and the nauseating stench from the pyres of the Inquisition have forced it to narrow its field. From a secular point of view there is, naturally, no point in making a virtue of distinguishing between authentic diabolical possession and hysterical simulation. That is a matter of interpretation, of the social consensus in the realm of the imaginary.

Demoniacal possession consists of a veritable shattering of the consciousness, linked with a strong sense of guilt (the possessed of Loudun). The presence of the spirit of evil calls for exorcism, which is undertaken by a qualified priest. The structural procedure thus conforms with the Tsonga model except in so far as the evil spirit, which is resolutely chased right away, is irremediable. The fundamental dualism of Christian thought forbids any contact with it, can tolerate no transformation of Evil into Good. This radical position is not without equivalents in Africa. The Fang of Gabon attribute sorcery to the presence within the body of the sorcerer (*nnem*) of a being that is fundamentally evil (*evu*); it assumes the material form of an animal resembling a crab or a scolopendra lodged within the viscera of the *nnem*.[56] The one possessed may be unaware of the 'possession', but he is none the less responsible for the evil caused by the *evu*, the vampire that feeds on the blood of its victims and devours their entrails. Exorcism accordingly becomes impossible: the evil can only be eliminated by reducing the corpse of the *nnem* to ashes. The solution is, after all, similar to that of the pyre, which the church appears to have practised more often where the second type of Satanic sorcerer was concerned, the type which we will refer to as 'contractual'.

In this second case, the sorcerer has voluntarily contracted a pact with the devil, and it is this alliance that confers magic powers on the beneficiary, who has excluded himself from the community of the faithful. The church explicitly acknowledges the existence of a 'Satanic marvel', seeing it as the antithesis to the divine miracle. As we know, both God and the devil have become extremely reticent in these respects, but the belief nevertheless constitutes an article of faith. The severity with which the church punished 'contractual' sorcerers or those believed to be such (Joan of Arc) stands in contrast to the leniency it demonstrates towards those possessed by the devil and not held to be responsible. This attitude is clearly inspired by the teaching of the Gospel in which Jesus, the miracle-worker, treats those possessed who display 'morbid disturbances related to madness'[57] as a skilled and charitable exorcist. It is not without interest to note that we are here adopting a strictly orthodox Catholic interpretation, which proves most valuable to anthropology: in the Gospel descriptions, 'diabolical possession is always accompanied by clinical signs characteristic of an abnormal state of the nervous system'.[58] This bodily epiphany, of which Africa provides so many examples, calls for a theological explanation of which Descartes himself would not have been ashamed: the activity of the devil comes into play 'at the point of intersection and liaison between the soul and the body'. To maintain the sacred—profane opposition in terms of a more modern psychology, the eminent author of this extremely interesting study concludes that 'the devil may take advantage of the disorder that a mental sickness may already have introduced into the composite human being; he may even cause and encourage this functional imbalance thanks to which he can insinuate and install himself at this point of least resistance'.[59] Theology clearly balks at purely and simply identifying possession and mental sickness in the Gospel.

The church has seen fit to promote the 'possession' theory of Satanic intervention. But the shamanistic theory of the contract of sorcery probably owes more to the extremely ancient pagan popular beliefs relating to the quest for magic power. However, there is also an element of shamanism in the attitude of the officially recognised mystics who, in their ecstasy, attempt an extraordinary synthesis of the two universal procedures that we have, until now, kept distinct from each other.

The fact is that, at the opposite pole of the Christian system, in the obscurity of divine light, John of the Cross appears in the guise of one dispossessed of an essential part of himself, engaged on his own account in a shamanistic quest for God. The great mystics are sick in their being, refusing to accept either nothingness or the regular procedures of the language of religion. Following an ascension during which they pass through a large number of shamanistic trials (the temptations of the devil), they find themselves suddenly plunged into the world of fusion-possession, in a position that is the symmetrical converse of that of the sorcerer who plunges into the abyss of sin. This extraordinary synthesis of the two 'paths', which archaic religions take care not to confuse, is described in unequivocal terms by John of the Cross: the devil wants to prevent the soul from attaining pure union with the one who is Spirit. With impeccable structural instinct, John also knows that (shamanistic) arrogance is a threat to whoever rises towards God at his own risk and peril. His struggle to solve this contradiction is what makes him the great poet of ecstasy: he is aggressive when faced with the devil who bars his mystical way, but humble and submissive before the God who is to 'possess' his famished soul 'using no created intermediary'.[60] The mechanism of the final possession is described in metaphorical terms which must certainly be taken seriously: 'God enters the soul and devours it.'

Theresa of Avila (who should on no account be confused with her pathetic, foolish namesake of Lisieux, exposed in so masterly a manner by Pierre Mabille)[61] engages in the same adventure but with a more openly admitted erotic connotation. She is a great lover who continues to pose the problem of the passion of love in a burning heretical context where possession and shamanism are consumed — supreme enigma — in the furnace of the human heart.

Notes

Introduction

1 Copenhagen, Brussels, Amsterdam.
2 The students who worked under Frans Olbrechts at Ghent had all moved in the direction of the study of African art. It will certainly not be forgotten that linguistic studies of the former Belgian Congo owe a great deal to the pioneer work of G. Hulstaert and a few others, before the flowering of the school of Tervuren under the direction of the much-lamented A. Meussen.
3 Heusch, 1954a.
4 *Idem*, 1955.
5 *Idem*, 1954b.
6 In 1975, during a mission organised in collaboration with the Institute for the National Museums of Zaïre, to which I should like to express my thanks.
7 Gluckman, 1962.
8 Lévi-Strauss, 1971, pp. 597–8.
9 Heusch, 1958.
10 *Idem*, 1972.
11 Burguière, 1971, p. vii.
12 Needham, 1971a.
13 *Idem*, 1977, p. 87; 1971a, p. xcix.
14 Korn, 1971.
15 Lévi-Strauss, 1973, p. 23.
16 Pouillon, 1966.
17 *Ibid*. p. 783.
18 Lévi-Strauss, 1962, p. 117.
19 Heusch, 1966, ch. 5.
20 I refer here to the studies of three Belgian investigators, Jean-Paul Colleyn, Danièle Jonckers and Philipe Jespers.
21 Heusch, 1975.
22 Lévi-Strauss, 1973, p. 40.
23 Marx, 1968, p. 313.
24 *Ibid*. p. 315.
25 Meillassoux, 1975, p. 14.
26 Godelier, 1974, p. 651.
27 Turnbull, 1962, p. 37.
28 Godelier, 1974, pp. 668–78.
29 *Idem*, 1966, p. 860.

30 Engels, 1964, p. ix.
31 Sahlins, 1976, p. 121; 1974, p. 78.
32 Jonckers and Colleyn, 1974, p. 47.
33 On this subject see Lizot's critique (1977).
34 Sahlins, 1976, p. 127; 1974, p. 83.
35 *Idem*, 1976, p. 172; 1974, p. 124.
36 *Idem*, 1976, pp. 180—1; 1974, p. 132. The French translation mentions erroneously the Melanesian chiefs, whereas the English text says many of the greatest African chiefs and all those of Polynesia.
37 Clastres, 1974.
38 Bonnafé, 1975.
39 Meillassoux (ed.), 1975.
40 Vansina, 1964b, p. 20.
41 Piault, 1975, p. 321.
42 Heusch, 1966.
43 Goody, 1971, ch. 2.
44 *Ibid.*, p. 19.
45 Heusch, 1958, 1962a and b, 1966, 1972.
46 I am in agreement here with the point of view recently put forward by A. Adler (1978).
47 D'Hertefelt and Coupez, 1964.
48 Cohen, 1977.
49 Vansina, 1964b, pp. 98—116.
50 Adler, 1978.
51 Clastres, 1976, p. 26.
52 *Ibid.*
53 Heusch, 1962a.
54 Sousberghe, 1963, p. 66.
55 Vansina, 1964b, p. 7; Adler, 1978, p. 29; Maquet, 1954, p. 25.
56 Deleuze and Guattari, 1972, p. 238.

Chapter 1. A defence and illustration of the structures of kinship

1 I should like to thank Claude Lévi-Strauss and Claude Tardits for the critical remarks they were kind enough to offer on a first draft of the unpublished text.
2 Van Wouden, 1935, p. 91.
3 Needham, 1958, p. 201.
4 Lévi-Strauss, 1969, p. xxxiii.
5 Needham, 1962, pp. 101—26; 1958.
6 Sperber, 1968.
7 Needham, 1962, p. 110.
8 Sousberghe, 1955, p. 62.
9 Heusch, 1971, pp. 72—85.
10 Sousberghe, 1955, p. 65.
11 Sperber, 1968, afterword, p. 113.
12 Rivière, 1966a, p. 555; Carter Lane, 1966, p. 198.
13 Sousberghe, 1955, p. 37.
14 Needham, 1958, p. 209; 1962, p. 111.
15 Sousberghe, 1955, p. 46.
16 Sperber, 1968, p. 181.

17 Sousberghe, 1955, p. 51.
18 *Ibid.* p. 65.
19 *Ibid.* pp. 44—5, 72—3.
20 *Ibid.* p. 39.
21 *Ibid.* p. 72.
22 *Ibid.* p. 39.
23 *Ibid.* p. 44.
24 *Ibid.* p. 45.
25 *Ibid.* p. 73.
26 *Ibid.* p. 74.
27 *Ibid.* p. 75.
28 *Ibid.* p. 74.
29 *Ibid.* p. 73.
30 *Ibid.* p. 75.
31 *Ibid.* p. 74.
32 *Ibid.* p. 73.
33 *Ibid.* p. 75.
34 *Ibid.* p. 74.
35 *Ibid.* p. 73.
36 *Idem*, 1963, pp. 23—32.
37 L. de Sousberghe points out here that the Pende often marry the daughter of a sister from their father's clan (1963, p. 26).
38 *Ibid.* p. 29.
39 *Idem*, 1955, p. 67.
40 *Ibid.* p. 52.
41 *Ibid.* pp. 49—50.
42 Lévi-Strauss, 1969, p. 433.
43 Carter Lane, 1966.
44 Rivière, 1966a and b.
45 *Ibid.*
46 Lévi-Strauss, 1969, p. 433.
47 Rivière, 1969, p. 62.
48 *Ibid.* p. 63.
49 *Ibid.* p. 64.
50 *Ibid.* p. 62.
51 *Ibid.* pp. 194, 179.
52 *Ibid.* p. 177.
53 *Ibid.* p. 181.
54 *Idem*, 1966a, p. 551.
55 *Idem*, 1969, p. 182.
56 *Ibid.* p. 194.
57 *Ibid.* p. 182.
58 *Idem*, 1966a, p. 551.
59 *Idem*, 1969, p. 73.
60 *Ibid.* p. 284.
61 *Idem*, 1966a, p. 552.
62 Lévi-Strauss, 1969, p. 434.
63 Rivière, 1969, p. 141.
64 *Ibid.* p. 142.
65 *Ibid.* pp. 67—8.
66 *Ibid.* p. 73.

67 Lévi-Strauss, 1969, p. 428.
68 *Ibid*. p. 429.
69 Rivière, 1966a, p. 555.
70 *Idem*, 1966b, p. 739.
71 Doutreloux, 1967, pp. 135–43.
72 Sousberghe, 1965, p. 406.
73 My own investigation.
74 Doutreloux, 1967, p. 136.
75 *Ibid*. p. 138.
76 *Ibid*.
77 *Ibid*. p. 141.
78 *Ibid*. p. 144.
79 *Ibid*.
80 *Ibid*. p. 145.
81 *Ibid*.
82 *Ibid*. p. 141.
83 *Ibid*.
84 *Ibid*.
85 *Ibid*. p. 136.
86 *Ibid*. p. 77.
87 *Ibid*. p. 145.
88 *Ibid*. p. 79.
89 *Ibid*.
90 *Ibid*.
91 *Ibid*. p. 98.
92 *Ibid*. p. 96.
93 *Ibid*. p. 77.
94 Bittremieux, 1923, pp. 550, 691.
95 Dartevelle, 1953.
96 Doutreloux, 1967, pp. 110–19.
97 *Ibid*. p. 145.
98 *Ibid*.
99 Lévi-Strauss, 1969, p. 117.
100 *Ibid*. p. 441.
101 *Ibid*.
102 *Ibid*.
103 *Ibid*.
104 *Ibid*. p. 117.
105 Tardits, 1974.
106 Richards, 1950, pp. 227–8.
107 Tardits, 1974, pp. 14–15.
108 *Ibid*. p. 14.
109 *Ibid*.
110 Richards and Tardits, 1974.
111 *Ibid*. p. 118.
112 *Ibid*. p. 113.
113 Sousberghe, 1955, pp. 22–3.
114 *Ibid*.
115 *Ibid*. p. 20.
116 *Ibid*. p. 19.
117 *Ibid*. p. 22.

118 *Ibid.* p. 27.
119 *Ibid.* pp. 78—92.
120 *Ibid.* p. 55.
121 Nimendaju, 1939.
122 Williams, 1932.
123 Rattray, 1969; Fortes, 1950.
124 Fortes, 1950, p. 279.
125 Rattray, 1924—5.
126 Lévi-Strauss, 1969, p. 110; Seligman, 1925.
127 Rattray, 1959 (1st edn 1927), p. 324.
128 *Ibid.* p. 322.
129 Fortes, 1970, p. 10.
130 *Ibid.* p. 19.
131 *Ibid.* p. 16.
132 *Ibid.* p. 31.
133 Fox, 1967, p. 101.
134 Augé, 1977, p. 102; see also Rattray, 1959, p. 321.
135 Fortes, 1950, p. 279.
136 *Ibid.* p. 265.
137 Lévi-Strauss, 1949, p. 144, following Herskovits, 1928, p. 719.
138 Kopytoff, 1977.
139 *Ibid.* p. 547.
140 *Ibid.* p. 551.
141 Rey, 1971.
142 *Ibid.* pp. 86—92.
143 *Ibid.* pp. 78, 127.
144 *Ibid.* p. 68.
145 *Ibid.* p. 111.
146 Sousberghe, 1955, p. 32.
147 Rey, 1971, pp. 110—11.
148 *Ibid.*
149 *Ibid.* p. 91.
150 Sousberghe, 1955, pp. 24—5; 1963, p. 31.
151 *Idem*, 1963, p. 31.
152 *Ibid.*
153 *Idem*, 1955, p. 20.
154 Rey, 1971, p. 113.
155 *Ibid.* p. 108.
156 *Ibid.* p. 79.
157 *Ibid.* pp. 110—14, 127.
158 Meillassoux, 1975, p. 47.
159 *Ibid.* p. 50.
160 Mitchell, 1956, pp. 199—200.
161 Lévi-Strauss, 1963, p. 322 n. 105.
162 Vansina, 1964b, p. 28.
163 Heusch, 1976.
164 Héritier, 1975.
165 Beattie, 1957 and 1958.
166 Biebuyck, 1953.
167 H.-A. Junod, 1936, I, pp. 207—73.
168 To be absolutely clear on this subject, it is indispensable to remember the

definition proposed by Lévi-Strauss, which I should like to adopt as my own: '[The] one and only criterion [of an elementary structure] rests in the fact that, preferred or prescribed, the spouse is the spouse solely because she belongs to an alliance category or stands in a certain kinship relationship to Ego. In other words, the imperative or desirable relationship is a function of the social structure. We enter the realm of complex structures when the reason for the preference or the prescription hinges on other considerations' (1969, p. xxxiv).

Chapter 2. Social structure and praxis among the Lele of the Kasai

1 This article first appeared in *L'Homme*, no. 3, 1964, pp. 87–109, on the subject of Mary Douglas's book *The Lele of the Kasai*, published for the International African Institute by Oxford University Press, 1963. All page references in my text are to this book.
2 Douglas, 1954.
3 Heusch, 1955.
4 Douglas, 1957 and 1955.
5 Lévi-Strauss, 1962.
6 Douglas, 1952.
7 Fig. 2.3 replaces the figure that appeared in the French publication of this essay (*Pourquoi l'épouser?* p. 61). My demonstration is in no way altered, but the original figure seemed to me to be based on too strong a hypothesis.
8 Douglas, 1952, p. 65.
9 Vansina, 1964a, p. 141.
10 *Ibid.* pp. 141–2.
11 Vansina, 1957, p. 487.
12 Vansina, 1954.
13 Heusch, 1958.
14 Douglas, 1962.
15 Heusch, 1963.
16 This paragraph does not appear in the original French edition.
17 This complementary note does not appear in the original French edition.
18 Lévi-Strauss, 1973, p. 130.
19 *Ibid.* p. 129.
20 Douglas, 1963, p. 115.
21 *Ibid.* p. 114.
22 Plaene, 1974, pp. 63–71.
23 Lévi-Strauss, 1973, p. 130.
24 De Plaene calls it 'primary' (*primaire*) (1974, p. 333).
25 Douglas, 1963, p. 118.
26 *Ibid.* p. 115.
27 Lévi-Strauss, 1973, p. 129.
28 *Ibid.* p. 135.
29 *Ibid.*
30 *Idem*, 1949, p. 143; 1969, p. 111.
31 *Idem*, 1949, pp. 61–2, 287; 1969, pp. 49, 228.
32 *Idem*, 1949, p. 576; 1969, p. 466.

Chapter 3. The debt of the maternal uncle

1 Marie, 1972, p. 15.

2 Marie, 1972.
3 *Ibid*. p. 15.
4 *Ibid*. p. 26.
5 H.-A. Junod, 1927, I, p. 117.
6 *Ibid*. p. 241.
7 *Ibid*. p. 242.
8 Lévi-Strauss, 1949, p. 581.
9 H.-A. Junod, 1927, I, p. 233.
10 *Ibid*. p. 262.
11 *Ibid*.
12 *Ibid*. p. 261.
13 *Ibid*. p. 294.
14 Krige and Krige, 1943, pp. 78, 149.
15 Griaule, 1954, p. 38.
16 Adler and Cartry, 1971, p. 14.
17 Heusch, 1978.
18 H.-A. Junod, 1927, I, p. 263.
19 Adler and Cartry, 1971.
20 Griaule, 1954.
21 H.-A. Junod, 1927, I, p. 162, II, p. 396.
22 *Ibid*. I, p. 268.
23 This lecture was delivered during autumn 1973 at the University of Cambridge and at the London School of Economics and Political Science, at the invitation of the British Academy.
24 Barnes, 1975.
25 Héritier, 1975, p. 98.
26 *Ibid*. p. 101.
27 *Ibid*. p. 107.
28 Needham, 1977, p. 115; 1971b, p. 15.
29 Héritier, 1975, p. 107.
30 Biebuyck, 1953.
31 Radcliffe-Brown, 1968, p. 123; H.-A. Junod, 1927, I, p. 32.
32 Radcliffe-Brown, 1968, p. 149.
33 Lévi-Strauss, 1969, p. xxxix.
34 Héritier, 1973, p. 124.
35 *Ibid*. p. 122.
36 *Ibid*. p. 125.
37 H.-A. Junod, 1927, I, p. 310.
38 *Ibid*. p. 254.
39 *Ibid*. p. 255.
40 *Ibid*. pp. 255—6.
41 Lévi-Strauss, 1949, p. 582.
42 Adler, 1976; Heusch, 1976.
43 Lévi-Strauss, 1969, ch. XXII.
44 Radcliffe-Brown, 1968, p. 149.
45 *Ibid*.
46 *Ibid*. pp. 73—92.

Chapter 4. Structure and history: views on the Kachin

1 Leach, 1954, p. 8.

 2 *Ibid.* p. 9.
 3 *Ibid.* p. 9.
 4 *Idem*, 1951, p. 45.
 5 *Idem*, 1954, p. 10.
 6 *Ibid.* p. 20.
 7 *Ibid.* p. 39.
 8 *Ibid.* p. 115.
 9 *Idem*, 1951, p. 44; 1954, p. 205.
10 *Idem*, 1954, p. 256.
11 *Idem*, 1951, pp. 40–5.
12 *Idem*, 1954, p. 160.
13 *Ibid.* p. 155.
14 *Ibid.* p. 187; *idem*, 1951, p. 41.
15 *Idem*, 1954, p. 162.
16 *Ibid.* p. 149.
17 *Ibid.* pp. 142–3.
18 *Ibid.* p. 149.
19 *Idem*, 1951, p. 43.
20 *Idem*, 1954, p. 45.
21 *Ibid.* pp. 116–17.
22 *Ibid.* p. 115.
23 *Ibid.* p. 116.
24 *Ibid.* p. 121.
25 *Ibid.*
26 *Ibid.* p. 122.
27 *Ibid.* pp. 204–7.
28 *Ibid.* pp. 169–70.
29 *Ibid.* p. 170.
30 *Idem*, 1951, p. 44.
31 *Ibid.*
32 *Ibid.* p. 45.
33 *Idem*, 1954, pp. 155–72.
34 *Ibid.* p. 87.
35 *Ibid.* p. 83.
36 *Ibid.* p. 78.
37 *Ibid.* p. 83.
38 *Ibid.* p. 81.
39 *Ibid.* p. 80.
40 *Ibid.* p. 84.
41 *Ibid.* p. 83.
42 *Ibid.* p. 169.
43 *Ibid.*
44 *Idem*, 1951, pp. 43–4.
45 *Idem*, 1954, p. 69.
46 *Ibid.* p. 95.
47 *Idem*, 1960, p. 10.
48 *Idem*, 1954, p. 77.
49 *Ibid.* p. 75.
50 *Ibid.* p. 77.
51 *Ibid.* p. 149.
52 *Ibid.* p. 205.

53 *Idem*, 1954, p. 205.
54 *Ibid*. pp. 204—5.
55 *Idem*, 1951, p. 43.
56 *Ibid*.
57 *Idem*, 1954, pp. 260—2.
58 *Ibid*. p. 206.
59 *Idem*, 1961, p. 84; 1951, pp. 41—3.
60 *Idem*, 1954, p. 206.
61 *Ibid*. p. 171.
62 *Ibid*. p. 162.
63 *Ibid*.
64 *Ibid*. p. 255.
65 *Ibid*. p. 223.
66 *Ibid*. p. 235.
67 *Ibid*. p. 256.
68 *Idem*, 1951, p. 45.
69 *Idem*, 1954, p. 190.
70 *Ibid*. p. 257.
71 *Ibid*. p. 256.
72 *Ibid*. p. 188.
73 Friedman, 1975, pp. 161—202.
74 *Ibid*. p. 167.
75 *Ibid*.
76 *Ibid*. p. 169.
77 *Ibid*. p. 170.
78 *Ibid*. p. 172.
79 *Ibid*. p. 178.
80 *Ibid*. pp. 170—1.
81 Leach, 1954, p. 164.
82 Sahlins, 1974, pp. 135—8.
83 Leach, 1954, p. 207.
84 Friedman, 1975, p. 172.
85 *Ibid*. p. 173.
86 *Ibid*. p. 173.
87 *Ibid*.
88 *Ibid*.
89 *Ibid*. p. 175.
90 Leach, 1954, p. 127.
91 Friedman, 1975, p. 180.
92 *Ibid*. p. 183.
93 *Ibid*. p. 185.
94 *Ibid*. p. 194.
95 *Ibid*. p. 196.

Chapter 5. Possession and shamanism

1 This text is adapted and expanded in vol. 2 of *Annales du Centre d'Etude des Religions* of the University of Brussels (Institute of Sociology), 1962, under the title 'Cultes de possession et religions initiaques de salut en Afrique'.
2 Several scholars are currently pursuing this interdisciplinary dialogue initiated some time ago in France by Dr Pidoux.

3   Eliade, 1951.
4   Bouteiller, 1950.
5   *Ibid*. p. 130.
6   Lévi-Strauss, 1963, p. 220.
7   *Ibid*. pp. 205ff.
8   Eliade, 1951, pp. 208–9.
9   H.-A. Junod, 1936, II, pp. 432–60.
10   Leiris, 1958.
11   Rouch, 1960, p. 217.
12   *Ibid*. p. 229.
13   See Heusch, 1962c (dedicated to Pierre Mabille).
14   Leiris, 1958, p. 17.
15   Métraux, 1958, pp. 172ff.
16   *Ibid*. p. 179.
17   Verger, 1957; Parrinder, 1950; Herskovits, 1938.
18   Herskovits, 1938, II, pp. 178–9.
19   *Ibid*. p. 170.
20   Parrinder, 1950, p. 107.
21   Herskovits, 1938, II, p. 180.
22   *Ibid*. p. 199.
23   Parrinder, 1950, p. 107.
24   Herskovits, 1938, II, p. 180.
25   *Ibid*. pp. 179ff.
26   Parrinder, 1950, pp. 107ff.
27   Verger, 1957, p. 72.
28   Herskovits, 1938, II, p. 187.

Chapter 6. The madness of the gods and the reason of men

1   Evans-Pritchard, 1965.
2   See Leach, 1961.
3   Van Wing, 1938.
4   Féjos, 1963.
5   Fortes, 1965.
6   Bataille, 1957.
7   Herskovits, 1938, I, pp. 375ff.
8   Ortigues and Ortigues, 1966.
9   Collomb and Zwingelstein, 1964.
10   Ortigues and Ortigues, 1966, p. 229.
11   *Ibid*.
12   *Ibid*. p. 265.
13   *Ibid*. p. 38.
14   Turner, 1953.
15   White, 1961.
16   *Ibid*. p. 50.
17   See ch. 5.
18   Lot-Falck, 1968, p. 45.
19   Foucault, 1962, p. 77.
20   Eliade, 1951, p. 113, following Shirokogorov.
21   H.-A. Junod, 1927, II, pp. 479–500.
22   *Ibid*. p. 420.

23 Burton, 1961, p. 58.
24 Nadel, 1946.
25 Callaway, 1965.
26 Van Wing, 1938, pp. 256—67.
27 Heusch, 1971, pp. 189—204.
28 Van Wing, 1938, pp. 262—4.
29 Tanner, 1955.
30 Lévi-Strauss, 1950.
31 Krige and Krige, 1943.
32 Leiris, 1958, p. 17.
33 Lewis, 1966.
34 Collomb and Martino, 1968.
35 Zempleni, 1966.
36 Heusch, 1971, pp. 170—87.
37 Lombard, 1967.
38 Rouch, 1960, pp. 281ff.
39 *Ibid.* p. 191.
40 Vansina, 1958.
41 Burton, 1961, pp. 50—60.
42 Nadel, 1946.
43 Heusch, 1966, pp. 249—353.
44 Gelfand, 1965.
45 Evans-Pritchard, 1956, pp. 287—310.
46 H.-P. Junod, 1934.
47 Rouch, 1960, p. 255.
48 Heusch, 1971, pp. 170—87.
49 Rouch, 1960, p. 290.
50 Heusch, 1971, pp. 170—87.
51 H.-A. Junod, 1927, II, pp. 504—18.
52 *Ibid.* pp. 529—30.
53 Van Wing, 1938, p. 123.
54 I am indebted to M. Meeussens for this information.
55 Heusch, 1971, pp. 174—5.
56 Etudes Carmélitaines, 1948, p. 337.
57 *Ibid.* p. 319.
58 *Ibid.* p. 324.
59 *Ibid.* p. 326.
60 *Ibid.* p. 88.
61 Mabille, 1937.

Bibliography

Adler, Alfred. 1973. 'Les jumeaux sont rois', *Homme*, 13, 1–2: 167–92.
    1976. 'Avunculat et mariage matrilatéral', *Homme*, 16, 4: 7–27.
    1978. 'Le pouvoir et l'interdit: aspects de la royauté sacrée chez les
    Mundang du Tchad', in *Systèmes de signes: textes réunis en hommage à
    Germaine Dieterlen*, pp. 25–40.
Adler, Alfred and Cartry, Michel. 1971. 'La transgression et sa dérision', *Homme*,
    11: 5–63.
Alexandre, P. and Binet, J. 1958. *Le groupe dit pahouin*. Paris.
Augé, Marc. 1977. *Pouvoirs de vie, pouvoirs de mort*. Paris.
Barnes, R.H. 1975. 'Elementary and complex structures', *Man*, 10, 3: 472–3.
Bataille, Georges. 1957. *L'érotisme*. Paris.
Beattie, J.H.M. 1957. 'Nyoro kinship', *Africa*, 27, 4: 317–40.
    1958. 'Nyoro marriage and affinity', *Africa*, 28, 1: 1–22.
Biebuyck, Daniel. 1953. 'Maternal uncles and sororal nephews among the Lega',
    in *Report of the Second Joint Conference on Research in the Social
    Sciences in East and Central Africa*, pp. 122–33. East African Institute of
    Social Research, Makerere College, Kampala, Uganda.
Bittremieux, L. 1923. *Mayombsch Idioticon*. Ghent.
Bonnafé, Pierre. n.d. *Un aspect religieux de l'idéologie lignagère: le Nkira des
    Kukuya du Congo-Brazzaville*. Laboratoire de Sociologie et de Géographie
    Humaine, Document de travail, no. 1. Paris.
    1973. 'Une grande fête de la vie et de la mort: le miyali, cérémonie funéraire
    d'un seigneur du ciel kukuya (Congo-Brazzaville)', *Homme*, 13, 1–2:
    7–166.
    1975. 'Les formes d'asservissement chez les Kukuya d'Afrique Centrale', in
    L'esclavage en Afrique précoloniale, ed. Claude Meillassoux, pp. 529–56.
    Paris.
Bouteiller, Marcelle. 1950. *Chamanisme et guérison magique*. Paris.
Burguière, André. 1971. 'Présentation', *Annales*, 26, nos. 3–4 (special no.,
    Histoire et structure).
Burton, W.F.P. 1971. *Luba Religion and Magic in Custom and Belief*. Annales du
    Musée Royal de l'Afrique Centrale, Tervuren.
Caillois, Roger. 1944. *La communion des forts*. Etudes sociologiques. Paris.
Callaway, C.H. 1965. 'Religion of the Amazulu', in *Source Book of Anthropol-
    ogy*, ed. A.L. Kroeber and T.T. Waterman. New York.
Carter Lane, Jean. 1966. 'A formal analysis of preferential marriage with the
    sister's daughter', *Man*, 1, 2: 185–200.
Clastres, Pierre. 1974. *La société contre l'Etat*. Paris.

Bibliography

1976. 'Preface', in Sahlins, 1976 (q.v.), pp. 11–30.

Cohen, Ronald. 1977. 'Oedipus Rex and Regina: the Queen Mother in Africa', *Africa*, 47, 1: 14–30.

Collomb, H. and Martino, P. 1968. *Possession et psychopathologie*. Mimeographed.

Collomb, H. and Zwingelstein, J. 1964. *Psychiatrica in Africa: clinical and social psychiatry and the problem of mental health in Africa*. Vancouver.

Dartevelle, Edmond. 1953. *Les 'N'zimbu', monnaie du Royaume du Congo*. Brussels.

Deleuze, Gilles and Guattari, Félix. 1972. *Capitalisme et schizophrénie: l'anti-Oedipe*. Paris.

D'Hertefelt, Marcel and Coupez, André. 1964. *La royauté sacrée de l'ancien Rwanda*. Tervuren.

Douglas, Mary. 1952. 'Alternate generations among the Lele of the Kasai, South West Congo', *Africa*, 22, 1: 59–65.

1954. 'The Lele of the Kasai', in *African Worlds*, pp. 1–26. Oxford.

1955. 'Social and religious symbolism of the Lele of the Kasai', *Zaïre*, 9, 4: 385–402.

1957. 'Animals in Lele religious symbolism', *Africa*, 27, 1: 46–58.

1962. 'Lele economy compared with the Bushong', in *Markets in Africa*, ed. Paul J. Bohannan and G. Dalton. Evanston, Ill.

1963. *The Lele of the Kasai*. International African Institute. Oxford.

Doutreloux, Albert. 1967. *L'ombre des fétiches, société et culture Yombe*. Louvain and Paris.

Eliade, Mircea. 1951. *Le chamanisme et les techniques archaïques de l'extase*. Paris.

Engels, Friedrich. 1946. *L'origine de la famille, de la propriété privée et l'Etat*. Paris.

Etudes Carmélitaines. 1948. *Satan*, ed. Desclée de Brouwer. N.p.

Evans-Pritchard, E.E. 1929. 'The study of kinship in primitive societies', *Man*, 29: 190–204.

1956. *Nuer Religion*. Oxford.

1965. *Theories of Primitive Religions*. Oxford.

Féjos, Paul. 1963. 'Magic, witchcraft and medical theory in primitive cultures', in *Man's Image in Medicine and Anthropology*, ed. Iago Gladstone. New York.

Fortes, Meyer. 1950. 'Kinship and marriage among the Ashanti', in *African Systems of Kinship and Marriage*, ed. A.R. Radcliffe-Brown and Daryll Forde, pp. 252–84. London, New York and Toronto.

1965. 'Some reflexions on ancestor worship', in *African Systems of Thought*, ed. M. Fortes and G. Dieterlen. Oxford.

1970. *Time and Social Structure and Other Essays*. London and New York.

Foucault, Michel. 1962. *Maladie mentale et psychologie*. Paris.

Fox, Robin. 1967. *Kinship and Marriage*. Harmondsworth.

Friedman, J. 1975. 'Dynamique et transformation du système tribal: l'exemple des Katchin', *Homme*, 15, 1: 63–98. Trans. as 'Tribes, states and transformation', in *Marxist Analyses and Social Anthropology*, ed. Maurice Bloch, pp. 161–202. London.

Gelfand, M. 1965. 'The Mhondoro cult of the Shona-speaking people of southern Africa', in *African Systems of Thought*, ed. M. Fortes and G. Dieterlen. Oxford.

209

Bibliography

Gluckman, Max. 1962. 'Les rites de passage', in *Essays on the Ritual of Social Relations*, ed. Max Gluckman, pp. 1—52. Manchester.

Godelier, Maurice. 1966. 'Système, structure et contradiction dans "Le Capital" ', *Temps Modernes*, 246: 828—64.

1971. 'Modes of production, kinship and demographic structures', in *Marxist Analyses and Social Anthropology*, ed. Maurice Bloch, pp. 3—27. London, 1975.

1974. 'Une anthropologie économique est-elle possible?', in *L'unité de l'homme*, ed. Edgar Morin and Massimo Piatelli-Palmarini, pp. 643—78. Paris.

Goody, Jack. 1959. 'The mother's brother and the sister's son in West Africa', *Journal of the Royal Anthropological Institute of Great Britain and Ireland*, 89: 61—88.

1971. *Technology, Tradition and the State in Africa*. London.

Griaule, Marcel. 1954. 'Remarques sur l'oncle utérin au Soudan', *Cahiers Internationaux de Sociologie*, 16: 35—49.

Hagenbucher-Sacripanti, Frank. 1973. *Les fondements spirituels du pouvoir au royaume de Loango*. Paris.

Héritier, Françoise. 1973. 'La paix et la pluie', *Homme*, 13, 3: 121—38.

1975. 'L'ordinateur et l'étude du fonctionnement matrimonial d'un système omaha', in *Les domaines de la parenté*, ed. Marc Augé, pp. 95—117. Paris.

Herskovits, M.J. 1928. 'The social organization of the Bush Negroes of Surinam', *Proceedings of the 23rd International Congress of Americanists*. New York.

1938. *Dahomey, an Ancient West African Kingdom*. 2 vols. New York.

Heusch, Luc de. 1954a. 'Eléments de potlatch chez les Hamba', *Africa*, 24, 4: 337—48.

1954b. 'Autorité et prestige dans la société tetela', *Zaïre*, 10: 1001—27.

1955. 'Valeur, monnaie et structuration sociale chez les Nkutshu (Kasai, Congo Belge)', *Revue de l'Institut de Sociologie* (Institut de Sociologie, Université Libre de Bruxelles), 1: 73—98.

1958. *Essais sur le symbolisme de l'inceste royal en Afrique*. Brussels.

1962a. 'Pour une dialectique de la sacralité du pouvoir en Afrique', *Annales du Centre d'Etude des Religions* (Institut de Sociologie, Université Libre de Bruxelles), 1: 15—47.

1962b. 'Aspects de la sacralité du pouvoir en Afrique', *Annales du Centre d'Etude des Religions* (Institut de Sociologie, Université Libre de Bruxelles), 1: 139—58.

1962c. 'Cultes de possession et religions initiatiques de salut en Afrique', *Annales du Centre d'Etude des Religions* (Institut de Sociologie, Université Libre de Bruxelles), 2: 127—67.

1963. 'Réflexions ethnologiques sur la technique', *Temps Modernes*, 211 (December).

1966. *Le Rwanda et la civilisation interlacustre: études d'anthropologie historique et structurale*. Brussels.

1971. *Pourquoi l'épouser? et autres essais*. Paris.

1972. *Le roi ivre ou l'origine de l'Etat*. Paris.

1975. 'Le roi, le forgeron et les premiers hommes dans l'ancienne société kongo', in *Systèmes de pensée en Afrique Noire*, bk 1: 165—77.

1976. 'Parenté et histoire en Afrique australe (réponse à Alfred Adler)', *Homme*, 16, 4: 29—47.

1978. 'La dette sacrée de l'oncle maternel: contribution à l'étude des structures complexes de la parenté', in *Systèmes de signes: textes réunis en hommage à Germaine Dieterlen*, pp. 271–98. Paris.

Jonckers, Danièle and Colleyn, Jean-Paul. 1974. 'La communauté familiale chez les Minyanka du Mali', *Journal de la Société des Africanistes*, 44, 1: 43–52.

Junod, Henri-A. 1927. *The Life of a South African Tribe*. 2 vols. Neuchâtel and London.

1936. *Moeurs et coutumes des Bantous: la vie d'une tribu sud-africaine*. 2 vols. Paris.

Junod, H.-P. 1934. 'Les cas de possession et d'exorcisme chez les Vandau', *Africa*, 7.

Kopytoff, Igor, 1977. 'Matrilinearity, residence and residential zones', *American Anthropologist*, 4, 3: 539–57.

Korn, Francis. 1971. 'A question of preference: the Iatmul case', in *Rethinking Kinship and Marriage*, ed. Rodney Needham, pp. 99–132. London.

Krige, E.J. and Krige, J.D. 1943. *The Realm of the Rain-Queen*. Oxford.

Leach, Edmund. 1951. 'The structural implications of matrilateral cross-cousin marriage', *Journal of the Royal Anthropological Institute of Great Britain and Ireland*, 81.

1954. *Political Systems of Highland Burma: a study of Kachin social structure*. London.

1960. 'Descent, filiation and affinity', *Man*, 60: 1–26, n. 6, pp. 9–10.

1961. *Rethinking Anthropology*. London.

1971. 'More about "Mama" and "Papa" ', in *Rethinking Kinship and Marriage*, ed. Rodney Needham, pp. 75–98. London.

1972. *Les systèmes politiques des hautes terres de Birmanie*. Paris (translation of *Political Systems of Highland Burma: a study of Kachin social structure*).

Leiris, Michel. 1958. *La possession et ses aspects théâtraux chez les Ethiopiens de Gondar. L'Homme: cahiers d'ethnologie, de géographie et de linguistique*. Paris.

Lévi-Strauss, Claude. 1949. *Les structures élémentaires de la parenté*. Paris.

1950. 'Introduction à l'oeuvre de Marcel Mauss', in M. Mauss, *Sociologie et anthropologie*. Paris.

1958. *Anthropologie structurale*. Paris.

1962. *La pensée sauvage*. Paris.

1963. *Structural Anthropology*, tr. Claire Jacobson and Brooke Grundfest Schoepf. New York and London.

1968. *Les structures élémentaires de la parenté*. 2nd edn. Paris and The Hague.

1969. *The Elementary Structures of Kinship*. 2nd edn. London.

1971. *L'homme nu*. Paris.

1973. *Anthropologie structurale deux*. Paris.

Lévi-Strauss, Claude, Augé, Marc and Godelier, Maurice. 1975. 'Anthropologie, histoire, idéologie', *Homme*, 15, 3–4: 177–88.

Lewis, I.M. 1966. 'Spirit possession and deprivation cults', *Journal of the Royal Anthropological Institute of Great Britain and Ireland*, 1, 3 (September).

Lizot, J. 1977. 'Population, resources and warfare among the Yanomami', *Man*, 12, 3–4: 497–517.

Lombard, J. 1967. 'Les cultes de possession en Afrique Noire et le Bori Hausa', *Psychopathologie Africaine*, 3, no. 3.

Lot-Falck, Eveline. 1968. 'Religions de l'Eurasie septentrionale et de l'Arctique',

Bibliography

in *Problèmes et méthodes d'histoire des religions*. Mélanges publiés par la Section des Sciences Religieuses, Centenaire de l'Ecole des Hautes Etudes. Paris.

Mabille, Pierre. 1937. *Thérèse de Lisieux*. Paris.

Maquet, J.J. 1954. *Le système des relations sociales dans le Ruanda ancien*. Tervuren.

Marie, Alain. 1972. 'Parenté, échange matrimonial et réciprocité', *Homme*, 12: 5–46.

Marx, Karl. 1968. 'Formes précapitalistes de la production', in *Oeuvres. Economie II*. Paris.

Meillassoux, Claude. 1975. *Femmes, greniers et capitaux*. Paris. (Trans. as *Maidens, Meal and Money*, tr. Felicity Edholm. Cambridge, 1980.)

Meillassoux, Claude (ed.). 1975. *L'esclavage en Afrique précoloniale*. Paris.

Métraux, Alfred. 1958. *Le vaudou haïtien*. Paris.

Mitchell, J. Clyde. 1949 (with M. Gluckman and J.A. Barnes). 'The village headman in British Central Africa', *Africa*, 19, no. 2.

1956. *The Yao Village: a study in the social structure of a Nyasaland tribe*. Manchester.

1959. 'The Yao of southern Nyasaland', in *Seven Tribes of British Central Africa*, ed. Elisabeth Colson and Max Gluckman, pp. 292–353. Manchester.

Nadel, S.F. 1946. 'A study of shamanism in the Nuba mountains', *Journal of the Royal Anthropological Institute of Great Britain and Ireland*, 76: 25–37.

Needham, Rodney. 1958. 'The formal analysis of prescriptive patrilateral cross-cousin marriage', *Southwestern Journal of Anthropology*, 14, 2: 199–219.

1962. *Structure and Sentiment: a test case in social anthropology*. Chicago.

1971a. 'Introduction', in *Rethinking Kinship and Marriage*, ed. Rodney Needham, pp. xiii–cxvii. London.

1971b. 'Remarks on the analysis of kinship and marriage', in *Rethinking Kinship and Marriage*, ed. Rodney Needham, pp. 1–34. London.

1977. 'Introduction', *La parenté en question* (translation of *Rethinking Kinship and Marriage*), pp. 15–131. Paris.

Nimendaju, C. 1939. *The Apinayé*. Catholic University of America, Anthropological Series, 8. Washington, D.C.

Ortigues, Marie-Cécile and Ortigues, Edmond. 1966. *Oedipe africain*. Paris.

Parrinder, Geoffrey, 1950. *La religion en Afrique occidentale (illustrée par les croyances et pratiques des Yorouba, des Akan et peuples apparentés)*. Paris.

Piault, Marc. 1975. 'Captifs du pouvoir et pouvoir des captifs', in *L'esclavage en Afrique précoloniale*, ed. Claude Meillassoux, pp. 321–50. Paris.

Plaene, Guy de. 1974. *Les structures d'autorité des Bayanzi*. Paris.

Pouillon, Jean. 1966. 'Problèmes du structuralisme. Présentation: un essai de définition', *Temps Modernes*, no. 246: 769–90.

Radcliffe-Brown, A.R. 1924. 'The mother's brother in South Africa', *South African Journal of Science*, 21. (Repr. in *Structure and Function in Primitive Society*. London, 1952.)

1968. *Structure et fonction dans la société primitive*. Paris.

Rattray, R.S. 1924–5. 'Ntoro and Abusua', *Journal of the African Society*, 24, no. 94.

1959 (1st edn 1927). *Religion and Art in Ashanti*. Accra-Kumasi and London.

1969 (1st edn 1923). *Ashanti*. Oxford.

Bibliography

Rey, Jean-Philippe. 1971. *Colonialisme, néo-colonialisme et transition au capitalisme: exemple de la 'Comilog' au Congo-Brazzaville*. Paris.

Richards, A.I. 1950. 'Some types of family structure amongst the Central Bantu', in *African Systems of Kinship and Marriage*, ed. A.R. Radcliffe-Brown and Daryll Forde, pp. 207–51. London, New York and Toronto.

Richards, A.I. and Tardits, Claude. 1974. 'A propos du mariage bemba', *Homme*, 14, 3–4: 111–18.

Rivière, Peter G. 1966a. 'A note on marriage with the sister's daughter', *Man*, 1, 4: 550–6.

1966b. 'Oblique discontinuous exchange: a new formal type of prescriptive alliance', *American Anthropologist*, 68, 3: 738–40.

1969. *Marriage among the Trio: a principle of social organization*. Oxford.

Rouch, Jean. 1960. *La religion et la magie Songhay*. Paris.

Sahlins, Marshall. 1974. *Stone Age Economics*. London.

1976. *Age de pierre, âge d'abondance: l'économie des sociétés primitives*. Paris (translation of *Stone Age Economics*).

Schapera, I. 1927. 'Customs relating to twins in South Africa', *Journal of the African Society*, no. 26.

Seligman, B.Z. 1925. 'Cross cousin marriage', *Man*, 25, no. 70.

Sousberghe, Louis de. 1955. *Structure de parenté et d'alliance d'après les formules pende (ba-Pende, Congo Belge)*. Brussels.

1958. 'Régime foncier ou tenure des terres chez les Pende', *Bulletin des séances de l'Académie Royale des Sciences Coloniales*, 4, 7: 1346–52.

1963. 'Les Pende: aspects des structures sociales et politiques', in L. de Sousberghe, B. Crine-Mavar, A. Doutreloux and J. de Loose, *Miscellanea ethnografica*, pp. 1–78. Tervuren.

1965. 'Cousins croisés et descendants: les systèmes du Rwanda et du Burundi comparés à ceux du Bas-Congo', *Africa*, 35, 4: 396–421.

Sperber, Dan. 1968. *Le structuralisme en anthropologie*. Paris. First published in *Qu'est-ce que le structuralisme?*, pp. 169–237. Paris, 1968.

Tanner, R.E.S. 1955. 'Hysteria in Sukuma medical practice', *Africa*, 25, no. 3.

Tardits, Claude. 1974. 'Prix de la femme et mariage entre cousins croisés: le cas des Bemba d'Afrique centrale', *Homme*, 14, 2: 5–30.

Turnbull, Colin M. 1962. *The Forest People: a study of the Pygmies of the Congo*. New York.

Turner, V.W. 1953. *Lunda Rites and Ceremonies*. Occasional Papers of the Rhodes–Livingstone Museum. Livingstone.

Vansina, Jan. 1954. 'Les valeurs culturelles des Bushong', *Zaïre*, 8, 9: 899–910.

1957. 'L'Etat kuba dans le cadre des institutions politiques africaines', *Zaïre*, 11, 5: 485–92.

1958. 'Les croyances religieuses des Kuba', *Zaïre*, 12, 7: 725–58.

1964a. Review of *The Lele of the Kasai, Journal of African History*, 5, 1: 141–2.

1964b. *Le Royaume kuba*. Tervuren.

Van Wing, J.R.P. 1938. *Etudes Bakongo*, vol. II: *Religions et magie*. Brussels.

Van Wouden, F.A.E. 1935. *Sociale structuur-typen in de Groote Oost*. Leiden.

Verger, Pierre. 1957. *Notes sur le culte des Orisa et Vodun à Bahia, la baie de Tous les Saints, au Brésil et à l'ancienne côte des Esclaves en Afrique*. Mémoires de l'Ifan. Dakar.

White, C.M.N. 1961. *Elements in Luvale Beliefs and Rituals*. Occasional Papers of the Rhodes–Livingstone Museum, 2. Manchester.

Bibliography

Williams, F.E. 1932. 'Sex affiliation and its implications', *Journal of the Royal Anthropological Institute of Great Britain and Ireland*, 62.

Zempleni, A. 1966. 'La dimension thérapeutique du culte des rab', *Psychopathologie*, 2, 3: 295–439.

Index

215

Index

Index

Maquet, Jacques, 1
Marie, Alain, 113
marriage
  complex forms, 8, 77, 79, 80, 81,
    112–26
  exchange of sisters, 16, 50, 52, 57, 59
  generalised exchange, 29, 37, 38, 41, 59,
    60, 61, 62, 70–80 passim, 96, 97, 98,
    106, 107, 109, 111, 120, 127, 130,
    134, 135, 139
  horizontal exchange, 106
  oblique discontinuous exchange, 43
  preferential, 30, 31, 32, 33
  prescriptive, 30, 31, 32, 33
  restricted (or direct) exchange, 29, 42,
    47, 49, 58, 59, 60, 76, 80, 81, 99,
    100, 106, 107, 109, 111, 120
  secondary preferential, 117, 118, 120,
    121, 124, 125, 126
  uxorilocal, 61–71 passim, 75, 76, 78,
    134
  vertical exchange, 106
  virilocal, 63, 67, 70–9 passim, 85, 98,
    111, 133
marriage with
  father's sister, 41, 43, 44, 49
  father's sister's daughter's daughter,
    49–60
  granddaughter, 35–40 passim, 86,
    89–99 passim, 104–11 passim
  mother's brother's daughter's daughter,
    50, 51, 57
  mother's brother's wife, 117, 118, 121,
    126
  sister's daughter, 43, 44, 46, 48
  wife's brother's daughter, 118, 120, 124,
    125, 126
  see also cross cousin
Martino, P., 183
Marx, Karl, 15, 17, 18, 20, 144, 146, 148
Marxism, 7, 15–20 passim, 74, 144–8
materialism (historical), *see* Marxism
matrilinearity, 43, 44, 60–81, 85
matrilocality, *see under* residence
Mauss, Marcel, 5, 8, 190
Mbala, 192
Mbata, 49
Mbum, 39
Mbuti, 16
Meillassoux, Claude, 15, 75
Melanesia, 6, 23, 111, 145
Métraux, Alfred, 152
Minyanka, 14, 17
Miwok, 126
model (structural), 22, 29, 32, 42, 43, 44,
  51, 53, 62, 64, 66, 67, 71, 76, 79,
  97, 121, 158

mode of production
  Asiatic, 19, 144–8
  domestic, 17, 18, 20, 23, 144
  lineage as, 72
  slavery as, 143
Mongo, 9
Monod, Jacques, 16
Moses, 187
Mundang, 24
Mundugumor, 110
mystics, 151, 164, 179, 195
myth, 13, 14, 113, 154

Nadel, S.F., 178, 186
Ndembu, 9, 15
Needham, Rodney, 11, 29, 31, 32, 34, 123
Nkutshu, 5
Nuba, 178, 186
Nuer, 187
Nyoro, 80, 186

Oedipus complex, 22, 170
Omaha system, 80, 118, 122, 123–6
Ortigues, Marie-Cécile and Edmond, 160,
  170, 178

pangolin, 104, 105, 106
Parrinder, Geoffrey, 161, 162, 163
patrilinearity, 43, 44, 45, 60, 61, 65, 71–81
  passim, 112, 117
patrilocality, *see under* residence
Pende, 13, 15, 20, 24, 31–42 passim, 48,
  49, 59, 63–6, 72–80 passim, 107–11
  passim
Piault, Marc, 21
polyandry, 85, 89, 90, 93, 99, 101
polygamy, 6, 7, 9, 19, 83, 89, 94, 102, 142
Polynesia, 18, 111
potlatch, 6, 7, 8, 131, 135, 137
Pouillon, Jean, 13
prestige, *see* wealth
primogeniture, 7, 140
prophets, 187
psychiatry, 152, 155, 158, 159, 177, 182,
  183, 188, 193
psychoanalysis, 153, 154, 158, 159, 160,
  167, 169, 170, 177
Pueblo, 153
Punu, 72, 73, 74
Purum, 123

Radcliffe-Brown, A.R., 2, 10, 11, 112, 126
Rattray, R.S., 68, 70
residence
  avunculocality, 61, 63, 64, 75, 76, 79
  disharmonic regime, 60, 63, 70–80
    passim

217